Millennial Mythmaking

Millennial Mythmaking

Essays on the Power of Science Fiction and Fantasy Literature, Films and Games

Edited by JOHN PERLICH *and* DAVID WHITT

McFarland & Company, Inc., Publishers
Jefferson, North Carolina, and London

LIBRARY OF CONGRESS CATALOGUING-IN-PUBLICATION DATA

Millennial mythmaking : essays on the power of science fiction
    and fantasy literature, films and games / edited by John Perlich
    and David Whitt.
            p.   cm.
    Includes bibliographical references and index.

    ISBN 978-0-7864-4562-2
    softcover : 50# alkaline paper ∞

    1. Myth in motion pictures.   2. Myth in literature.
    3. Fantasy films— History and criticism.   4. Science fiction
    films— History and criticism.   5. Fantasy fiction — History and
    criticism.   6. Science fiction — History and criticism.   I. Perlich,
    John R.   II. Whitt, David.
    PN1995.9.F36M56   2010
    700'.415 — dc22   2009046357

British Library cataloguing data are available

Front cover: Digital illustration ©2010 Blend Images

Manufactured in the United States of America

McFarland & Company, Inc., Publishers
    Box 611, Jefferson, North Carolina 28640
    www.mcfarlandpub.com

For Caprica, Caiden & Kelyn

Acknowledgments

Once again we have many people to thank for the completion of this volume. In addition to the love and support from our family and friends we would like to extend special thanks to the following individuals.

Dave would like to thank Dr. Sara Jane Dietzman for her assistance translating one of the only scenes in *The Triplets of Belleville* with French dialogue, his brother Joe for his research prowess finding a single sentence in *Harry Potter and the Goblet of Fire*, Rachelle Kamrath for her patience and tolerating his sci-fi geekiness, and of course, Johnny P.

John would like to thank his wife and daughters (Jessica, Caiden and Kelyn) for unbounded support; Guillermo Del Toro for an amazing story; and Dave (from "The John and Dave Show").

We would also like to thank our co-contributors for their enthusiasm and hard work throughout this process. Editing your own work is difficult enough, but editing someone else's has its own unique challenges. We appreciate each author's openness to our suggestions, especially those who made changes right up until the last minute.

Table of Contents

No Boundaries

Preface

"There and Back Again..."
JOHN PERLICH *and* DAVID WHITT

Curious readers will wonder about the intentionality of the editors' allusion to the "real" title of J. R. R. Tolkien's *The Hobbit* as an opening device for our preface. In an attempt to capture the essence of his journey, Bilbo Baggins settles upon the phrase *There and Back Again* as a summary of his adventure. In many ways, his title is appropriate as an explanation for the book you are now reading. This volume is actually a continuation of previous work. We completed a project — similar to and yet unique from the present work — and so it could be said that we have been "there." After a brief return to our normal lives ("back") we decided to embark on another "grand adventure"[1] ("again"). To contextualize this project we should articulate the writing process with regard to several issues: our topic (modern mythology), how we became interested in this subject, and what specifically the present work addresses. Through this discussion it should be clear to the reader that our work is inspired by several scholars in key areas of inquiry.

THE JOURNEY BEGINS

December, 2007 — two small but surprisingly heavy shipping boxes arrive from Switzerland at our respective institutions of higher learning in Nebraska 104 miles apart. We carefully slice open our packages and fold back the top which reveals several shrink-wrapped hard covered books. We each remove the top book from the pile, take off the clear protective covering, gaze at the cover, and flip through the pages. Months of work staring at computer screens, late-night phone calls, and countless email attachments were now officially over. The fruits of our labor, a book about comparative mythology titled *Sith, Slayers, Stargates, and Cyborgs: Modern Mythology in the New Millennium* which we co-edited and contributed chapters to, was finally in our hands. Now it was time for a well-deserved break to enjoy the holidays, recharge for the spring semester, and turn our attention to other academic pursuits.

Initially, we both thought that after *Sith, Slayers, Stargates, and Cyborgs (SSSC)* was released we would take off a year or more to watch sales and see if there was even an audience for this subject matter. Our hope was that if the book did well we would eventually do another, and then perhaps even a third to complete our "trilogy." However, one of us had a different idea; only a few months into 2008. John surprisingly declared that we should begin exploring the possibility of another book immediately — striking while the iron was hot so to speak, to take advantage of the many science fiction and fantasy texts emerging within popular culture (e.g., *X-Men Origins: Wolverine, Star Trek, Terminator Salvation, Up, Night at the Museum: Battle of the Smithsonian, Transformers: Revenge of the Fallen, Land of the Lost, Harry Potter and the Half-Blood Prince, G.I. Joe: The Rise of Cobra, Twilight: New Moon, Avatar,* and, of course, *The Hobbit* [in production at the time]). Clearly the explosion of this genre resonates with the sour economic climate that feeds an impulse toward escapism — but we contend there is more to this "stuff" than satiating a desire to get away.[2] Initially a bit reluctant to jump back into the process of writing and editing, Dave was quickly won over by John's enthusiasm and the process of soliciting a publisher, submitting a call for papers, and figuring out what we would each write about began again.

Our growth from naïve book publishing novices to an efficient editorial team (at least we hope so) was somewhat like the mythic characters we and several other authors examine in our final collaboration *SSSC* as well as this volume. However, ours was obviously not a hero's quest filled with exciting adventures, though our experience did parallel mythic scholar Joseph Campbell's odyssey of separation, initiation, and return; ours was an academic journey with unique trials and struggles. The process of completing a book loosely reflects Campbell's stages in the monomyth: we answered the call to adventure (the challenge of editing, contributing chapters to and publishing a book), had hero partners (our talented co-authors), were given assistance by wise and helpful guides (colleagues who have been through the publishing process), navigated a labyrinth (editing numerous chapters with their many rewrites), experienced sacrifice (time with friends and family), conquered the powers of darkness (word processing and Internet server glitches), and finally received a boon at the end of our adventure (publication). This story has achieved a sort of mythic quality for us, providing inspiration and guidance throughout the process of creating this volume of comparative mythology.

REVISITED: WHY STUDY MYTH?

The power of stories is undeniable. All civilizations, ancient and modern, have used tales to share and preserve their history, religion, and culture. Atkinson (1995) states, "There is power in storytelling that can transform our

lives. Traditional stories, myths, and fairy tales ... stories told from generation to generation carry this power in the enduring values and lessons about
living life deeply that they pass on" (p. 3). This is why we study legends, para-
bles, narratives, yarns, anecdotes, and chronicles. Myth in particular is a
unique form of storytelling. According to Leeming (1998) the word myth
"comes via *mythos* from the Greek root (mu) meaning to make a sound with
the mouth and is thus basic to human existence as we know it" (p. 3). Before
the invention of the alphabet ancient civilizations used the spoken word to
not only communicate with each another, but also pass down personal and
cultural histories from one generation to the next. Some of these stories were
mythic tales of mighty heroes and their epic adventures. Others were creation
myths about how the gods, people, and animals came to be. Over the centuries these stories, generated from all corners of the world, became part of a
much larger and vibrant mythic chorus, or what Campbell (1991) called "the
music of the spheres" or "the song of the universe" (p. xvi). Some songs in this
universe are more recognizable than others. For example, Homer's *Iliad* and
Odyssey are arguably the most widely celebrated myths, still popular over two
thousand years later. Other myths, like those of the Navaho Indians of North
America, Australian Aboriginals, or various African tribes, are perhaps less
well known, but are still culturally meaningful.

However, the study of mythology extends beyond ancient stories and lost
civilizations. Contemporary myths, particularly science fiction and fantasy
texts, can provide socio-cultural commentary on who we are, what we have
created, and where we may be going. Voytilla (1999) argued, "Science Fiction
and Fantasy are our New Mythology, and provide an important canvas that
allows us to explore society's issues" (p. 260). Not surprisingly many authors
in the present volume draw upon traditional mythic archetypes and themes
to analyze contemporary science fiction and fantasy texts. In doing so these
authors provide a unique perspective into the human experience, which has
always been the purpose of mythology.

Overview

The chapters within are divided into three sections—"Contrasting Colors," "New Champions," and "No Boundaries"—each section containing
essays that investigate similar themes. The first and most loosely affiliated
group, "Contrasting Colors," combines the works of three author-teams:
Cronn-Mills and Samens, Edwards and Klosa, and Besel and Smith Besel.
Kirsten Cronn-Mills and Jessica Samens' literal investigation of color as a
meaningful signifier in the *Harry Potter* book series articulates a semiotic symbolic analysis that connects the meaning of color with archtypical roots. Binary
colors, like black and white, take on a more figurative meaning in the essay
by Jason Edwards and Brian Klosa, who deconstruct and challenge one of the
more primary structures studied in rhetoric, mythology, and comparative

myth — the aspects of good and evil. Carried to another level of abstraction, by tracing the development of the *Planet of the Apes* mythology, Richard Besel and Reneé Smith Besel articulate significant implications regarding class, culture, color and race. Together, these three chapters complicate simple binaries, and yet are not irreconcilable with previous works that summarize the interrelatedness of these poles. As Campbell explained to Moyers (1991), "the basic mythological motif that originally all was one, and then there was separation.... So now the eternal is somehow away from us, and we have to find some way to get back in touch with it" (p. 62). As a group, the authors provide keen insight regarding classic forces in myth and mythology.

While the point of comparative mythology is often to describe similarities in mythic structures, there is value in delineating differences as well. "New Champions" provides the reader with a comprehensive treatment in alternative forms of odyssey, mythic-journey, and hero(ine). Dee Goertz's analysis of Chihiro's quest in the Japanese anime *Spirited Away*; David Whitt's study of Madame Souza's journey in the French animated film *The Triplets of Belleville*; and John Perlich's deconstruction of Ofelia's transformation in the Academy Award–winning Spanish-language film *Pan's Labyrinth* all provide a glimpse of new, and globally representative, faces in the eternal amalgam known as *The Hero with a Thousand Faces* (Campbell, 1968).

"No Boundaries" opens the door to additional possibilities in the study of creative mythology. It is fitting that our final section implies that more work can be done in the analysis of mythic structures. After reading Baker's essay on the mythic import of actors and actresses, Gorsevski's arguments regarding implications of the digital frontier, and Chipman's ideas regarding cognitive transcendence, we hope the reader will see this volume not as completing, but instead initiating, dialogue regarding the role of mythology and new myth in the twenty-first century and beyond. — David Whitt and John Perlich.

NOTES

1. The "grand adventure" was used as a persuasive device by Gandalf when he solcited Bilbo's assistance and convinced him to leave the comforts of home.

2. Our use of the term "stuff" in relation to mythology is an intentional reference to the conversation between Bill Moyers and Joseph Campbell (1991, p. xii) in *The Power of Myth*.

REFERENCES

Atkinson, R. (1995). *The gift of stories: Practical and spiritual applications of autobiography, life stories, and personal mythmaking.* Bergin and Garvey: Westport, CT.

Campbell, J. (1968). *The hero with a thousand faces.* Princeton, N.J.: Princeton University Press.

Campbell, J. & Moyers, B. (1991). *The power of myth.* New York: Anchor Books.

Leeming, D. A. (1998). *Mythology: The voyage of the hero.* New York: Oxford University Press.

Voytilla, S. (1995). *Myth and the Movies: Discovering the Mythic Structure of 50 Unforgettable Films.* Studio City, CA: Michael Wiese Productions.

Contrasting Colors

1

Sorting Heroic Choices: Green and Red in the Harry Potter Septology

KIRSTIN CRONN-MILLS *and* JESSICA SAMENS

The job of myth is to help humans explain our experiences. Myths are guidebooks, of sorts, that explain how humans act, how things work, and how human culture has evolved. According to Malgorzata Zdybiewska (2004), "Myths, whether in the form of tales, legends or traditional folktales, have the power not only to entertain and excite but also to enrich one's imagination. They offer an explanation of the past and modern worlds" (¶ 6). William Doty (1996) argues, "Mythic themes and subjects *matter* (author's italics); they represent powerful significances because their discourse, like that of poetry and symbolic diction generally, gestures toward suprarational values that cannot easily be reduced to the arithmetic and pragmatic languages of economics and technology" (p. 449). In other words, myths are stories that explain our complicated human experience. Sharing our myths helps us understand large issues that are difficult to articulate. What is love? What is a hero? How do humans understand the nature of evil? This chapter explores the mythic nature of the Harry Potter septology and how Harry's hero's journey moves him from child to adult (another large, complicated human situation). Following Doty's nod to things that cannot be easily reduced, J.K. Rowling chooses to use green and red as defining symbols within her story. The meanings of these colors are not easily simplified, and Rowling uses varied objects of both red and green to signal particular beliefs within Harry's story.

We formulated the ideas in this chapter based on discussions with students and fellow fans about Rowling's use of color in her books.[1,2] Our theory: Rowling uses color to represent various levels of power and choice in her books. Harry's identity is actively shaped by the colors green and red as the series proceeds because these colors (green more so than red) are the ultimate representations of choice, appearing in mythic ways throughout the series. This chapter sketches a mythological perspective of Harry's character, explores a very general analysis of color before providing a connection to color in myth, and then explains our interpretation of red and green in the series.

Some relevant disclaimers: First, this chapter assumes a reader has familiarity with all seven volumes of the series, and this analysis contains spoilers. We apologize to those not familiar with the series, but the spoilers are necessary to our argument. Relevant passages quoted in the chapter will be given as much context as possible. Also, books will be referred to by their "traditional" abbreviations, which is the second half of the title after the "the." For example, *Harry Potter and the Sorcerer's Stone* will be called *SS* or *Sorcerer's Stone*. These abbreviations are used in the online fan community as well as in other Harry Potter scholarship. For the sake of page number clarity, hardcover and soft cover designations will be made on our works cited page. Additionally, we will not be able to provide every example of color use (green, red, or otherwise) in the Harry Potter series—we would have to write our own book to do that.

One final disclaimer: The most important colors of the series are really the ones of Gilderoy Lockhart's robes in *Harry Potter and the Chamber of Secrets,* because they started Kirstin's quest to examine color within the septology. Gilderoy Lockhart is the new Defense Against the Dark Arts teacher introduced in *Chamber of Secrets* (DADA teachers change for each book), and when Kirstin was re-reading the book she was struck by how often Rowling referred to Lockhart's robes. His robes are described, at various times, as forget-me-not blue (matching his eyes) (p. 59), turquoise (p. 89), mauve (p. 113), jade-green (p. 173), plum (p. 189), and pink (p. 236). All these different colors piqued Kirstin's interest, because Rowling leaves nothing to chance in Harry's universe. Kirstin decided the colors were to indicate the "prettiness" of Lockhart and his inability to be anything *but* pretty. His lack of depth is obvious in the text; his intellectual dullness combined with his extreme vanity is reflected in the colors of his robes. So, she wondered, if Rowling used color this way (in *COS*) how might she use color throughout the rest of the series? Thus the hunt for color symbolism began, and our interest in the color green and red began to emerge.

HARRY'S MYTHOLOGICAL IDENTITY

It is no secret that Harry is a hero—in fact, he is the quintessential Joseph Campbell hero of the monomyth. Campbell's (1968) definition of the hero is familiar to most individuals studying literature and/or myth —"a hero ventures forth from the world of common day into a region of supernatural wonder: fabulous forces are there encountered and a decisive victory is won: the hero comes back from this mysterious adventure with the power to bestow boons on his fellow man" (p. 30). He extends his definition in his interviews with Bill Moyers (1988)—"[e]ven in popular novels, the main character is a hero or heroine who has found or done something beyond the normal range of achievement and experience. A hero is someone who has given his or her life to something bigger than oneself" (p. 123). Rowling has left specific clues that she has shaped Harry as a monomythic hero. The earliest clue is his literal invitation, found early on in *Harry Potter and the Sorcerer's Stone*, to embark on his hero's journey—"Harry stretched out his hand at last to take the yellowish envelope addressed in emerald green to Mr. H. Potter, the Floor, Hut-on-the-Rock, The Sea" (p. 51). Singularity is another feature of a monomythic hero, and Rowling clearly shapes Harry as such: he is the Boy Who Lived, and the only person to survive the Killing Curse (Avada Kedavra, represented by a green flash). The heroes that Campbell discusses are singular heroes: Osiris, Buddha, Jesus, Apollo, King Arthur, Daniel Boone. Christopher Vogler (1998) mentions "group-oriented heroes" (p. 42), but spends more time discussing "loner heroes" (p. 43), whose "natural habitat is the wilderness, their natural state is solitude" (p. 43). Harry's natural habitat has been the wilderness of his horrible treatment by the Dursleys, his abusive and neglectful aunt, uncle and cousin. Harry went to live with the Dursleys after his parents were killed by Lord Voldemort, the villain of the septology, so Harry's solitude is well established in the first thirty pages of the series. In a CBBC interview, Rowling recognizes Harry as a singular hero, claiming she killed Sirius in *Order of the Phoenix* so Harry would have to go it alone—"It is more satisfying, I think, for the reader if the hero has to go on alone, and to give him too much support makes his job too easy" (*News Round*, July, 2005, ¶ 75).

There is discussion to be had about whether or not Harry is "playing" the hero—as much is said by Hermione (*GOF* and *OOP*) and Voldemort (*OOP* and *DH*)—but that discussion is outside the scope of this chapter. For our purposes, we choose to identify Harry as a reluctant, loner hero. Even if he has delusions of grandeur (no different than any other child—we cannot forget Harry is a child), the ultimate outcome is the same; Harry completes his hero's journey and wizardkind is strengthened by his return.

We must also note that Rowling has created seven individual hero's journeys inside Harry's singular hero's journey. Each book can be seen as a hero's journey because there is always "separation-initiation-return," which Campbell calls the "nuclear unit" of the monomyth (1968, p. 30). For each of Harry's seven adventures, he must separate from the Muggle (non–Wizarding) world, be initiated into each individual book's trials and tribulations, then return to the Dursleys' house for the summer. He does this seven times over in the course of his journey from the cupboard under the stairs to the final battle of the Second Wizarding War. The series has a singular boon—the ultimate defeat of Voldemort—but each book has its own boon. For example, he gains new knowledge to pass to Ron Weasley and Hermione Granger, his best friends, and he defeats the shade of Voldemort in *Sorcerer's Stone*. In *Chamber of Secrets*, the basilisk is destroyed and safety from the Heir of Slytherin is momentarily restored. These smaller boons continue as the series progresses, and they move him closer to his final triumph in *Deathly Hallows*.

The Hero as Choice-Maker

Entertainment Weekly listed Harry as #4 on a recent list of Top Twenty heroes, in part for "deploying his secret weapons: love, loyalty, and the good ol' Expelliarmus" (Bernardin, Collis, Jensen, Nashawaty, Rottenberg, Schwartz, Snierson, Spines, Svetkey, Tucker, Vary, 2009, p. 34). In another article in the magazine, Jensen (2009) argues for Potter as a hero we should watch closely:

> We need more from pop culture than just seeing good guys and bad guys in action — we need to see how they're made. Case in point: Harry Potter. J. K. Rowling's seven-book saga took us deep inside the boy wizard's trial-and-error transformation from a world-wounded young boy to a young man who saves the world without compromising himself or his values. We believed it, because Rowling — and Harry — did the hard work of proving it [p. 33].

"Trial-and-error transformation" follows with Campbell's descriptions of a hero's journey. But the presence of trial and error also indicates how the hero makes choices as s/he goes through the hero's journey.

For example, choice is an integral part of the hero's journey through the "refusal of the call." In Harry's case, he had to decide whether or not to believe the claim of his first magical friend, Hogwarts gamekeeper Rubeus Hagrid, who makes the preposterous claim of Harry's wizard identity after the Dursleys had provided him with ten years' worth of evidence to the contrary. Once Harry sees the green-inked envelopes (*SS*, p. 39), he knows there is something unique and unusual about his life. But to believe one is a wizard? The leap is large. Trusting Hagrid's claim is Harry's first big choice, and his first big step forward into his true identity. Heroes also must decide, as their journey continues, whether to move forward or step back. The reward/boon is forward, but so are incredible trials and hardships. Safety is behind the hero, but in a premature return, the hero has to live with the possibility of regret.

According to Vogler (1998), "At the root, the idea of hero is connected with self-sacrifice" (p. 35). Whether or not to sacrifice him/herself is the ultimate choice of the hero, and it is a choice Harry must make as well. His final decision is evident in the last two hundred pages of the last novel, *Harry Potter and the Deathly Hallows*. Close to the end of the book, Aberforth Dumbledore (Professor Dumbledore's brother) warns Harry against a possible return to Hogwarts. Harry's response to Aberforth shows us his choice: "I'm going to keep going until I succeed — or I die. Don't think I don't know how this might end. I've known for years" (*DH*, p. 569). Even though Hermione reminds him, "You don't have to do everything alone, Harry" (*DH*, p. 583), just as others have reminded him throughout the series, Harry chooses to fight the final battle himself.

For Harry, another part of his self-sacrifice involves the choice to hold himself apart from others. Harry loner-hero status arises at several points within the series. Hermione's quote is evidence of that projection, as is his decision to break off his budding romance with Ginny (*HBP*, p. 646) once he realizes he must fight Voldemort to his or Voldemort's death. He is alone in the middle of the Dursleys at the beginning of each book, and even as his friends journey with him through all seven books, Harry remains alone in his mind. Finally, as he walks to his possible death, he is surrounded by the shades of his parents, James and Lily, and his godfather Sirius Black, the people who left him alone in life.

Harry is so convinced of his solitude that he misses the impact of his choices. Because of his choices to tell the truth about Voldemort's return (end of *GOF*, all of *OOP*) and to fight the Dark Lord's growing power (*HBP* and *DH*), Harry becomes the symbol of the good still left in the world despite Voldemort's evil takeover. While Harry, Ron, and Hermione are on the run from Voldemort in *Deathly Hallows*, they hear "Potterwatch," a radio show done by Harry's supporters. During the show, they hear commentary by Remus Lupin, a friend of James Potter and former teacher at Hogwarts. Lupin points out the significance of Harry's choices—"'The Boy Who Lived' remains a symbol of everything for which we are fighting: the triumph of good, the power of innocence, the need to keep fighting" (p. 441). Even though Harry thinks people have sacrificed themselves for him, they have actually allowed their deaths by fighting for the most significant choice Harry has made — to remain on the side of love and goodness. Even if he cannot see how his choices matter, Harry Potter continues to give the Wizarding world hope. A person could ask for nothing more in a hero.

COLOR THEORY AND COLOR IN MYTHOLOGY

Just as particular elements of the monomyth are relevant to Harry's character, particular elements of color theory are relevant to Rowling's textual decisions that specifically illustrate Harry's battle against Voldemort. Rowling's use of colors, specifically green and red, signals the reader to pay attention to particular items within the books. Green and red objects take an active role in shaping Harry's identity as a hero, and the colors act as guideposts for the reader to understand the ideological choices Harry must make. The best example of green and red in the Harry Potter series is one even a casual fan knows: Harry's eyes are green and Voldemort's eyes are red. But examples of red and green objects abound in the series (green more so than red, in our view). Given the unusually high occurrence of green and red, it bears examination as to why these colors appear so often (purple and gold, another set of complimentary colors, also appear quite often, but they are not as emotionally charged throughout the series as red and green are). First, however, we will analyze color in mythology. Then we will explore how Rowling conceives of choice throughout the series as represented by color.

The significance of color in our world is well established, and a larger discussion of color is beyond the scope of this chapter. However, because red and green as colors have cultural significance attached to them, that significance bears examination here. According to Boggs and Petrie (2004), color is "the special quality of light reflected from a given surface" (p. 204). Boggs and Petrie go on to note that "[c]olor not only is seen but is felt emotionally by each viewer and is therefore subject to his or her personal interpretation" (p. 204). If you combine that personal interpretation with variations of pigment and light (including variations in saturation, intensity, and hue), everyone will come to their own conclusions about particular shades of color. As well, Boggs and Petrie distinguish between *local* color and *atmospheric* color (p. 206). The color of one object by itself (local) will seem different than an object of the same color amongst its peers (atmospheric). The examples they give are leaves — one leaf on a table is different than many leaves on a tree (p. 206).

In many cultures (e.g., the United States), red can be interpreted in several ways: love — Valentine's Day, hearts, intimacy and passion; help — fire trucks, the red cross on first-aid kits, the idea of courage; danger — fire, blood, red lights, stop signs. These particular instances are all atmospheric and we need the context of the holiday, or the fact that we are driving, to interpret the color red. Local contexts of red occur in different ways for different individuals. For example, a red shirt may represent a gift given by a loved one. Red is considered a "warm" color, representing feelings of heat, fire, and intensity.

Our cultural interpretations of green also vary. Green may mean: luck — leprechauns, money; negative emotion — "green with envy"; nature — trees, grass, "going green" for the planet. Once again, these are atmospheric instances of the color; we will all have different instances of "local" green. Green is considered a "cool" color, indicating feelings of calm and comfort. We do not have to look very far into these colors to notice the same thing the rest of this chapter will point out: a color can evoke emotional responses provoked by the dialectical poles on both ends of the spectrum of "good" and "bad."

Additionally, red and green are significant as colors because of their position on the color wheel because they are opposites. Opposites on the color wheel are considered complementary colors, and are often used in combination with each other because they look nice together (orange/blue, green/red, purple/yellow). What is most significant about complimentary colors relates to what happens when the pigments are combined. When mixed together in equal proportion, complementary colors produce a neutral color, such as grey, black, or white. This piece of information is significant to our argument.

Green and red have appeared as noteworthy colors in other examples of children's stories. In the film *The Wizard of Oz*, the Wicked Witch of the West is green, as is the Emerald City. Dorothy's slippers are, of course, ruby red. In the animated film *Shrek*, Shrek is a green ogre, and Princess Fiona is green in her ogre incarnation. Fiona also wears a green dress for the entire film, in both her human and ogre forms. Shrek and Fiona's nemesis, Lord Farquaad, wears red throughout the film. In both stories, the colors are ambiguous. Dorothy's shoes are "good," because they can take her home. But the Wicked Witch and the Emerald City are both green — are they both "bad"? Even though Shrek is originally cast as a mean, angry ogre from a horrible swamp, he turns out to be a good guy, as does the ogre incarnation of Fiona, who is also green. But Fiona hides her secret through 90% of the film — or does she? Does her green dress give her secret away? We can never be sure.

In America, the most prominent example of the combination of red and green is the representation of Christmas. Even when the colors are paired together at other times of the year, we still tend to interpret them as "Christmas." The colors have been "assigned," so to speak, to that time of year, and their color combination is not applied elsewhere (another example of atmospheric color designation). Many reasons have been given for why red and green are the traditional Christmas colors. Most of the explanations relate to beliefs about holly and mistletoe. In the dark of the year at the pagan Winter Solstice, the red berries and green leaves of both plants represented the hope that spring will return. Some sources claim evergreen boughs also represent the hope of spring. Christmas red has also been related to the blood of Jesus and Jesus' importance to the Christian Christmas season (Gardiner and Robinson, 2004, ¶ 1, ¶ 6).

Multiple meanings for colors are not unusual. Umberto Eco (2004) claims that color symbolism in Medieval times "could have two opposite meanings depending on the context in which [the color] was seen" (p. 121). Eco also points out some contradictions about red from that time: "In the same way red surcoats [garments worn over a knight's armor] and caparisons [drapes over horses] expressed courage and nobility ... red was also the color of executioners and harlots" (p. 123). In Gary R. Varner's (2007) exploration of green related to fairy mythology, he claims green is associated with both fertility and the supernatural. Even though green is a symbol of divinity and is a sacred color in some religions, Varner also argues the early Christian church saw green as associated with paganism, which then morphed into green as a representation of evil (p. 57) as Christianity continued to grow. Early Christians were afraid of nature as its own powerful entity, and nature's dominant color came to represent that fear.

It makes sense that color has worked its way into stories as representations of these early ideas. Medieval literature has used the color green in several stories, from the original Green Man to the famous *Sir Gawain and the Green Knight*. No one is sure who the original Green Man was, though he was connected with nature and vegetation. The Green Man has been represented at various times as The Jolly Green Giant, Pan, a wild man of the woods, the boogey man, the noble savage, Puck, and an herbalist (Patterson, 2005, ¶ 1–19). We see the Green Man echoed (though not directly) in the Green Knight, with his green hair and beard, which are compared to grass (Benson, 1965, p. 63). In a translation of the 1611 text, the Green Knight has green clothes, green hair, and green saddle trimmings. Even the "hair of the horse's head was of green" (*Sir Gawaine*, ¶ 9). As well, the Green Knight had red eyes, which he "rolled ... about" in frustration while waiting for greetings from Arthur's court (*Sir Gawaine*, ¶ 14).

In the tale, Sir Gawain is approached by the Green Knight at Arthur's Round Table. The Green Knight offers a challenge of allowing anyone to give him one blow to the head with an axe, provided the Green Knight can come back one year later and do the same to him. Sir Gawain accepts the offer and beheads the Green Knight. The Green Knight picks up his head and tells Gawain to find him in a year at the Green Chapel. Gawain thus becomes a marked man who must fulfill the promise he made to the Green Knight (Parker, 2007, p. 272). Harry's situation is similar. One man is marked to come back and battle the other, though the circumstances are different, and Harry is chosen without his knowledge or consent. Just like Sir Gawain and the Green Knight, both Harry and Voldemort understand their fate and choose to complete their given tasks.

When Gawain travels to battle the Green Knight, he stays first in a castle along the way. While staying at the castle, Gawain is tempted by the lady of the castle, who offers him kisses and a green belt. Knights wear green belts to remember the loyalty and honor in the vows they have taken (Parker, 2007, p. 274). Gawain accepts the belt as well as the kisses. When he goes to battle the Green Knight, he discovers the lady actually belongs to the Green Knight. Sir Gawain is mortified by his cowardice, because he has betrayed his knightly vow of virtue. Finally, the Green Knight is revealed to Sir Gawain as a man named Bertilak. Bertilak was bewitched by Morgan Le Fay and asked to test the Knights of the Round Table (National Endowment for the Humanities, sec. 7, ¶ 1).

Aside from the battle, there are other similarities between Harry's and Gawain's journeys. In his journey to and from the Green Knight, Gawain discovers the Knight's shape-shifting powers after he transforms back to Bertilak. Harry discovers a similar ability in Voldemort as the series progresses — Voldemort morphs from a face on the back of another man's head (*SS*) to a snake-like man (*GOF*) to a snake-like man who can fly (*DH*). Neither Harry nor Gawain knows of the supernatural powers Voldemort and the Green Knight possess, making the heroes' tasks even more complex. Furthermore, in the same way Harry is convinced of Voldemort's evil, Gawain is convinced that the Green Knight is corrupt. But we cannot know for sure if the Green Knight is "good" or "bad." Other pertinent questions include: What is the meaning of the Green Knight's red eyes? Do they indicate an evil soul? A bloodthirsty nature? Something else? We cannot really know.

As a final color note, there are many fans who claim Rowling is exploring the process of alchemy as she moves through the series, and those alchemical possibilities are explored in her characters' names. According to Cicero and Cicero (1995), metals change into gold as they pass through four different color stages: black, white, yellow, and red (p. 272). As we know, Albus (white) Dumbledore, Sirius Black (black), and Rubeus (red) Hagrid have significant effects on Harry as he completes his hero's journey. Their names may, in fact, mark them as alchemical agents for Harry's personality. The color green (especially emerald green) also figures into the alchemical theories floating around in the online Potterverse. While these theories seem very wise to us, they are outside the scope of this chapter.

POWER, CHOICE, AND COLOR IN THE HARRY POTTER SERIES

Rowling establishes the power of choice very early in the series. In *Sorcerer's Stone*, Harry is Sorted (the capital "S" in Rowling's text notes the importance of the act) into his house, the group of people who will become, as Professor McGonagall notes, "something like your family" (p. 114). Though the explicit characteristics of each house are not defined until *Goblet of Fire* during a Sorting Hat song (p. 177), Harry has no desire to be associated with Slytherins, prompted by meeting Draco Malfoy (*SS*, p. 77–79, p. 108–110), son of a former Death Eater and a Slytherin legacy (*SS*, p. 77), and discovering that Lord Voldemort was also a Slytherin (*SS*, p. 107). As well, Harry knows that the Weasley family members have all been Gryffindors (*SS*, p 106). Hermione also expresses an interest in Gryffindor because it was Dumbledore's house (*SS*, p. 106). Though he has no point of reference other than the people he's met, he knows what he does not want based on those facts alone.

When the Sorting Hat is placed on Harry's head, it must decide what to do with him:

> Difficult. Very difficult. Plenty of courage, I see. Not a bad mind, either. There's talent, oh my goodness, yes— and a nice thirst to prove yourself, now that's interesting.... So where shall I put you? [p. 121].

Harry's immediate response is "Not Slytherin" (p. 121). The Sorting Hat replies, noting Harry's choice:

> Not Slytherin, eh?.... Are you sure? You could be great, you know, it's all here in your head, and Slytherin will help you on the way to greatness, no doubt about that— no? Well, if you're sure— better be GRYFFINDOR! [p. 121].

The importance of choice is fully established with this decision. Sorting is one of the defining moments of a young witch or wizard's life, and previous to

Harry's attempt to influence the Sorting Hat, no indication is given that the Sorting Hat's mind can be changed — the Sorting Hat places you according to what it sees in your personality, and the Sorting Hat sees both Gryffindor bravery (*GOF*, p. 177) and Slytherin ambition (*GOF*, p. 177) within Harry's mind, so a choice must be made. However, Harry is the one to make it, not the Sorting Hat.

The significance of Harry's choice again becomes clear in the epilogue to the series, which takes place nineteen years after the death of Lord Voldemort. By this time, Harry is married to Ginny Weasley, and they have three children: Lily, James, and Albus. In a conversation with his youngest son, Harry comforts him as Al worries about being Sorted into Slytherin:

> "It doesn't matter to us, Al. But if it matters to you, you'll be able to choose Gryffindor over Slytherin. The Sorting Hat takes your choice into account."
> "Really?"
> "It did for me," said Harry.
> He had never told any of his children that before, and he saw the wonder in Albus's face when he said it [*Deathly Hallows*, p. 758].

Though we never discover his fate at Hogwarts, we know Harry's son Albus understands we all have abilities to make choices for our future — and our choices matter.

Albus Dumbledore is the headmaster at Hogwarts. One of the most powerful wizards in his world, Dumbledore serves as Harry's champion and mentors him through Harry's hero's journey(s). In many ways, Rowling uses Dumbledore as the moral voice of the series. To that end, Dumbledore articulates the power of choice at the end of *Chamber of Secrets*. At the end of the book, Dumbledore and Harry are discussing Tom Riddle's claims of similarity between the two boys, claims made by Tom in the Chamber of Secrets at the end of *COS* (Tom Riddle is Lord Voldemort's given name). Dumbledore explains to Harry how Voldemort left some of himself when he gave Harry his scar. Because of this revelation, Harry confesses to Dumbledore the Sorting Hat wanted to put him in Slytherin, and Harry is now convinced the Sorting Hat was right. But Dumbledore pushes Harry to discover why the Sorting Hat did what it did:

> "Yet the Sorting Hat placed you in Gryffindor. You know why that was. Think."
> "It only put me in Gryffindor," said Harry in a defeated voice, "because I asked not to go in Slytherin...."
> "*Exactly*," said Dumbledore, beaming once more. "Which makes you *very different* from Tom Riddle. It is our choices, Harry, that show what we truly are, far more than our abilities" [p. 333, italics are Rowling's].

Dumbledore's statement is Rowling's most explicit commentary on the power of choice. While choice is explored again and again throughout the series, Dumbledore sums up her position less than 650 pages into the (approximately) 4200-page journey.

How Red and Green Focus Rowling's Concept of Choice and Identity

Choice and identity intersect with color by the way the colors red and green are laid out in the books. Each time Harry — and by proxy, the reader — encounters an object that is green or red, the object represents an ideological choice Harry must make: is this object "good" or "bad" for him? How will the object help or hinder Harry on his way to the ultimate boon of defeating Voldemort? As Harry makes his choices, he grows in his identity as hero.

As readers know, Harry's green eyes are always balanced against Voldemort's red eyes, and Gryffindor, whose house colors are scarlet and gold (*SS*, p. 306), is always balanced against Slytherin, whose house colors are green and silver (*SS*, p. 306). However, red and green appear again and again in the book in static and dynamic ways. Some instances of green are not significant: when Kreacher (the house elf in the ancestral House of Black) tells his sad tale and gets snot everywhere (*DH*, p. 192–200), we expect the snot to be green. In general, however, each time Rowling mentions red or green, she has a reason for tagging an object with either color. To be clear, Rowling does not tag each and every object with a color. Not everyone's robes are described, nor does every spell have a shower of colored sparks. Even Voldemort's snake/Horcrux, Nagini, receives no color description. When Rowling does mention the color of an object, she wants us to notice it.

To keep things organized, we will list pertinent examples of red and green from each book, and do our analysis of these instances directly after each list. As a general construct for the series, we contend Rowling's choice of green or red must be interpreted through the significance and context of the object, or its "atmospheric" color. Something interpreted as "good" can be green (McGonagall's robes) or red (Weasley hair). Something interpreted as "bad" can be green (the potion that injures Dumbledore) or red (Mundungus Fletcher's hair). "Good" and "bad," of course, are relative terms.

Rowling's textual choice to mix up the references is unique and intriguing. Given that she starts readers out with clear references to Harry's green and Voldemort's red eyes, it would seem she has made her stand: green is good, and red is bad. However, just as in life, Harry has to choose how various objects are allied (or not) to his cause. Can he trust the family with red hair? What about the man with a green-velvet-covered belly? Those choices contribute to his growth as he moves from a neglected eleven-year-old boy to a seventeen-year-old young man who ends the Second Wizarding War.

Sorcerer's Stone *Examples of Green and Red*

In *Sorcerer's Stone*, Rowling lays the groundwork for a series mythology. In doing so she establishes some perpetual instances of green and red that include Harry's green eyes (p. 20); the Weasley family and their "flaming red hair" (p. 92); Voldemort's "glaring red eyes" (p. 293); the green and silver of the House of Slytherin (p. 306); the scarlet and gold of the House of Gryffindor (p. 306). These instances of green and red occur consistently throughout the series. Harry's eyes are especially important because they are his mother's eyes, and represent a tie to Harry's past. As well, they are a feature everyone remembers about Lily Evans Potter (p. 47), and everyone remembers Lily with loving thoughts (except Harry's Aunt Petunia, but exploring her feelings belongs to another discussion). Harry's green eyes are also significant because they "color" everything — they represent his perception of the world. For Harry's eyes, that perception includes growth. Voldemort's eyes are the same way — they "color" everything with tinges of revenge, hatred, and blood.

SS also sets us up to see the deadly Avada Kedavra curse, long before we know what it is. First, Harry remembers, "a blinding flash of green light and a burning pain on his forehead," which he assumes is from the car crash that killed his parents, "though he couldn't imagine where all the green light came from" (p. 29). Then, when Hagrid tells him the actual circumstances of his parents' death, Harry sees a "blinding flash of green light, more clearly than he had ever remembered it before" (p. 56). Harry sees it again the first night he's at Hogwarts, in a dream: "then Malfoy turned into the hook-nosed teacher, Snape, whose laugh became high and cold — there was a burst of green light and Harry woke, sweating and shaking" (p. 130).

There are other notable instances of green and red throughout SS: the "wild-looking old woman dressed all in green [who] waved merrily at him once on a bus" (p. 30); the emerald-green ink on Harry's invitation to Hogwarts (p. 51); the green smoke that billows out of Harry's Gringotts bank vault (p. 75); the emerald-green robes of Professor McGonagall (p. 113), the stern and brilliant head of Gryffindor; Harry's emerald-green hand-knitted Christmas sweater from Mrs. Weasley (p. 200), the woman who gives him motherly love throughout the series; Hagrid's red and green spark signals in the hunt for the unicorn in the Forbidden Forest (p. 251). We have several instances of "good" green balanced against Slytherin's "bad" green, a few instances of indeterminate green, and two "good" instances of red balanced against Voldemort's "bad" red eyes. We also have one "stoplight" red/green pairing (red sparks mean we are in trouble, green sparks mean we found the unicorn). As well, many of these early instances are "emerald green." We do not know if this is a reference to Slytherin's emeralds in the hourglass in the Great Hall, or if this is just one possible shade of green Rowling uses. It has been suggested by fans that emerald green is part of Rowling's alchemical symbolism (Andrea, 2009).

In *Sorcerer's Stone*, we have a significant instance of red and green together — the combination of Lily's green eyes and her red hair, first seen in the Mirror of Erised (p. 208). Because our sympathies are already established for Harry and his mother, we do not see either red or green as "evil" as applied to Lily, so our first interpretation of this combination is a positive one. SS also provides us with one other significant instance of red and green: the phoenix feather inside Voldemort's wand. When Ollivander muses over the wand that picked Harry, he gives us this piece of information: "It so happens that the phoenix whose tail feather is in your wand, gave another feather — just one other. It is very curious indeed that you should be destined for this wand when its brother — why, its brother gave you that scar" (p. 85).

At this point in the series, we have not met Fawkes, Dumbledore's phoenix. Fawkes is a "crimson" (*COS*, p. 207) bird who lives in Dumbledore's office. Even though Fawkes is not a Gryffindor, his red becomes associated with a Gryffindor's bravery, in part because Dumbledore was assumed to be a Gryffindor (*SS*, p. 106) and in part because he helps Harry fight the basilisk in *Chamber of Secrets*, bringing Harry Godric Gryffindor's sword (concealed in the Sorting Hat) so Harry may slay the snake. Dumbledore confirms that it is Fawkes' feather in each wand at the end of *Goblet of Fire*. In a scene in his office, with Fawkes present, Dumbledore explains: "Harry's wand and Voldemort's wand share cores. Each of them contains a feather from the tail of the same phoenix.... *This* phoenix, in fact ... Mr. Ollivander wrote to tell me you had bought the second wand, the moment you left his shop four years ago" (p. 697). Thus, even though Voldemort and his wand represent the "evil" green of the House of Slytherin, Fawkes' contribution of Gryffindor-like red remains deep within Voldemort's wand. This red/green reference is far more ambiguous than Lily's combination of the colors.

As we examine the instances of green and red throughout the series, it is important to note that the tension between the sides ("good"/"evil," or "right"/"wrong") is almost as important as the sides themselves. Without the tension, we would not be able to make any choice at all. As Lavoie (2003) argues in her discussion of Hogwarts houses, "Gryffindor and Slytherin need one another as worthy rivals" (p. 39). If we did not have a rivalry of red and green as represented by these two houses (also the two male-founded houses), we would not have an opportunity to make a choice between them. Rowling does provide multifaceted themes in other parts of the series (How do we listen to authority? How do we construct a family?), but on the topic of good/evil or right/wrong, she seems to believe in choice. Even for Severus Snape, one of her most morally ambiguous characters, she still believes he has made a choice for a particular side.

One note before we proceed to other books: instances of red and green are neither hidden nor prominent. They are just ... there. The big ones (Weasley hair, Harry's/Voldemort's eyes, Slytherin/Gryffindor, Avada Kedavra) are established as touchstones in Potterworld, and become "givens" as the series goes along. Smaller instances, on the other hand, are everywhere. The colors seem insignificant until you consider the number of times they recur and the types of objects that are described by either color.

Chamber of Secrets *Examples of Green and Red*

In *COS*, the instances of red and green still serve both functions: they establish series mythology and provide instances of both "good" and "evil." For *COS*, green and red are significant in several spots: the house-elf Dobby's green eyes (p. 12); Mr. Weasley's green robes (p. 38); the "emerald green" flames created by Floo powder (p. 47) which allow a witch or wizard to travel from fireplace to fireplace; the red Howler (a letter of reprimand) Ron receives from home (p. 87); Professor Flitwick's "throbbing green boil" created by Ron's broken wand (p. 104); Dumbledore's crimson and gold phoenix, Fawkes (p. 207) A "ruby-red sky" outside the Headmaster's window in Riddle's diary memory (p. 243); Dumbledore's auburn (red) hair as a younger man (p. 245); Minister of Magic Cornelius Fudge's scarlet tie and lime-green bowler hat (p. 261); the basilisk's "poisonous" green skin, shed on the floor of the Chamber of Secrets (p. 303); the poisonously green basilisk and the crimson Fawkes as they fight in the Chamber (p. 318); the rubies in the hilt of the sword of Godric Gryffindor (p. 320).

Rowling gives us additional groundwork-establishing "good" and "bad" examples of color: Dobby's green eyes, Fawkes' red fathers, the basilisk's green skin. However, some of the red/green messages are deeper than they appear. For example, Floo powder transforms regular red-hot fire into cool emerald green flames that do not harm anyone and act as transportation. As well, even though Dobby's eyes are green, just like Harry's, he is an example of "bad" green, because his former masters are the Malfoys, one of the series' most prominent examples of a Slytherin family. We must also consider how Rowling gave Cornelius Fudge, the slightly incompetent Minister of Magic, both green and red clothes the first time we meet him in the series. As fans know, Fudge reveals his positive and negative qualities as the series progresses.

Another color side note: it is no accident that both green-eyed Lily and green-eyed Dobby give their lives for Harry Potter. Even though the sacrifice these characters make for Harry seems to be the ultimate reference to green as "good," it is still balanced against the green of Voldemort's Slytherin heritage. In fact, Lily's and Dobby's sacrifices were required because of Voldemort.

Prisoner of Azkaban *Examples of Green and Red*

By the time we get to *Prisoner of Azkaban*, most of the significant green/ red mythology is set. In this book, Rowling creates some foreshadowing with her color designations. Some notable examples of red and green are as follows: the "green and leathery" Monster Book of Monsters (p. 12), a textbook for Hagrid's Care of Magical Creatures class; "Dark green" cars and drivers wearing "suit[s] of emerald velvet" from the Ministry of Magic, summoned by Mr. Weasley (p. 70) to take the family to the train station; Professor

Trelawney's "long emerald earrings" (p. 103); Neville's potion in Potions class, which is supposed to be "bright acid green," though it turns orange (p. 125); Neville's grandmother's dress, which is "green, normally," and her "big red" handbag, as worn by Professor Snape after Neville's boggart (a shape-shifting ghost) has been *riddikulus*-ed (p. 135); fellow Gryffindor Seamus Finnegan's boggart as it turns into a "green-tinged" banshee (p. 137); the "sickly green" grindylow (a water creature) with green teeth in Professor Lupin's office (p. 154); Professor Trelawney's "green sequined dress" for the occasion of Christmas Day, "making her look more than ever like a glittering, over-sized dragonfly" (p. 228); Neville's scarlet Howler from his grandmother (p. 271). Though this book does not set any precedents as to "good" and "bad" red and green, we do see two figures with significant red and green involvement (mostly green): fellow (red) Gryffindor Neville Longbottom and Sybil Trelawney, the Divination teacher. Their identities, instead of Harry's, are the focus of this book's red and green instances.

At this point in the series, Neville and Professor Trelawney both hold indeterminate roles. Rowling's application of green to Neville (with one instance of red) in *POA* does not tell us anything except to point out Neville as an important character. Most readers tend to view Neville as a bumbling oaf until they finish *Order of the Phoenix*. In *OOP*, Neville proves to be a solid member of Dumbledore's Army, the student group who fights against a cruel teacher. In *Deathly Hallows*, Neville is almost as much a hero as Harry is, leading the student opposition forces at Hogwarts and pulling Gryffindor's sword out of the Sorting Hat (just as Harry did in *COS*) to slay Nagini, the last remaining Horcrux. Only a true, brave Gryffindor can pull the sword from the Sorting Hat, so Neville's "good" red is ultimately demonstrated by this act. In *POA*, Rowling's green reminds us to pay attention to this additional budding hero. She begins demonstrating his "good" red with the green references assigned to both him and his grandmother.

Trelawney's green also points out her importance. In this book, we see both Professor McGonagall and Hermione (the smartest women of the series) ridicule Trelawney's divination skills. However, this is the book where Trelawney makes her second accurate prediction, that the Dark Lord would regain one of his servants (p. 324). Peter Pettigrew, who has been disguised as Ron Weasley's rat, Scabbers, up to this point, does indeed return to Voldemort before the book is over (her first accurate prediction is explored in *Order of the Phoenix*, claiming Harry as the one the Dark Lord must defeat in order to live, p. 841). Though she is cast as a dingbat who knows nothing, Trelawney reveals significant information for readers through her predictions. We must also point out that Neville and Professor Trelawney's green references are intertwined. Had Voldemort not anointed Harry as the Chosen One, the prophecy of Voldemort's demise could have been applied to Neville Longbottom. He "matches" the prophecy with the exception of being marked by the Dark Lord.

If we look back at the instances of red and green thus far, all have some impact on Harry's identity. Whether it's the affection of the red-haired Weasley family, the suspicions aroused by Fudge and his lime-green bowler (and the green Ministry cars), or his help from Fawkes the scarlet phoenix in defeating the poisonous green basilisk, Harry is influenced by green and red in every book. Though we have not discussed it here, Quidditch is also significant to the color scheme of the book. Harry's life as a (red) Gryffindor Seeker is consumed by his need to defeat his (green) Slytherin opponents.

Goblet of Fire *Examples of Green and Red*

In this book, red and green show up at regular intervals. Some significant examples: the green shamrocks (p. 82) which cover the tents of Ireland's Quidditch team supporters; the red, white, and green Bulgarian flag (p. 83); the scarlet robes of the Bulgarian National Quidditch players, and the "green blur" of the Irish National Quidditch team members (p. 105); the "emerald stars" and the "greenish smoke" that comprise the Dark Mark cast at the Quidditch World Cup (p. 128); Dumbledore's "deep green robes embroidered with many stars and moons" at the start of term banquet (p. 175); the glowing red "Support Cedric Diggory — The REAL Hogwarts Champion" badge that change to a glowing green "Potter Stinks" badge (p. 297–8); Reporter Rita Skeeter's "scarlet-taloned fingers" (p. 303) and her "acid-green" Quick-Quotes quill (p. 304); Triwizard champions Fleur Delacour's "Welsh Green" and Viktor Krum "scarlet Chinese Fireball" dragon models, used in the first task of the Triwizard Tournament (p. 350); Dobby's handmade Christmas gift to Harry of a "bright red" left sock and a green right sock (p. 409); the "grayish-green" gillyweed that allows Harry to complete his second task (p. 491); the "long, wild, dark-green hair" of the merpeople in the lake (p. 497); the Avada Kedavra's "blast of green light" that kills Cedric Diggory (p. 638); the "dark, raw, reddish black" Voldemort who is dumped into the cauldron with Harry's blood (p. 640); the "vivid red tattoo" on Wormtail's arm that represents the Dark Mark (p. 645); the jets of green light (Avada Kedavra) and red light (Expelliarmus) from Voldemort's and Harry's wands (p. 663). It must be noted that blood begins to appear as a red element starting with *GOF*. Though we do not expect human blood to be any color but red, we believe it matters as an instance of red in the series.

In *Goblet of Fire*, we see more joint instances of red and green. At this point, we have decided on the following interpretations of these pairs: Ireland and Bulgaria: the binary of victory/defeat; Fleur and Krum's dragons: the binary of man/woman; Rita Skeeter's fingernails and quill: the binary of truth/lie; "Support Cedric" and "Potter Stinks" badges: the binary of hero/villain. Most significantly, we have the jets of light the Avada Kedavra and Expelliarmus make when Harry and Voldemort fight in the graveyard. Surprisingly, they create a "narrow beam of light … neither red nor green, but bright, deep gold" (p. 663). This binary can be interpreted as good/evil, obviously, but why do the spells combine to make gold? This passage helps convince fans of Rowling's alchemical intentions.

A note needs to be made about the green of Avada Kedavra. In *GOF*, Rowling lets Mad-Eye Moody explain Avada Kedavra to Harry's class during a Defense Against the Dark Arts lesson. Moody demonstrates the curse on a spider. The moment marks the first time Harry has seen the curse performed. There is "a flash of blinding green light and a rushing sound" (p. 216) before the spider drops dead. Then Harry a moment of insight:

> So that was how his parents had died ... exactly like that spider. Had they been unblemished and unmarked too? Had they simply seen the flash of green light and heard the rush of speeding death, before life was wiped from their bodies? [p. 216].

Finally he has the pieces all together for the puzzle initiated with the green flashes we see in *SS*. The horrible details of his parents' deaths are complete.

At this point, we could speculate that Harry's identity has been shaped negatively by the color green. After all, his parents were killed by a green spell. But what about Harry's green eyes? Rowling is still indeterminate about which color means "bad" and which color means "good." Both green and red have garnered those labels. *Goblet of Fire* marks the middle of the series. In hero's journey terms, the return of Voldemort marks the moment of Harry's descent into the underworld of the most difficult trials. Vogler (1998) calls it the "approach to the inmost cave," because in the inmost cave, the hero passes into the "very center of the Hero's Journey" (p. 145). With Harry's descent, the journey (and the series) becomes darker and more deadly.

Order of the Phoenix *Examples of Green and Red*

This particular book shows us the beginning of the Second Wizarding War. Some of the red and green references are, again, more casual. Some of the references relate to elements of that war: Emmeline Vance's emerald-green shawl (p. 49); Mundungus Fletcher's "matted ginger hair," coupled with the "billowing clouds of greenish smoke" from his pipe (p. 81); the "olive-green walls" and "moss-green velvet curtains" in the drawing room of 12 Grimmauld Place (p. 101); the "large, pale toad" that is Dolores Umbridge (p. 146); Ron's Draught of Peace potion that spits green sparks (p. 233); Umbridge's "green tweed cloak that greatly enhanced her resemblance to a giant toad" (p. 414); the "green nylon pinafore" on the mannequin in the storefront that marks the entrance to St. Mungo's Hospital for Magical Maladies and Injuries (p. 483); the healers of St. Mungo's who wear "lime-green robes" (p. 484); the red headline letters across Harry's picture in his tell-all article for *The Quibbler* (p. 579), a Wizarding world publication; the "vast mossy boulder" that is Hagrid's half-brother (and giant) Grawp's head and Grawp's greenish-brown eyes (p. 693); the "enormous glass tank of deep-green water" which holds brains in the Department of Mysteries (p. 772), tucked deep inside the Ministry of Magic; the "red-gold blur" of the X Hermione uses to mark doors in the Department of Mysteries (p. 772); the jet of red light from a Stunning Spell (p. 801); the jet of green light from Avada Kedavra (p. 803); the "cool line of pale green along the horizon" signaling the dawn of the day after Sirius is killed (p. 820).

The red and green references here seem to signal opposites sides of war, with no set decision about which side is winning. Number 12 Grimmauld Place is decked out in green because it belonged to the Black family, an upstanding Slytherin family and one of the families on Voldemort's side during the First Wizarding War ("bad"). At the same time, St. Mungo's Hospital has green robes for its healers ("good"). Emmeline Vance, an Order of the Phoenix member, comes to escort Harry from the Dursley's house in a green shawl ("good"), but Dolores Umbridge, the sadistic Defense against the Dark Arts teacher in *OOP*, is referred to as a toad over and over again, and she wears green to heighten the reference ("bad").

We have another important set of green/red opposites in Mundungus Fletcher, an Order of the Phoenix member who doubles as a con man. Though he seems useful to the Order as a spy, we discover he has traitor tendencies as well as the series proceeds. Another red/green opposite is the jets of light that fly around during the battle between the Order of the Phoenix and the Death Eaters in the Department of Mysteries. Though none of them collide to produce a gold arc, their colors are still important.

Half-Blood Prince *Examples of Green and Red*

As the Second Wizarding War progresses, the green and red references continue to be important: Green Floo powder flames in the Muggle Prime Minister's office (p. 3); Cornelius Fudge's lime-green bowler (p. 4); Molly Weasley's "old green dressing gown" (p. 81); Draco Malfoy's soon-to-be-purchased robes in Madam Malkin's (p. 112); new Potions professor Horace Slughorn's "green velvet-covered belly" (p. 142); a lime-green Fanged Frisbee (p. 172); the "greenish glitter" of the cursed opal necklace (p. 250); the "unpleasantly pulsating green object" that is a Snargaluff pod (p. 280), found in a particular kind of tree stump that comes complete with "pale green worms" inside (p. 283); the "red gleam" in the young Tom Riddle's eyes (p. 436); the "crimson velvet" inside the box that contained house founder Salazar Slytherin's locket when it belonged to Hepzibah Smith (p. 437); Dumbledore's blood that opens the entrance of the cave where the Horcrux lies (a Horcrux is a vessel for part of Voldemort's soul; Voldemort has split his soul into seven pieces in order to make it harder for him to be killed) (p. 560); the greenish light from the basin of poison that contains the Horcrux (p. 560); the "coppery green chain" that tethers the green boat to the edge of the lakeshore (p. 563); the "emerald liquid" in the basin that contains the Horcrux (p. 567); the "blazing green skulls" of the Dark Mark cast over Hogwarts (p. 581); the Avada Kedavra cast by Snape that sends Dumbledore to his death (p. 596); the rubies that represent Gryffindor House points strewn all over the floor of the Great Hall (p. 601); Madame Pomfrey's "harsh-smelling green ointment" she uses to treat Bill Weasley after Fenrir Greyback's attack (p. 613).

Surprisingly, Draco Malfoy rejects his green robes a few pages later (p. 114) as he complains about Madame Malkin's treatment while they are in her store. It is possible to see this act as a rejection of the negativity of green. Given that he has been ordered by Voldemort to murder Dumbledore (though that information is not revealed until the end of the book), we can understand why Malfoy might want to reject both Voldemort and their shared Slytherin (green) heritage. And, as we learn through the book's climax, Malfoy is not up to the task of murder. In the Wizarding world, murder is another instance of green, because it is indicated by Avada Kedavra's green flash of light.

The red and green references in this book indicate danger at some level. Of this list, the only possibly non-hazardous green or red items are Molly Weasley's bathrobe and the Fanged Frisbee, which is confiscated by Hermione as she's using her prefect powers. Draco Malfoy's robes are not without danger because they belong to Malfoy, nor is Slughorn's green belly non-hazardous, because he is the one who tells Tom Riddle how to create Horcruxes. At the time he reveals that information to Riddle, Slughorn is the Head of House for Slytherin as well. The Snargaluff pods are more disgusting than dangerous, but Snargaluff pods become a weapon in the final battle for Hogwarts in *Deathly Hallows*—a weapon for Harry's side.

In fact, many of the other green objects in this list represent death — the ultimate hazard — in one way or another. We first see the opal necklace in *Chamber of Secrets*, in Borgin and Burkes with a note next to it that says "*Caution: Do Not Touch. Cursed — Has Claimed The Lives of Nineteen Muggle Owners To Date*" (p. 52). In *Half-Blood Prince*, Katie Bell is only severely injured by the necklace because she touched it with a gloved hand. We as readers also assume the poison in the basin will cause Dumbledore's death; it is no accident Rowling made the poison emerald green. As it turns out, readers are wrong about the poison. Avada Kedavra (cast by Severus Snape) causes Dumbledore's death, and the death is duly noted by the green Dark Mark above the castle, though the mark is cast before the murder happens.

In one of the book's pivotal scenes, Rowling also creates two complex red/green pairs. As we near the book's climax, Harry and Dumbledore have traveled to a remote cave in the hopes of recovering one of Voldemort's Horcruxes. For this scene, Rowling has chosen that the chain to raise and lower the green boat, the transportation to the Horcrux, will be copper. Copper is a reddish metal, and when copper ages, it gains a green patina. That color combination is useful here, because Harry's identity is completely altered by the copper chain and the green boat. This pairing is her first red/green combination of the final conflict, and this combination leads Harry to one of the most profound moments of change within the series.

Throughout *Half-Blood Prince*, Dumbledore treats Harry with adult-like respect as the pair piece together Voldemort's plan to create Horcruxes and remain immortal. However, when Harry and Dumbledore pull up the green boat with the copper chain and travel to the island where Voldemort has hidden a Horcrux, Harry takes the final step toward adulthood, though he is unaware of how pivotal the moment will be. As we discover, Harry must keep his wits about him while Dumbledore cannot, and Harry must parent his mentor as his mentor becomes child-like.

Once they arrive on the island, Dumbledore makes Harry swear to follow his earlier promise (pp. 550–551) — no matter what Dumbledore orders, Harry must do it. Harry reluctantly swears the vow again. Then, we as readers squirm as the second red/green pair is realized: Harry's and Dumbledore's (red) Gryffindor bravery is tortured by Voldemort's hideous green potion. At one point in the scene, Dumbledore is in agony, and Harry must force him forward:

> "You ... you can't stop, Professor," said Harry. "You've got to keep drinking, remember? You told me you had to keep drinking. Here...." Hating himself, repulsed by what he was doing, Harry forced the goblet back toward Dumbledore's mouth and tipped it, so that Dumbledore drank the remainder of the potion inside. (p. 571) ... "This will make it stop, Professor," Harry said, his voice cracking as he tipped the seventh glass of potion into Dumbledore's mouth [p. 572].

As the scene goes on, Dumbledore becomes more and more helpless, and Harry must continue to coax him to drink the potion, as a father might help a child take a horrible-tasting medicine. As Dumbledore moans and cries, Harry comforts him, just as a parent would: "Nothings happening to you, you're safe, it isn't real, I swear it isn't real — take this, now, take this...." (p. 572).

Harry's identity shifts in these moments. Now he is the adult, directing the man who has directed him so often over the last six years. With this scene, Harry moves from boy to man. In the course of the series, no greater identity shift happens for him.

Deathly Hallows *as the Unification of Choice and Power*

By the time a reader gets to *Deathly Hallows*, the prevalence of green and red may be apparent. At the least, a reader has noticed the red and green of Harry's and Voldemort's eyes, and how their eye color is the opposite of their house color. A reader has probably also noticed the color of Avada Kedavra and the consequences of its green flash. For the final book, Rowling creates several red and green pairs that take those initial green and red instances a step further. These new red and green combinations show us her definitive approach to choice and identity.

As we explore Rowling's constructions, we must first return to *Sorcerer's*

Stone. In a touchstone quotation from the end of the book, choice morphs into power. In the chapter "The Man With Two Faces" (the chapter name is significant for more than its description of the situation), Rowling reveals to us Voldemort's current incarnation: as a face on the back of Professor Quirrell's head. As Quirrell is explaining how he came to have Voldemort within him, he says, "A foolish young man I was then, full of ridiculous ideas about good and evil. Lord Voldemort showed me how wrong I was. There is no good and evil, there is only power, and those too weak to seek it" (*SS*, p. 291). Usually, "good" and "evil" are presented as an either/or choice. We have no other option but to select one or the other. However, Quirrell's quotation morphs the two into another entity: power. His statement shows us the binaries of good and evil are opposite side of the same coin of power, and both are equally powerful. The choice to direct that power towards good or evil is represented by Rowling's red and green color choices throughout the book.

The two-sides-one-coin option of good and evil is also represented in this chapter of *Sorcerer's Stone* by the "blood-red stone" (p. 292) Voldemort so desperately desires. Harry pulls the Sorcerer's Stone out of his pocket in the Mirror of Erised as Voldemort is trying to find where Dumbledore hid it. Later, when Dumbledore and Harry discuss the Sorcerer's Stone, Dumbledore is very clear that the stone is both good and bad: "You know the stone was really not such a wonderful thing. As much money and life as you could want! The two things most human beings would choose above all — the trouble is, humans do have a knack of choosing precisely those things that are worst for them" (p. 297).

These two examples from *Sorcerer's Stone* are brought full circle in *Deathly Hallows*. In her last Harry Potter book, Rowling unites many different objects and ideas, including her red and green examples, to end the series with one last thought about choice — no matter which side you are on, it is all the same thing. What matters is where you direct your power.

Deathly Hallows *Examples of Green and Red.* For this book, we will focus on the unifying examples of red and green rather than the smaller ones. Several times Rowling places red and green in direct contact: the "red rose with a simpering face in the middle of its petals ... strangled by a green weed with fangs and a scowl" on the front cover of a pamphlet about Mudbloods "and The Dangers They Pose to a Peaceful Pure-Blood Society" (p. 249); the red blood from Ron's Splinched arm (p. 269) and the green smoke the Essence of Dittany makes when it heals his arm ("splinching" happens when a wizard or witch Disapparates then Apparates elsewhere with a missing body part) (p. 270); the red rubies of Gryffindor's sword destroying Slytherin's emerald-encrusted locket (p. 377); the "small green shoots forcing their way up through the red earth of Dobby's grave" (p. 522); the "deep green mountains and lakes coppery in the sunset," visible as the trio rides the Gringotts dragon (p. 546); the "green into red" stare between Harry and Voldemort during their final battle (p. 738). Even though the green printing on the front of Dumbledore's horrible biography by Rita Skeeter bears mentioning (p. 252), as does the time Ron's eyes flash scarlet as he destroys the Horcrux (p. 377), as does the image of the Slytherin House-points emeralds spilled all over the Great Hall floor (p. 646, echoing the Gryffindor rubies spilled in the Great Hall In *HBP*), these larger red-green pairs deserve our focus. Here we have binaries similar to the ones in *GOF*. Ron's horribly mangled arm is bleeding red, but the healing herbal potion applied to his arm creates green smoke as well as the binary of sick/well. The red rose cowering from the green weed creates the binary of beauty/ugliness, or delicacy/coarseness. Once again, Rowling is showing us that both green and red can be "good" and "evil." But this time around, the meaning is deeper.

Discovering the true importance of these pairs relies on three things: remembering our quote from Professor Quirrell, thinking back to our color theory, and focusing on two more quotations from *Deathly Hallows*. As Harry is watching the memories Snape gave him as Snape's last gesture, Harry sees this conversation between Dumbledore and Snape. Dumbledore is speaking first:

> "Lord Voldemort's soul, maimed as it is, cannot bear close contact with a soul like Harry's. Like a tongue on frozen steel, like flesh in flame —"
> "Souls? We were talking of minds!"
> "In the case of Harry and Lord Voldemort, to speak of one is to speak of the other" [p. 685].

To speak of their minds is to speak of their souls. To extend the idea, to speak of Harry is to speak of Voldemort.

The other significant quotation comes as Harry and Dumbledore converse at King's Cross, after Harry has "died." Dumbledore is speaking first:

> "He took your blood and rebuilt his living body with it! Your blood in his veins, Harry, Lily's protection inside both of you! He tethered you to life while he lives!"
> "I live … while he lives? But I thought … I thought it was the other way round! I thought we both had to die? Or is it the same thing?" [p. 709].

These two quotations give us the proof that Rowling meant what she said in *Sorcerer's Stone* about good, evil and power. Any two-sided entity — life and death, good and evil — is really the same thing. We can focus on either side of the coin — the red earth of Dobby's grave or the green shoots coming up from it — but the coin remains a singularity. The slippery nature of "good" and "evil" remain constant if we realize that they are opposite sides of the same entity. The wandmaker Mr. Ollivander says as much when he discusses Voldemort's wand with Harry: "After all, He-Who-Must-Not-Be-Named did great things — terrible, yes, but great" (*SS*, p. 85). The destruction Voldemort created was horrific, but the ability to create such destruction has a greatness — of scale, of force — within it.

By the time we come to the end of the series, members of the House of Slytherin also reveal some binaries. At various times we are confronted with members of that house whom we could consider on the "evil" side of green,

Lord Voldemort and the Malfoys most notably. However, we also have one indeterminate member of the house that joins the series closer to its end: Horace Slughorn, a former Head of House (*HBP*, p. 70) who was partial to Tom Riddle and Regulus Black (also a known Death Eater, *HBP*, p. 70) as well as Gryffindor student Lily Evans (*HBP*, p. 70). We see Slughorn's "green velvet-covered belly" (p. 142) at the beginning of *Half-Blood Prince*, and we know he is the one to tell Tom Riddle how to create Horcruxes, as we mentioned before. But Dumbledore also trusted him enough to ask him to return to Hogwarts as the Potions master (*HBP*, p. 69, p. 74), and Rowling has created Dumbledore to be unerring in his judgment of those around him. Finally we see Slughorn in the last battle for Hogwarts in "emerald pajamas" (p. 734), fighting against his old protégé Tom Riddle, storming up the front steps of Hogwarts along with all the other friends and families who return to help Harry (p. 734). Despite Slughorn's association with "evil" green, he becomes an example of "good" green in the end.

The best example of a red/green duality within the House of Slytherin is Severus Snape, a former Death Eater who renounces Voldemort once he learns Voldemort has killed the love of his life — Lily Evans (*DH*, p. 678). At the beginning of the series, Harry is utterly convinced (as are readers) that Snape is out to make his life as miserable as possible. Snape is nothing but mean and rude to Harry. Snape even kills Dumbledore (*HBP*, p. 596) as supposedly the ultimate "proof" of his evil. But, as readers discover in *Deathly Hallows*, the larger plan was one of intense bravery, a Gryffindor trait. As we learn, Snape is so distraught by the news of Lily's death, he begs Dumbledore to do everything Dumbledore can to protect Harry (*DH*, p. 678–9). As Harry grows at Hogwarts, Snape is horrible to him because of his dislike for James. Despite his contempt for Harry and his father (and his unresolved grief for Lily), Snape's decision to care for Lily's son continues as the Second Wizarding War begins. As soon as Voldemort's return is confirmed in *Goblet of Fire*, Dumbledore dispatches Snape to Voldemort's side, and Snape's double agency begins (p. 713). Eventually, Snape sends Gryffindor's sword to Harry and Ron in the forest, so they can destroy Slytherin's locket (*DH*, p. 690). Snape's love for Lily remains so strong that, despite his dislike for Harry, in the last moments of Snape's life he asks Harry to look at him, so he may gaze into Lily's eyes one last time (*DH*, p. 658).

Snape's bravery is epitomized in the epilogue to the series. The proof is Harry's son Albus, whose middle name is Severus. When Al and Harry are discussing Al's impending meeting with the Sorting Hat, Harry remarks, "you were named for two headmasters of Hogwarts. One of them was a Slytherin and he was probably the bravest man I ever knew" (*DH*, p. 758). Even though the red of Gryffindor is never applied to Snape (with the exception of Snape's protection of Gryffindor's sword (*DH*, p. 689), Snape is as much a Gryffindor as Harry is. Dumbledore realizes this fact as well. While they are discussing Snape's possible need to return to Voldemort's side, he mentions to Snape, "You know, I sometimes think we Sort too soon..." (*DH*, p. 680).

If Harry and Voldemort are two sides of the same coin, what makes up their singularity? Many things: great talent, power, dead parents, a Muggle-born mother, "brother" wands (*SS*, p. 85), strong ambition, and choices made —for opposite sides. Despite his sad and difficult childhood, Harry chooses to embrace the good in the world. Voldemort's childhood in the orphanage drives him to see the world as a negative place. The Sorting Hat could have chosen to place Tom Riddle in Gryffindor for his bravery in surviving the orphanage. The Hat could have placed Harry in Slytherin for his ambition to be great. Each could be the other, except for his choices. Harry and Voldemort, in their similar backgrounds and their green/red eyes combined with their red/green houses, create a singularity, a singularity neutralized by its opposite side. Red and green combined, after all, create gray.

CONCLUSIONS

Harry's identity is shaped by choice in every book. Each time he chooses to trust (or not) an individual, a situation, or his own intuition, he is making decisions about who he is and what he stands for. According to Abrahams (2003), "*Identity* has become the encompassing term for cultural, social, and spiritual wholeness" (p. 198). How do humans make themselves whole? No one can say, but we can presume, we make choices toward wholeness every day, just as Harry does, though *our* wholeness probably does not include defeating the dark wizard who killed our parents. Even if we do not know whether our choices are "good," "evil," or even heroic, we can say we are choosing *something* every moment of every day. Our entire identity is a matter of choice, and J.K. Rowling's Harry Potter series is one long meditation on the power of our choices.

As Varner (2007) indicates, myth is a product of the unconscious mind, "a mind that stretches between cultures, times, and geographic locations" (p. 1). Just as the Green Knight was a product of the late fourteenth century, Harry is a product of the late twentieth century, and both carry the concerns of their times. However, both myths unite as they employ a color as a guiding feature, and the universality of the hero's journey is moved to new heights by incorporating colors as guideposts within it.

As we have noted elsewhere in the chapter, Harry's choice to trust a red or green object shapes his journey as he grows from boy to man and moves more clearly into his hero's identity. Rowling's use of color is a useful and easily identifiable way to "deepen" the meaning of the object, and because Rowling only gives colors to objects that are truly important in Harry's world, green and red remain significant throughout the story. Mrs. Weasley is important to Harry as his stand-in mother and mother of his best friend, but her green dressing gown (*HBP*) signals a commitment to Harry and his cause, because she helps in the fight against Voldemort as well as welcoming Harry into her family. In the case of Fawkes, Dumbledore's crimson phoenix, his significance is deepened by his red color as well as his attachment to the red that symbolizes Godric Gryffindor's bravery. Fawkes is the one who brings Harry the Sorting Hat, and Gryffindor's sword within the hat, which Harry uses to slay the basilisk. Fawkes's bravery in helping Harry fight the basilisk adds to Harry's bravery. Mrs. Weasley and Fawkes would still be important to the series as a whole, but their colors mark them as significant catalysts in Harry's growth.

As well, the two colors give us an easily tracked pattern for readers to identify significant information within the texts. If we encounter a green or red object, we can speculate how it relates to the entire story: does the object (or what it represents) foster Harry's growth? Does the object stand in his way? How does the object shape Harry's journey? Rowling has left us, in essence, colored clues to understanding the meta-messages of the myth, starting with Harry's green and Voldemort's red eyes.

Varner (2007) notes that the Estonian word for "fairy" (*vo_o*) translates as "green," but also "sacred," "holy," "evil," and "anger" (p. 56). If the word "green" can contain so many linguistic possibilities, the color as a symbol can contain just as many ideas, and Rowling has capitalized on this opportunity. Varner also claims that "green is symbolic of both life and death" (p. 56), opposite sides of the same coin of existence. The Harry Potter series is consistent with this idea as well. Rowling has done a masterful job at creating a new set of myths that develop both characters and conflicts using color as tools to understand the mythology. Zdybiewska (2004) agrees with our idea:

> Is the Harry Potter series a new myth? The answer is yes. The myth that will help the new generation of young readers understand ancient riddles of life. It will also enable them to escape unpleasant, scary everyday reality.... Harry Potter is not an ordinary boy because the power of his imagination will enable him to believe in himself and win the battle for a better life. The moral of the tale is that the most important magic comes from inside of each of us [¶ 9].

If the job of myth is to help us understand the world's possibilities, and how the magic inside of us shapes our experiences, Rowling shows us a new path (both literally and figuratively a magical journey) toward understanding the human adventure of growing up.

To echo Dumbledore, it is our choices that make us who we are. Had your authors not chosen to pick up *Harry Potter and the Sorcerer's Stone*, we could not celebrate the joy of Harry and his adventures with other fans. We definitely would not have noticed Rowling's uses of red and green, and we could not have written this chapter. In deciding whether or not to accompany Harry on his hero's journey, we are sure we chose correctly.

NOTES

1. Kirstin Cronn-Mills: *Harry Potter and the Sorcerer's Stone* was published in the United States in the fall of 1998, and I missed it. Completely. I had a brand new baby and was spending all my time learning to be a mom. I finally met Harry in the spring of 2003, and I devoured the first four books in less than two weeks. Then I joined the impatient hoard waiting for *Harry Potter and the Order of the Phoenix* to come out in June of that year. After I had fallen for Harry, I convinced my dean (I teach at a small two-year community and tech college) to let me begin teaching a special topics literature class. In the summer of 2004, the first ENGL 201: Mythos of Harry Potter class was launched. That class has expanded to include all seven books (approximately 4200 hardcover pages in one semester — not advisable for the faint-hearted). One semester is never enough time to spend on the series (films are not included because of time), but it still provides an introduction to the literary version of the Harry Potter phenomenon for fans as well as the uninitiated. About fifty percent of the students come to the first class meeting with all the texts read (of course!). The other fifty percent manage to finish most of the books. I am proud to report that no student has ever told me they hate Harry by the end of the class. In fact, most students are completely in love with him by the time they write their final exam."

2. Jessica Samens: I was not a Harry Potter fan. In fact, there was nothing in life I could guarantee I disliked more than Harry Potter. For years, my friends and classmates had been telling me I would be in love with the story after the first few pages. I had no desire to immerse myself in a world where witches and wizards were real and fantasy becomes reality. However, in an attempt to avoid working on my thesis in graduate school, I came across *Harry Potter and the Sorcerer's Stone* on television. As a true procrastinator, I chose to spend a few minutes watching the movie, hoping to prove to myself that my dislike of Harry Potter was justified. Two hours later, I was on my way to a local bookstore to purchase the first book. After reading the first five books within a week, I was hooked. My fellow fans helped foster this need, from having book discussions to taking Kirstin's Harry Potter course. A couple months later, *Harry Potter and the Half-Blood Prince* made its debut, which opened up a whole new world of Harry Potter for me. The chance to experience the sixth book's release with other fans helped me understand the significance and influence this book had on its readers. It was finally apparent to me what my friends had been saying all along.

REFERENCES

Abrahams, B. (2003). Identity. In B. Feintuch (Ed), *Eight words for the study of expressive culture* (pp. 198–222). Urbana: University of Illinois Press.

Andrea, H. (2009). Emerald eyes? Request from Hans Andrea. In *The Hogwarts professor*. Retrieved 21 April 2009 from http://hogwartsprofessor.com/?p=832

Benson, L. (1965). *Art and tradition in Sir Gawain and the Green Knight* (pp. 56–109). New Brunswick, NJ: Rutgers University Press.

Bernardin, M., Collis, C., Jensen, J., Nashawaty, C., Rottenberg, J., Schwartz, M., Snierson, D., Spines, C., Svetkey, B., Tucker, K., & Vary, A. B. (2009, April 3). The top 20 heroes. *Entertainment Weekly, 1041,* 25–28.

Boggs, J., & Petrie, D.W. (2004). *The art of watching films.* (6th ed.). McGraw-Hill.

Campbell, J. (1968). *The hero with a thousand faces* (2nd ed.). Bollengen Series XVII. Princeton, NJ: Princeton University Press.

Campbell, J., & Moyers, B. (1988). *The power of myth.* New York: Doubleday.

CBBC. Read the full J. K. Rowling interview. July 18 2005. In *CBBC News Round.* Retrieved 17 April 2009 from http://news.bbc.co.uk/cbbcnews/hi/newsid_4690000/newsid_4690800/4690885.stm

Cicero, C., & Cicero, S. T. (1995). *Self-initiation into the golden dawn tradition: a complete curriculum of study for both the solitary magician and the working magical group.* Woodbury, MN: Llewellyn Worldwide.

Doty, W. G. (1996). Myth. In T. Enos (Ed.), *Encyclopedia of rhetoric and composition: communication from ancient times to the information age* (pp. 449–452). New York: Garland Publishing.

Gardiner, S., & Robinson, D. Why are red and green the colors of Christmas. (2004–2008). In *Christmas light source.* Retrieved 2 May 2009 from https://www.christmas-light-source.com/Why-are-Red-and-Green-the-Colors-of-Christmas_ep_52-1.html

Jensen, J. (2009, April 3). Heroes & villains. *Entertainment Weekly, 1041,* 31–33.

Lavoie, C. (2003). Safe as houses: sorting and school houses at Hogwarts. In G. Anatol (Ed.), *Reading Harry Potter: critical essays* (pp. 35–49). Westport, CT: Praeger.

National Endowment for the Humanities. Symmetry in Sir Gawain and the Green Knight. In *Edsitement.* Retrieved 23 April 2009 from http://edsitement.neh.gov/view_lesson_plan.asp?id=601

Parker, J., Mills, A., & Stanton, J. (2007). *Mythology: myths, legends, and fantasies* (pp. 270–278). Capetown: Stuik.

Patterson, B. (2005). The mystery of the green man. In *The green men of Coventry.* Retrieved 21 April 2009 from http://www.birch.streamlinetrial.co.uk/greenmen/story.html

Rowling, J. K. (1998). *Harry Potter and the sorcerer's stone.* New York: Scholastic.

_____. (1999). *Harry Potter and the chamber of secrets.* New York: Scholastic.

_____. (1999). *Harry Potter and the prisoner of Azkaban.* New York: Scholastic.

_____. (2000). *Harry Potter and the goblet of fire.* New York: Scholastic.

_____. (2003). *Harry Potter and the order of the phoenix.* New York: Scholastic.

_____. (2005). *Harry Potter and the half-blood prince.* New York: Scholastic.

_____. (2007). *Harry Potter and the deathly hallows.* New York: Scholastic.

Sir Gawaine and the Green Knight. In M. Fulstone (Ed.), *Sir Gawaine (Gwalchmai).* Retrieved 21 April 2009 from http://glenavalon.com/gawaingreenknight01.html

Eco, U. (Ed.). (2004). *History of beauty.* (A. McEwen, Trans). New York: Rizzoli.

Varner, G.R. (2007). *Creatures in the mist: little people, wild men, and spirit beings around the world. A study in comparative mythology.* New York: Algora.

Vogler, C. (1998). *The writer's journey: mythic structure for writers* (2nd ed.). Studio City, CA: Michael Wiese Productions.

Zdybiewska, M. (2004). Harry Potter—a new myth. In *British study web pages: myths, legends, fantasy....* Retrieved 2 May 2009 from http://elt.britcoun.org.pl/elt/b_hpmyth.htm.

2

The Complexity of Evil in Modern Mythology: The Evolution of the Wicked Witch of the West

JASON EDWARDS *and* BRIAN KLOSA

There are many moments which a parent eagerly awaits for in their children's lives. One of these moments is the costume their child will playfully select for Trick or Treat during Halloween. The vision of a smiling youngster in a cute costume running from house to house in the elusive search for mountains of candy is one of the joyful perks of having kids. Little did we know that a Halloween costume would serve as an appropriate opening anecdote for this chapter.

For Halloween 2007, Brian's daughter Megan, dressed up as a witch. Her outfit was complete with green face paint, a black pointed hat, and even a hand held green tinseled broom. However, this energetic three-year old was quick to gleefully announce to the world that she was not a witch, but was in fact dressed as Elphaba, otherwise known as the iconic Wicked Witch of the West from *The Wizard of Oz*. Certainly, this declaration would not come as a surprise to the many people that know Brian. He and his wife Aimee have avidly introduced their daughter to the award-winning Broadway musical *Wicked* by having her read books on the star character and spending countless hours in mini-vans singing the popular songs of the show such as "The Wizard and I," "Popular," and "Defying Gravity." However, upon further reflection Megan's fascination and love of Elphaba pointed to a larger conundrum. The authors of this chapter can remember when the Wicked Witch of the West scared us to death as children. She is consistently rated one of the most frightening villains in the history of literature, film, and television. For example, the American Film Institute ranked the Wicked Witch of the West as the fourth scariest film character on their 100 Heroes and Villains list. Thus, it begs the question of how can we account for this reinvention of the Wicked Witch of the West?

The answer to that question is our larger inquiry in this chapter. The Wicked Witch of the West is part of the fantasy story of Oz that many have become familiar with over the years. Inevitably, stories of fantasy, like their science fiction counterparts, are structured and embedded with mythic imagery. These fantasy narratives often have clear dichotomies of good and evil, light and dark, black and white, right and wrong. There are lucid heroes and villains, along with bit characters. These mythic fantasy narratives serve to simplify the world around us and demonstrate who is undoubtedly good and clearly evil. When analyzing these narratives, scholars primarily focus on the heroes and their (re) enactment within the narrative. For example, Cochran and Edwards (2008) demonstrate how the television show *Buffy the Vampire Slayer* revises both the myth of the hero's quest and how that hero is (re)cast.

Yet heroes are not the only important characters within fantasy texts. Villains— those that are evil — are just as important to any fantasy storyline. Cole (2006) asserted that evil is a central concept within mythic narratives. He explained, "each time we describe someone as evil we are placing them within a mythological narrative, giving them a special role to play in human history. Evil, in this sense, is the grandest of all narratives" (p. 19). Without Satan there is no real Christian narrative. Without evil villains such as The Joker and Penguin, there is no Batman. Without Deceptions there are no Autobots. Without Cobra there is no G.I. Joe. Hence, evil is a necessity within mythic story arcs.

Conversely, modern fantasy texts offer greater complexity as to what constitutes evil. Returning to the *Buffy* example, we find in the early seasons of *Buffy* that she fights vampires, demons, and the like with reckless abandon. These creatures are presented as nothing more than one-dimensional foils to her larger goal of destroying that season's "Big Bad." As the series progressed, however, the idea of evil becomes more multifaceted. More and more we come to find that vampires and demons have a world of their own, unseen to "normal" humanity, where they have businesses and perform services. The vampires Angel and Spike become allies (and lovers) of Buffy, as she and her friends battle larger demonic forces. As the Buffy example illustrates, the clear-cut evil character of the myths of old are being recast into more composite and complicated characters of present. In turn, this added complexity redefines the story arcs of modern fantasy texts.

Our examination is indicative of how modern fantasy texts are complicating the notion of evil. Modern texts often challenge audiences by shifting the narrative format found in traditional fantasy stories. While the good vs. evil motif still exists, it is often altered. The nature of the protagonist and antagonist is completely changed if not reversed. Basically, what was once considered evil is now good and what was once good turns to evil.

In this chapter, we turn to how the Wicked Witch of the West also serves to offer a many-sided view of the myth of evil. As our opening anecdote suggests, the Wicked Witch of the West is no longer the malevolent character she once was. Her archetype as the personification of evil was originally planted within L. Frank Baum's *The Wonderful Wizard of Oz (1900)*, but escalated with the movie *The Wizard of Oz (1939)*. Seventy years later, Geoffrey Maguire's book *Wicked (1995)* and the subsequent hit musical have altered the Land of Oz by changing some familiar characters (i.e. the Wizard) and introducing a more ambiguously evil, if not sympathetic and even heroic Wicked Witch of the West. This results in a broader spectrum of images to see this iconic character. This continuum not only presents a more comprehensive fantasy narrative of Oz, but a more multifaceted and complicated image of the Witch.

Exploring the complexity of evil as it appears in the character development of the Wicked Witch of the West offers the opportunity to see how myths are being redefined. This redefinition is important because it is reflective of the more complex world in which we live. While President George W. Bush would have liked us to believe in a simple world of good vs. evil (i.e. you are either with us or against us), the reality will always be that what is and is not evil cannot be as cut and dry as they would appear. Modern fantasy texts reflect this complexity and by examining an instance of how these texts complicate the idea of evil, we come to understand that these more modern narratives perform a similar function as the older stories. They help us to comprehend the world around us and, because of that, continue to perform their timeless task.

To that end, we begin with a basic theoretical discussion of myth and evil's place within it. Then we analyze how the image of the Wicked Witch of the West has changed over the years. We focus on L. Frank Baum's original conception of the Wicked Witch of the West and how the movie cemented her role as the epitome of evil. Then we consider Geoffrey Maguire's book and the impact of the musical. Finally, we end with some conclusions regarding evil, myth, and fantasy.

UNDERSTANDING MYTH AND EVIL

Myth is a common form of discourse. In fact, Campbell (1949/2008) argues that some myths and their functions cut across all cultures and societies. At their most basic level, myths are narratives that contain a plotline with characters that constitute heroes, villains, and bystanders. Yet not all narratives are myths. A narrative of the happenings of one's day, for example, is not mythic in nature because myths involve stories that are engrained in the specific political and social culture of a particular society, stories that articulate the society's beliefs, dilemmas, and values (Rushing and Frentz, 2005). Myths, then, offer us a way to frame the reality of our situation. When we humans use them, our myths function in a variety of ways.

For our discussion here, the most important function of myths is that they provide people a way of knowing and living our contemporary experience (Nimmo and Combs, 1980). Often these stories, such as the frontier myth, the myth of the American dream, and the myth of the hero's quest are adapted and recast to meet present circumstances. At times, both individuals and communities are struck by some form of disorder: a natural disaster, an attack by another nation, a specific illness, a downturn in the economy, or any other disturbance to the regularity of life. It is then when myths develop or are invoked to offer a means of coping. The overall story, the characters, and the lessons that can be derived from the myth offer a vocabulary to simplify and comprehend the world around us. The world is often too complicated to grasp — too much information, too many people, too many countries, simply too many factors to manage all at once. Myths give our world structure so that individually and collectively we can better realize the opportunities available to us, the challenges that may pose a threat to our success, and the limitations within which we must work to accomplish an objective.

Within all mythic narratives there are a variety of characters involved. There are heroes, sidekicks, bit characters, and ultimately villains. As we noted earlier, most readings of myth tend to focus on the protagonist and his/her growth throughout the mythic journey. However, the villain and his/her evil nature is just as important as the heroic triumph that seem to inevitably come with most fantasy narratives (Cole, 2006). Evil, and the characters that embody it, are portrayed as having a number of different characteristics. Jewett and Lawrence (2002, 2004) note that evil is a cosmic counterforce that must be stopped by good. Within many fantasy story arcs there is a clear polarity between good and evil. There is no compromise. There is no neutrality. Villains are portrayed as having vast and cunning powers, where they use that power for their own wicked ends. Many of these evil characters are selfish, have no concern for others, and will use any means necessary to achieve their goals.

These characters are manifest in a number of areas. Perhaps, most prominently, in political discourse, particularly in justifications for sending American forces into combat. One of the strategies used by rhetors, particularly American presidents, is the articulation of the myth of American Exceptionalism, also termed the myth of mission (Bostdorff, 1994; Edwards, 2008). The use of the mission myth creates an us versus them dichotomy within political rhetoric. The president casts American actions as defensive, rational, and conducted for the protection of others. The United States is out to defend freedom, democracy, and lives of innocents. By contrast, he characterizes the United States' adversary as a diabolical savage that is out to harm America and its allies. The actions of this enemy deserve nothing but revulsion from any rational actor (Ivie, 1980, 2004). Actions that would generate such as response could be, but not limited to: driving families from their homes, destroying property incessantly, and engaging in concerted campaigns of rape, torture, and murder. This discourse serves to rhetorically strip them of any humanity they may have, while revealing they are the epitome of evil. It is a classic construction that is oft repeated in American history and can still be found in the discourse surrounding the current conflicts in Iraq and Afghanistan.

Popular culture is also a prominent space for constructing the nature of evil. For example, Baumeister (1999) argued that popular culture (books, television, and movies), similar to presidential discourse, have heightened the dualities between good and evil. Cartoons, according to Baumeister, have replaced fairy tales and stories for teaching children about the world. Cartoons, such as *Transformers* and *G.I Joe* portray stark and simple battles between good and evil. Within these shows, villains are portrayed as outsiders who are trying to generate chaos against those that stand for order and peace. These villains inflict deliberate harm on innocents and take pleasure from that harm. Evil is conducted for evil's sake. Jewett and Lawrence (1977, 2004) support this basic argument. They argue that U.S. popular culture, at least through the 1980s, follows a singular American monomyth. That storyline looks something like this: A community is a harmonious paradise that is threatened by evil. The dastardly villains carry out a campaign of terror that cannot be stopped by normal institutions. Out of this threat a selfless hero appears to aid the community. With the help of others and fate, the hero is able to defeat the diabolical enemy and restore harmony to paradise. Ultimately, however, popular culture often relies and portrays evil in stark dualities that should be clear to viewers.

These sources yield basic guidelines when attempting to define and recognize evil and myth. Specifically, within a myth's story arc there is a constructed cosmology between good and evil. The story often provides a lucid, if not simplistic, view of who is in the right and who is in the wrong. This dichotomy becomes more apparent when one defines the basic characteristics of the villains within the story. Evil characters are constructed as one-dimensional. There is no depth to their experience. Their purpose is self-preservation, self-interest, and wicked in nature. They are easily recognized based on wanton acts of cruelty they perform without regard to whom their victims are.

The Wicked Witch of the West, as she was originally presented, upholds these basic characteristics, as we will demonstrate. However, the later manifestations of that character in Maguire's (1995) text and the subsequent musical present a multifaceted, perhaps more realistic, view concerning the nature of evil in myth. In doing so, this complexity may help some to better understand the multifaceted world we inhabit.

CONSTRUCTING THE WICKED WITCH
OF THE WEST AS EVIL

We begin our examination of the Wicked Witch of the West by comparing her original conception in L. Frank Baum's (1900) book *The Wonderful Wizard of Oz* and the 1939 film *The Wizard of Oz*. In Baum's book, the seeds of the Witch's evil nature are laid, but they are not clearly developed. It is the film that constructs her as the epitome of iniquity. Specifically, we compare Baum's work and *The Wizard of Oz* around four critical differences that we argue demarcate the evil nature of the Witch and cause her evil "stock" to rise. First, is the amount of initial interaction between Dorothy and the Witch. Second, is the Witch's motive for obtaining the magical slippers. The third is how Dorothy is treated when she is a prisoner of the Witch. The final difference is how the Witch is killed.

The first element that demarcates the Witch's evil to rise is the amount of time that the hero and villain interact. Within most fantasy story arcs, the hero and villain must interrelate for the plot to surface, develop and reach its ultimate conclusion. In Baum's book (1900/1995), however, there is little contact between hero and villain. The Witch is only mentioned twice in random passing by other minor characters and Dorothy and the Witch only meet in one confrontation. Baum clearly demarcates the Witch as evil, but there is no specific detail to describe her evil nature. By contrast, *The Wizard of Oz* (Fleming, 1939) clearly demonstrates the Wicked Witch of the West's evil nature through her interactions with Dorothy. Initially, she torments and terrorizes the character by demanding answers about the death of her sister. When the Witch appears, she shouts at Dorothy:

> Who killed my sister? Who killed the Witch of the East? Was it you? Answer Me!
> Glinda: Leave her alone!
> Witch: You stay out of this. I'm here for vengeance! So it was you, was it? You killed her ... didn't you?
> Dorothy: No-no! It was accident! I didn't mean to kill anybody ... really I didn't it!
> Witch: Didn't mean it, eh? Accident, eh? Well, my little pretty, I can cause accidents, too—and this is how I do it! ...

Then after an unsuccessful attempt at getting the ruby slippers, the Witch tells Dorothy:

> Very well—I'll bide my time—and as for your fine lady, it's true, I can't attend to you here, but just try to stay out of my way, just try. I'll get you my pretty, and your little dog, too!

Moreover, when Dorothy and the Scarecrow save the Tin Man, the Witch reappears on the yellow brick road. She threatens them by stating she will stuff a mattress with the Scarecrow and make a beehive out of the Tin Man. Then she proceeds to accost the Scarecrow by throwing a ball of fire at him and setting him on fire. Finally, she appears over the Emerald City as she terrorizes and commands "Surrender Dorothy." None of these scenes appear in the Baum book. These confrontations suggest the Witch is obsessed with capturing and killing Dorothy to fulfill her own selfish desires. As a result, we can clearly see who is good and who is wicked.

A second element that constructs the Witch as evil is the motivation for obtaining the magical talisman of the shoes/slippers. In the Baum book, the Witch is clearly aware of the power of the silver shoes (ruby slippers in the movie). She is the leader of a group of people called the Winkies in the western part of Oz, but the source of her power, the flying monkey golden cap, has been exhausted. In order to preserve her power, the Witch desires to replace that power with the power of the shoes. But in the book there is no clear indication that she desires to see harm come to Dorothy. The Witch does verbally threaten to beat Dorothy but she never follows through with her scheme. Instead, she attempts to trick Dorothy into gaining possession of the silver shoes. Thus, in Baum's book, there is a rationale for the Witch to go after Dorothy. In the film, the Witch desires the ruby slippers, but only wants them for her own sake. Her motivation appears to be nothing more than naked power. In order to obtain those slippers, the Witch attempts a number of diabolical actions by attacking Dorothy and her companions, putting her to sleep (and in all probability killing her) with magic potions, and locking her up and attempting murder to receive the boon. The Witch goes to great lengths to achieve her goal. Her motivations and actions give her the appearance as incarnate evil. There is no attempt to rationalize her behavior. She is merely selfish and one dimensional. She commits wanton acts of destruction and will harm innocents no matter the cost. The combination of her attempts to do harm to Dorothy, along with Dorothy's noble quest to return home, only serve to reinforce her appearance as a malevolent entity.

A third element of evil is the treatment that Dorothy receives as a prisoner of the Wicked Witch of the West. In both the book and the film, Dorothy is captured by flying monkeys. However, in Baum's book, Dorothy is made to do manual labor. She cleans pots, scrubs floors, and is treated as a menial servant. Although she is mistreated, her life is never portrayed as in danger. By contrast, the film treatment of Dorothy as a prisoner reinforces the one dimensional evil nature of the Wicked Witch of the West. Dorothy is locked into a room by herself. In one of the most terrifying scenes from the film, the Witch turns over an hourglass filled with red sand, telling her:

> You've been more trouble to me than you're worth, one way or another — but it'll soon be over now!

The Witch picks up an hour glass— turns it over — speaks:

> Do you see that? That's how much longer you've got to be alive! And it isn't that long, my pretty. It isn't long!

A clearly petrified Dorothy is crying and desperate for help. In her state, Dorothy sees the image of her Auntie Em. Auntie Em shouts:

Dorothy, Dorothy, where are you? It's me — it's Auntie Em. We're trying to find you. Where are you?

Dorothy replies and pleads with her to rescue her:

I — I'm here in Oz, Auntie Em. I'm locked in the Witch's Castle and I'm trying to get home to you, Auntie Em. Oh, Auntie Em, don't go away! I'm frightened! Come back! Come back!

Then the Witch appears cackling:

Auntie Em — Auntie Em — come back! I'll give you Auntie Em, my pretty!

In this short scene, the Witch's attempted murder, along with the psychological torture and taunting of her meek and innocent victim crystallizes her evil nature because it gives the appearance of a menacing, heartless entity. The only conclusion that can be drawn from this particular scene is the Witch is the epitome of evil.

A final component that causes the Witch's evil "stock" to rise is her death scene. In both the Baum book and the 1939 film the Wicked Witch is killed by Dorothy throwing a bucket of water on her. In the book, the fatal scene occurs in a kitchen. In an attempt to obtain the silver slippers, the Witch creates an invisible bar which Dorothy trips over and one of the shoes falls off. In a rage over the loss of her shoe, Dorothy picks up a bucket of water and throws it at her captor. Here, Dorothy's motive is embarrassment and vengeance, not an attempt to save the life of her companion, Scarecrow; whereas, in the film, the Witch's demise is brought about by Dorothy's desire to undue evil actions. After a chase scene through her castle, Dorothy, the Cowardly Lion, Scarecrow, and Tin Man, are trapped by the Witch and her troops. In a menacing fashion, the Witch seeks to torment them further. She states:

Well — ring around the rosy — a pocket full of spears! Thought you'd be pretty foxy didn't you? We'll I'm going to start in on you right here — one after the other! And the last to go will see the first three go before her! And your mangy little dog too!

Here, the Witch raises her broomstick to a candelabra, lights the straw on fire, and directs it toward the Scarecrow, shouting:

How about a little fire, Scarecrow?

The Scarecrow is on fire, shouting:

Help! I'm burning! I'm burning! I'm burning! Help! Help!

To save her friend, Dorothy picks up the bucket of water, douses the flame, but ends up killing the Wicked Witch of the West. The dichotomy between Dorothy and the Witch is clear. Similar to a president's portrayal of American actions in war, Dorothy's actions are not done out of malice, but defending the life of a fellow friend. Clearly, she represents good. In contrast, the Witch clearly wanted to harm innocent lives. By attacking innocents, the Witch is stripped of any hint of humanity. No rational, civilized person would attack others without some good reason. The only conclusion one can reach is that the film version of the Wicked Witch of the West is a representative of evil.

These differences between the book and the film clearly suggest that Witch is reduced to nothing but her "Wicked" nature. In the Baum book, the Witch is only a minor character. She appears in two quick references and in only one chapter in the entire book. Her appearances do not lend themselves to the development of a grand plot of good versus evil. Rather, the focus of his book is more on the exploration of the Land of Oz and following our heroes on their travels through this colorful and picturesque place. Moreover, when Baum does describe the Wicked Witch within the narrative, he does not offer a clearly definable villain. Baum offers explanations for the Witch's behavior, serving to rationalize her actions. She is the ruler of a land. She wants to maintain her position of her power. There is no clear indication for the wanton destruction of innocents for innocent's sake. Based on this idea, one must question if the Witch, as portrayed in the Baum book, is evil. People are scared of her. She does subjugate her people. When she sees Dorothy and her small group coming into her land she does send three waves of animals to try to rid her lands of them. However, the Witch simply views these visitors as a hostile threat. She is defending her territory. While not angelic, her actions can be justified. She dies because a child has a tantrum. One cannot excuse the behavior of the Witch for tricking Dorothy but then again Dorothy is not presented in a clear, heroic fashion. None of these actions suggest evil in the sense that the conveyor of a mythic text would expect evil to emerge.

In the film, the Wicked Witch of the West is clearly a major character. Hero and villain are on screen together a number of times and when their images are juxtaposed against one another the struggle between good and evil is clearly developed and focused. Moreover, in the film version of Oz, the Witch displays the one dimensional all encompassing nature of evil. Without question, the intense visual images of the Witch in the 1939 film combined with the plot variations have cemented her image as one of the most evil characters in any mythical text. She is ugly with green skin, a cackling voice, and intemperate demeanor. She is obsessive in obtaining her desires and uses her powers (conjuring fire, flying on broomstick, magically appearing out thin air, and growing deadly poppies) for evil. Just about everyone in the film (and the two authors growing up) are afraid of her. Generations of Americans have viewed the film and have been scared by those images for she is portrayed as a heartless killer, who terrorizes and torments her victims. Thus, one can only come to one conclusion: she is evil.

COMPLICATING THE WICKED WITCH OF THE WEST

As we have seen from the previous section, the movie adaptation of

Baum's book presents a simple and clear myth of good and evil. Dorothy and her companions are portrayed as innocent, loyal, and courageous. The Wizard represents a man who is a bumbler and a fool, but tries to do good for his subjects and fulfill the wishes of the Cowardly Lion, Scarecrow, Tin Man, and Dorothy. The Wicked Witch of the West is presented as a one-dimensional character, who is malicious, frightening, and has no regard for others. She commits wanton acts of cruelty and attempts murder against innocents for her own selfish designs (to obtain the silver shoes/ruby slippers). Her selfish acts of destruction reveal her evil character.

By contrast Gregory Maguire's (1995) book *Wicked* and the musical adapted from it obscure the myth of evil. Creating this complexity in the Wicked Witch of the West appears to have been an active goal behind Maguire's writing. In a variety of interviews, Maguire has stated that he was inspired to reconsider the nature of evil when he saw how politicians were portraying Saddam Hussein during the first Gulf War. He stated that experience got him "interested in the nature of evil, and whether one really could be born bad ... when I realized that nobody had ever written about the second most evil character in our collective American subconscious, the Wicked Witch of the West, I thought I had experienced a small moment of inspiration" (*Wicked the Musical* in London, 2006, ¶ 8).

Before we specify how this "inspiration" modifies typical conventions of evil, we want to provide the reader a bit of the plot and character description to help them contextualize our findings. The book itself contains five sections, all of which sequentially track the trajectory of the life of the Wicked Witch of the West. In the first part of the book, Maguire reveals that the Witch's real name is Elphaba. Like her film counterpart, she is green but we discover that it is because of a skin disorder. Elphaba, born and raised in Munchkinland, is raised primarily by father, Frex — her mother died while giving birth to her sister — comes to have an extremely rough childhood. She is neglected, mocked by those around her for appearance, and her father favors her sister, Nessarose. Yet, this experience appears to make Elphaba only stronger. She becomes a defender of her homeland, extremely patriotic, and a critic of how the Wizard of Oz is subjugating his fellow countrymen.

As the novel progresses, Elphaba attends Shiz University in Emerald City. It is here that she meets many of the main characters of the novel. Elphaba becomes the roommate of Galinda (later Glinda) — who is from a privileged and charmed family. These two, although opposite in every way, come to form a strong friendship. Here, she becomes friends with Boq (later the TinMan), Fiyero (eventually her lover), and Dr. Dillamond — who is a talking goat (an Animal), a professor at Shiz, and a mentor to Elphaba.[1] It is also at Shiz where Elphaba becomes an activist and protector of others. She advocates on behalf of others who are weaker than her and works with Dr. Dillamond to prove that there is no difference between human beings and Animals. When Dillamond is murdered, presumably by Madame Morrible — headmistress at Shiz and a close associate of the Wizard — Elphaba becomes hardened in her political views and ramps up her political activity.

Over the next three parts, Maguire chronicles Elphaba's growth into the "evil" witch. A few years after leaving Shiz University, Elphaba has become an active part of the movement that seeks to free the Animals and overthrow the Wizard. It is here where she reunites with Fiyero. Although Fiyero is married to Sarima, Elphaba and Fiyero engage in a short, passionate, and ultimately tragic love affair. During their affair, Elphaba finally has the opportunity to fulfill her task in the movement: kill Madame Morrible. However, her plan is thwarted by a group of children interfering with her ability to fire. Fiyero, who had followed Elphaba, proceeds to go back to their apartment. It is here where he is kidnapped by the Wizard's secret police and subsequently murdered. Upon learning the news, Elphaba becomes mute from grief and enters a nunnery.

A few years after Elphaba enters a nunnery, she travels to the Vinkus, meeting Fiyero's wife and children (Irji, Manek, and Nor). Elphaba is also traveling with a boy, Liir, whom she claims is no relation. Over the next year and a half, Elphaba, Liir, and later Nanny stay at the castle Kiamo Ko with Sarima, her sisters, and her children, becoming an unexpected familial unit. Elphaba tries to tell Sarima about the affair, seeking her forgiveness, but Sarima refuses to talk about her husband. Eventually, Elphaba is called away from the Vinkus by her father, who has asked Elphaba to return to Munckinland to talk with her sister about her leadership of Munchkinland. After settling things with her father and Nessarose, Elphaba returns to find that the Vinkus has been invaded by the Wizard's soldiers and that Sarima, her sisters, and her children are gone, presumably captured and murdered.

In the final part of the book, we are told that a storm has visited Munchkinland, which dropped a house upon Nessarose that killed her. The house contained a young girl named Dorothy and her dog Toto. After her sister's funeral, Elphaba learns that Glinda had sent Dorothy to the Wizard, presumably so he could send her back to Kansas. Elphaba also learns that Glinda has given Dorothy her sister's silver shoes, which were promised to her by her father. On her way back to the Vinkus, Elphaba stops at Shiz University to finally finish her task of killing Madame Morrible. However, she arrives too late because the old headmistress has passed away. Elphaba returns to Kiamo Ko and learns that Dorothy has been sent by the Wizard and her friends to kill her. When Dorothy arrives at the castle, after several trials and tribulations, she tells Elphaba that the Wizard did send her to kill her, but that she wanted to apologize to the Witch for killing her sister. Elphaba becomes furious; waving her burning broom around and accidentally sets herself on fire. Seeing this, Dorothy tries to put out the fire with a bucket of water, but the water ends up killing Elphaba. Dorothy returns to the Wizard with evidence of Elphaba's demise, presumably returning to Kansas.

Now that we have a brief summary to the text, we turn to how this book reworks the classic story of good and evil within the Land of Oz. It does so in two ways. First, Maguire's (1995) construction of evil is tenuous and ambiguous. One particular conversation that Elphaba has with other characters is representative of this definition. The dialogue occurs when Elphaba traveled to Shiz to confront and kill Madame Morrible for her horrible actions. Finding Madame Morrible dead, Elphaba makes it appear as if she has been murdered and admit her "crime" to someone who will immediately tell the authorities. Ultimately, she confesses to her old schoolmate, Avaric. After a brief conversation, Avaric invites her to stay for dinner. It is during dinner, despite the objections of Avaric's wife, that the talk turns to the subject of evil. Avaric and his guests all put forth a number of different suggestions for what constitutes wickedness. Avaric argues that evil "isn't *doing* bad things, its *feeling* bad about them afterwards" (p. 473; emphasis in original). Another guest calls it an "affliction of the psyche, like vanity or greed" (p. 473). A different guest explains that it is "an absence of good, that's all…. The nature of the world is to be calm, and enhance and support life, and evil is an absence of the inclination of matter to be at peace" (p. 473). Another guest, who is an artist, makes the point that evil is "an other. It's not *us*" (p. 474). Other guests attempt to argue that evil is "an attribute," "metaphysical," "physical," "inanely corporeal," "moral at its heart — the selection of vice over virtue," and it is "act, not an appetite" (p. 474). Ultimately, as Elphaba is leaving she declares to Avaric that

> The real thing about evil … isn't any of what you said. You figure out one side of it — the human side, say — and the eternal side goes into shadow. Or vice versa. It's like the old saw: What does a dragon in its shell look like? Well no one could ever tell, for as soon as you break the shell to see, the dragon is no longer in its shell. The real disaster of this inquiry is that it is the nature of evil to be *secret* [p. 475; emphasis in original].

Notice none of these characters provide a definitive notion of evil, which is a contradiction to many treatments of good and evil. As we noted earlier, most narratives provide clear dichotomies of what constitutes good and what represents evil. When Maguire was writing this text, President George H.W. Bush and the media offered a clear and definitive picture of Saddam Hussein as evil. People knew he was evil through descriptions of his actions (see Bates, 2004). In the previous section, we noted how *The Wizard of Oz* presents a clear picture of evil nature of the Wicked Witch of the West. By contrast, Maguire's world offers no clear attributes, no clear meaning of what the nature of true evil is. Its disposition is, as Elphaba put it, "to be secret." Elphaba's conversations concerning evil and its attributes question and undermine the fundamental logic of the traditional fantasy story arc. In doing so, the clarity of evil within the fantasy narrative becomes opaque and complex.

Maguire (1995) does not only demonstrate that there is no clear definition of evil, but through Elphaba he questions the entire mythic cosmology of good and evil. For example, Elphaba tells Fiyero that there is no one "higher plan" no true "cosmology" to the universe (p. 254). In another section of the text, after

Sarima tells her daughter, Nor, a "true" story about the Witch and the fox babies, Elphaba castigates Sarima for telling Nor a story that has an afterlife to it. As she put it, "I think that's shameful, even if it's just a story, to propose an afterlife for evil.... Any afterlife notion is a manipulation and a sop. It's shameful the way the unionists and the pagans both keep talking up about hell for intimidation and the airy Other Land for reward" (p. 348; emphasis in original). For Maguire (via Elphaba), it is apparent that evil is not part of a clear "cosmology." The very nature of traditional cosmological forces is called into question. Evil is created through "manipulation" and by implication can be countered with different constructions of good and evil. Ultimately, Elphaba's questioning of what constitutes evil and its cosmic origins challenges one of the fundamental precepts of the myth of evil within fantasy narratives— that it (evil) is clear and definable. Kind of the "I know it when I see it" argument. Evil, as Maguire represents it, is not clear. It is a product of "manipulation" and construction, rather than innate to nature. By questioning the nature of evil, Maguire redefines an understanding of evil within myth. This redefinition provides a new way to understand the world around us. The ultimate conclusion being that a simplistic good versus evil dichotomy will no longer suffice for modern mythology. Rather, modern myths must adapt to contemporary circumstances, resulting in narratives that suggest more nuance, more depth, and a more "realistic" way of knowing and living for our contemporary experience.

The second way that Maguire (1995) presents a more multifaceted view of evil is through his character development, particularly as it relates to the Wizard and to the Wicked Witch of the West. In Baum's original novels and the movie, the Wizard is presented as an intelligent, kind-hearted, if not a bumbling fool of a leader who ultimately grants the wishes of the Cowardly Lion, Scarecrow, and Tin Man. Moreover, he demonstrates selflessness with his mission to take Dorothy back to Oz himself. Unfortunately, things go awry for Dorothy, but the Wizard is presented as a character who attempts to do good. Maguire, on the other hand, portrays the Wizard as a cruel, murderous tyrant who is out for his own self-interested gains. Maguire alludes to a number of the activities that create this image. According to his account, the Wizard came to power in a coup d'état, where he overthrew the royal family of Oz, killed its members, and exiled the rightful heir to the throne to the outland regions of Oz. The Wizard's declarations circumscribed the civil liberties, initially of Animals, but later on of all people of Oz. The Wizard conducted military campaigns against Munchkinland and the Vinkus, in the name of reunifying all of Oz. Yet, his brand of reunification involved the burning of villages, the slaughter of animals, the raping of women, and the massacring of innocents. The Wizard ordered the kidnapping, capture, and eventual murder of Fiyero and attempted to murder Elphaba as well. The Wizard could only be described, as Elphaba noted, as "a monster" (p. 456). From Maguire's account and based on the earlier criteria we discussed regarding myth and evil, the conclusion must be that the Wizard is the archetype of evil.

On the other hand, the Wicked Witch of the West is a much more sympathetic and even heroic character in *Wicked*. In creating more depth for the character, Maguire presents the Witch going against her stereotypical "evil" nature through his vivid portrayals of selfless acts she performs. In each section of the book, save for the first one[2], the Witch works for goals larger than herself that will benefit others. She becomes a sympathetic and heroic figure as she builds friendships, falls in love with Fiyero, fights for the freedom of Animals, and attempts to oppose the Wizard. But her attempts to save others clearly illustrate how evil is complicated within the story arc of *Wicked*.

One definitive example[3] can be found in the second section of the book, "Gillikin," where Elphaba is sitting in her life sciences class. The professor, Doctor Nikidik, brings in a lion cub (the Cowardly Lion) and asks the class whether this cub is an Animal or an animal. Elphaba, clearly disturbed by a lion cub being used for a public experiment, shouts to the doctor "the question you asked was whether who can tell if this is an Animal or an animal. It seems to me the answer to the question is that its mother can. Where is its mother?" (Maguire, 1995, p. 186). Doctor Nikidik proceeds to dismiss her question and ask it again. Elphaba again asks where the mother is. Nikidik continues to dismiss her. She sits down, revealing to Boq "it doesn't seem right to me for the sake of a science lesson to drag a cub in here without its mother. Look how terrified it is. It *is* shivering. And it can't be cold" (p. 187; emphasis in original). When the professor proceeds to pull out a hammer and a syringe with the apparent goal of experimenting on the cub in front of the class, half a dozen students jump up and yell at Nikidik to discontinue his test. The end result was two girls rescuing the cub, Nikidik walking off the stage from his lecture, and Boq remarking to Elphaba "you felt for the beast didn't you? Elphie, you're trembling. I don't mean this in an insulting way, but you're nearly gone white with passion" (p. 188).

This example, along with her other selfless acts of "saving" others, reveal that the Wicked Witch of the West is not the embodiment of evil as she has been portrayed to be. Elphaba has a "passion" for speaking up for others that cannot speak for themselves. She tried to rescue the lion cub, convince the Wizard to stop his brutal campaign against the Animals, and win Nor's release. These attempts at redemption, in combination with her friendships, her capacity to love others, her attempts to seek forgiveness from Sarima for her affair with Fiyero, all point to a character that is much more sympathetic, if not in many respects heroic. By giving the Wicked Witch of the West the capacity to demonstrate love and selflessness, Maguire has offered a character with much more depth that certainly recasts and adds much more complexity to this classic character. But perhaps more importantly, he has recast the very notion of evil with fantasy narratives. In modern mythology, evil is not all it appears to be: what was once familiar becomes different; what once was simple is more complex; what once were clear demarcations of good and evil get turned on their head. The Wizard has much more capacity for evil than the Witch ever could; and ultimately she becomes the hero. The breadth and depth that Maguire displays in describing Elphaba's deeds not only diminishes her evil nature, but really makes her the hero of Oz.

Wicked: The Musical

Before we conclude, we would like to briefly comment on another text that complicates the Wicked Witch of the West's evil nature: the musical *Wicked*. In a way that is similar to how *The Wizard of Oz* creates the Wicked Witch of the West as the icon of evil, the stage production of *Wicked* humanizes this character in a dramatic fashion. Although the visual images of a green Witch offer a vision of an "Other," when Elphaba makes her initial entrance on stage she is a shown as a vibrant young teenager running on stage with a long black braid and a killer smile that generates warmth and energy. One can instantly recognize the positive nature that emanates from Elphaba. In fact, when both authors have seen a number of productions of *Wicked*, audiences immediately offer a rousing ovation to the Witch as she enters. This is a far cry from the initial film entrance of the Wicked Witch of the West who appears in a cloud of smoke, broomstick in hand, scaring young children such as ourselves.

But it is not just the energetic nature of Elphaba's appearance that humanizes the Wicked Witch of the West. Rather, it is the beauty of the musical numbers, the lyrical content, which provide the emotional, mental and other humanizing aspects of the Witch. For example, the first song sung by Elphaba entitled "The Wizard and I," is a moving number that describes how a young impressionable girl feels that she has finally been accepted. Elphaba dreams of the Wizard of Oz's greatness and how they will work together as a team for the betterment of Oz. The song speaks of dreams of hope, acceptance, and the desire to be more human.

Other songs in the musical also humanize Elphaba. In "I'm Not That Girl" she describes the heartfelt pain she experiences as the man she secretly has a crush on, rejects her, and begins dating her roommate Galinda. The lyrics clearly show a young woman lamenting over never finding love. The audience can easily identify with the powerful and realistic emotions of hopelessness, despair and loneliness, which provides a glimpse to the breadth and depth of the character by showcasing her as a complexity of emotions, not as a one-dimensional creature that has been demonstrated before. The tune "One Short Day" allows the audience to see two young and excited girls and share in their wonderment as they visit the awe-inspiring Emerald City. Additionally, this song cements the friendship between the two central characters of Galinda and Elphaba. The song "As Long As You're Mine" is a love song where the Witch and her lover Fieryo are seducing one another. The cumulative effect of these songs is they offer an account of a complex, highly likable, compassionate character full of hopes, anxieties and dreams, not the iconic evil of the Wicked Witch of the West that we have come to know. No one would think of a witch singing love songs, acceptance, and getting excited about visiting the big city. By doing so, the character of Elphaba endows a more well-rounded picture of the iconic Wicked Witch of the West and makes it more difficult to think of her as evil.

What truly humanizes the Wicked Witch of the West, at least in the context of the musical, is the theme of friendship that is a common thread throughout the production. Friendship entails receiving mutual enjoyment and satisfaction from another person's company. Friends help, console, and turn to each other for advice during times of peril. The musical centers on the developing friendship between Elphaba and Glinda and how they attempt to overcome a number of obstacles. One of the final songs, "For Good" serves as a microcosm for that theme of friendship. The two characters meet for the last time and seize the opportunity to share how important they are to each other. Elphaba tells Glinda that she has had an indelible impact on her life. Even though they may never meet again, she tells Glinda she will always be with her. As the song progresses, Elphaba wants to clear the air with her friend, asking for forgiveness for her hurtful deeds, just as she did in the book. Ultimately, the two friends declare that their lives have changed for the better because they knew each other. Here and throughout the musical, Elphaba makes a heart felt disclosure to her one and only true friend. She asks for forgiveness for all of the things that may have hurt people. Evil does not ask for forgiveness. Evil takes and destroys without any pause for consequence to others. Evil divides and conquers, creating division not unity. One cannot picture the Wicked Witch of the West in the 1939 film asking Dorothy and her friends to excuse her terrorism. By declaring her fidelity to Glinda and asking for absolution, Elphaba attempts reconciliation. Reconciliation involves uniting parties so that both can live in peace. Peace does not typically generate evil. Through her friendship with Glinda, Elphaba offers a lesson of how disparate parties can find common ground, live together in harmony, and even come to prosper with one another. Ultimately, the visual nature of the stage production and the accompanying music suggest that the evil nature of the Wicked Witch of the West is removed altogether.

Conclusions

In this chapter, we have argued that the Wicked Witch of the West has evolved from an icon of evil to one of sympathy and even heroism in her modern incarnations. The seeds of evil were planted in L. Frank Baum's book, *The Wonderful Wizard of Oz*, but escalated in the film version of the book. This film created a one-dimensional character that will stop at nothing for her selfish ends. Geoffrey Maguire's book *Wicked* and the subsequent musical have served to turn the Land of Oz on its head. What was once good is now evil and vice versa. We come to know the Wicked Witch of the West as having a name, fighting for the rights of others, finding friendship and falling love, and just trying to be accepted by others. From this analysis, we can draw conclusions about the nature of evil within modern mythology.

First, the modern fantasy narrative of Oz, as told by Maguire, should make us question that nature of what constitutes evil. Many of us are presented a variety of narratives where we could discern characters, actions, and storylines that what would be considered "good" and "evil." Surely, the actions of the Devil or Adolf Hitler cannot be considered in a positive light. Those examples aside, our exploration of the Wicked Witch of the West shows what constitutes evil is much more than the simple binary our political leaders want us to believe in. Rather, evil is not necessarily innate to the world, but it is a judgment based upon viewing the actions of others. We are not stating that one cannot judge certain actions as evil. Certainly, the attacks by Al-Qaeda or the atrocities of Darfur can be considered evil. However, we are arguing that in order to make those judgments, one should understand and tell the breadth and depth of the story. If the United States wishes to condemn Al-Qaeda or another enemy then we must demand the other side of the story. What precipitated such action to call for the condemnation of the Other? What are the reasons for the Other to commit actions that we would consider to be "evil"? We must ask and demand answers to these kinds of questions in order to make full judgments about the world around and what constitutes proper action. For what appears to be evil may in fact be part of a larger story, as Maguire's novel demonstrates. The Wicked Witch of the West's evolution offers an important cautionary tale of getting the whole story before making judgments. If not, it can lead to disastrous consequences, such as in our current standing within the Middle East and throughout the world.

Second, our analysis reveals that evil within modern mythological narratives need to be recast and adapted. As Cochran and Edwards (2008) have shown, modern mythological stories complicate, adapt, and even break traditional myths. The evolution of the Wicked Witch of the West offers a complicated and complex vision of what constitutes evil in myth, but in doing so it offers a more realistic vision of evil and a richer story that can offer life lessons. Scholars would be remiss if they did not further investigate how books, plays, television, and film are transgressing stories of old and recasting them to help us comprehend the world around us, but perhaps in a more realistic notion.

Finally, our analysis reveals that the visual mediums of film, television, or a live stage production seem to amplify feelings of good and evil. As we noted earlier, it was not until the Wicked Witch of the West's appearance of film that she became an icon of evil. Seventy years later, Maguire's book supplies a well-rounded and complicated view of the Witch, but she is certainly not portrayed as someone who is wholly good and likeable. Yet with the musical, the Witch is presented as a solely sympathetic and likeable character who only wants to find acceptance, friendship, and love. There is really no semblance of evil that is presented within the musical. Thus, the visual medium of the play's production makes Elphaba even more heroic. The ambiguity between good and evil that comes through in the book is removed. In some respects, the musical returns the myth of good and evil that underlies the Land of Oz to a more simplistic, less complicated notion, but evil and good just happened to be turned on their heads. Future scholarship should examine how mythic stories are changed when they are presented through a visual medium. Are the myths that are embedded within these stories changed? Do they become amplified and even simplified through visual mediums? If so, why? What is it about visual rhetoric that offers a more visceral response for mythic narratives than ones embedded in literature?

The Wicked Witch of the West is an iconic figure in literature, film, television, and now on stage. As future generations grapple with the magnificent Land of Oz, you can bet that her image will continue to evolve and change. Perhaps, she will return to being the iconic image of evil or perhaps her hero status will only grow. Only time will tell how she her "Wicked" nature is presented into the future.

NOTES

1. For those not familiar with the book, Maguire makes a distinction between Animals and animals. Animals, like Doctor Dillamond, are creatures that can talk, think aloud, reason, make scientific discoveries, etc. They work in various professions, such as education, and contribute to the culture and wealth of a society. In some respects, they are equal to the human beings they work with. On the other hand, animals are controlled by humans and used as instruments for various purposes.

2. We see no evidence of Elphaba performing selfless acts in the first section, "Munckinlanders," because it only encapsulates the first two years of her life.

3. There are other examples of where Elphaba tries to "save" others. For example, in the section "Gillikin," Elphaba begs the Wizard to reconsider his policies against the Animals because it is "immoral" (p. 224; see pages 218–226). Another example can be found in the final section of the book where the Wizard asks for an audience with Elphaba (pp. 446–454). After a brief confrontation, Elphaba finds that the Wizard has made Nor (Fiyero's daughter) his slave. The Witch begs the Wizard to release Nor into her custody, but he will not bargain. Attempting to save the lives of others is certainly not a quality most evil characters possess

REFERENCES

Baum, L. F. (1900/1995). *The wonderful wizard of Oz*. New York: Penguin Classics.

Bates, B. R. (2004). Audiences, metaphors, and the Persian Gulf War. *Communication Studies, 55,* 447–463.

Baumeister, R. F. (1999). *Evil: Inside human violence and cruelty*. New York: Holt Paperbacks.

Bostdorff, D. M. (1994). *The presidency and the rhetoric of foreign crisis*. Columbia, SC: University of South Carolina Press.

Campbell, J. (1949/2008). *The hero with a thousand faces, 3rd edition*. New York: Third World Library.

Cole, P. (2006). *The myth of evil: Demonizing the enemy*. Westport, CT: Praeger.

Cochran, T. R., and Edwards, J. A. (2008). *Buffy the Vampire Slayer* and the quest story: Revising the hero, reshaping the myth. In J. Perlich and D. Whitt (Eds.) *Sith, slayers, stargates, and cyborgs: Modern mythology in the new millennium* (pp. 145–169). New York: Peter Lang.

Cote, D. (2005). *Wicked the grimmerie: A behind the scenes look at the hit Broadway musical*. New York: Hyperion.

Edwards, J. A. (2008). *Navigating the post-cold war world: President Clinton's foreign policy rhetoric*. Lanham, MD: Lexington Books.

Freed, A. (producer) and Fleming, V. (director). (1939). *The wizard of Oz* [Film]. Hollywood, CA: Metro-Goldwyn Mayer.

Gregory Maguire and the novel wicked. (2007). *Wicked* the musical in London. http://www.wickedwestend.co.uk/articles-reviews/wicked-gregory-maguire.htm. Accessed May 6, 2008.

Ivie, R. L. (1980). Images of savagery in American justifications of war. *Communication Monographs, 47*, 279–294.

_____. (2004). Democracy, war and decivilizing metaphors of American insecurity. In F.A. Beer and C. De Landtsheer (Eds.) *Metaphorical world politics* (pp. 75–90). East Lansing, MI: Michigan State University Press.

Jewett, R., and Lawrence, J. S. (1977). *The American monomyth*. Lanham, MD: University Press of America.

_____, and Lawrence, J. S. (2002). *The myth of the American superhero*. Grand Rapids, MI: William B. Eerdmans Publishing.

_____, and Lawrence, J. S. (2004). *Captain America and the crusade against evil: The dilemma against zealous nationalism*. Grand Rapids, MI: William B. Eerdmans Publishing.

Maguire, G. (1995). *Wicked: The life and times of the Wicked Witch of the West*. New York: Harper.

Nimmo, D., and Combs, J. E. (1980). Subliminal politics: Myth and mythmakers in America. Englewood Cliffs, NJ: Prentice-Hall, Inc.

Rushing, J. H., and Frentz, T. S. (2005). The mythic perspective. In J. Kuypers (Ed.) *The art of rhetorical criticism* (pp. 241–269). New York: Allyn and Bacon.

3

Polysemous Myth:
Incongruity in Planet
of the Apes

RICHARD BESEL *and* RENEÉ SMITH BESEL

In the late 1960s—an era of free love, race riots, political assassinations, growing environmental concern and war—a film emerged as a mythic symbol of American values. It highlighted the very controversies with which Americans themselves were struggling, but it did so with dazzling costumes and make-up, ingenious set designs and musical score, and memorable casting and humor. This unlikely iconic film was *Planet of the Apes* (1968), starring Charlton Heston.

The original *Apes* movie is now a story with which generations of film-watchers are familiar: Four astronauts—George Taylor (Charlton Heston), Dodge (Jeff Burton), Landon (Robert Gunner) and Stewart (Dianne Stanley)—depart Cape Kennedy in the twentieth century to embark on an intergalactic journey that takes them forward in space and time. Awakening from a deep-space hibernation, Taylor, Dodge and Landon discover their female companion did not survive the journey and that their ship is crashing into a body of water. With barely enough time to read their instruments and discern that they have arrived on a planet in the constellation Orion 2,000 years in the future, the trio escapes to dry land with a few rations and basic survival equipment. After traversing barren land for days, the three stumble across a race of primitive, nomadic, mute humans who are trying to avoid capture from Ape soldiers on horseback. Taylor and Landon are injured, while Dodge is killed during the slave-hunt. Reversing the role of human dominion over apes in contemporary society, Sterling's Apes confine the humans to cages for use in zoos or medical experiments. Trying to communicate with Ape animal psychologist Dr. Zira (Kim Hunter), Taylor reveals he can understand the Apes as well as read and write. Dr. Zira encourages Taylor to tell his unique story, much to the dismay of Dr. Zaius (Maurice Evans), Minister of Science and Keeper of the Faith, who pronounces Taylor's tale of far-off planets and space-crafts absurd. When Taylor discloses that he can also speak, Dr. Zaius puts Taylor, Dr. Zira and Dr. Zira's fiancé, Cornelius (Roddy McDowall) all on trial for crimes against the faith, for the inferiority of humans is integral to the Apes' religion. Realizing the only way to salvage their careers and their lives is to prove the truth, Dr. Zira concocts a plan to free Taylor and escape to an archeological site in the Forbidden Zone, where Cornelius reveals several arti-facts that pre-date the Apes' sacred religious scrolls, including a talking human doll. The group concludes that Apes evolved from humans, and humans were, at one point, the dominant race. Taylor and a nomad he has fallen in love with, Nova (Linda Harrison), escape on horseback, when Taylor sees a familiar sight — the Statue of Liberty — almost entirely buried in sand. He realizes then that he has been on Earth all along and that humans destroyed both their planet and their race.

Despite Heston's fame and a screenplay by *Twilight Zone* creator Rod Sterling, critical reviews of the film were mixed. Renata Adler of the *New York Times*, wrote, "It is no good at all, but fun, at moments, to watch" (1968a, p. 55) and, "The serious moral message ... is a complete failure, as are the sus-pense on which the plot depends and an ending that is repeated a number of times in case any anthropoid in the audience may have missed it" (Adler, 1968b, d1). Roger Ebert (1968) of the *Chicago Sun–Times* noted that the film "is not great" (¶ 6) but that it "seems to have found its audience" (¶ 3) and called the film "quickly paced" (¶ 9) and "completely entertaining" (¶ 9). Meanwhile, *Variety* magazine said, "*Planet of the Apes* is an amazing film. A political-sociological allegory, cast in the mold of futuristic science-fiction, it is an intriguing blend of chilling satire, a sometimes ludicrous juxtaposition of human and apes mores, optimism, and pessimism" (1968, p. A1).

With such reviews and a largely unknown cast, no one, not even pro-ducer Arthur P. Jacobs, was prepared for the commercial success they had on their hands (Berardinelli, 2001a). Yet *Planet of the Apes* emerged as the first science fiction/fantasy film to truly launch a franchise. Not only did *Planet of the Apes* spawn four theatrical sequels, it was the basis for a short-lived 1970s television series, a Saturday morning TV cartoon, countless books, comic books, and other spin-off material — not to mention the "action figures," cos-tumes, lunch boxes, and various other paraphernalia that are now mandatory to the success of any would-be blockbuster (Berardinelli, 2001b). In addition, *Planet of the Apes*, directed by Franklin Schaffner, was nominated for two Academy Awards (Best Costume Design and Best Original Score), while make-up designer John Chambers won an Oscar for his work in the movie (Booker, 2006). Yet, there was more to this movie than just outstanding visual effects. It donned a political voice with implications for the very issues Americans were debating upon the film's release in 1968.

Given the way the movie engaged issues such as race relations, animal rights, nuclear war and class conflict, *Planet of the Apes* came to be recognized as a modern-day myth, a fable used to "resolve contradictions of some sort or address important questions which a culture is asking about itself" (McGuire, 1977, p. 3). In other words, the film helped audiences face their uncomfortable cultural anxieties. As Greene (1998) noted about the 1968 movie and its 1970s sequels:

> The makers of the *Apes* films created fictional spaces whose social tensions resembled those then dominating the United States. They inserted characters in those spaces whose ideologies, passions, and fears duplicated the ideologies, passions, and fears of generations of Americans.... The films were attempts to explore the meanings of those cleavages and understand what they said about the character of the society and its people both as US Citizens and as human beings [p. 9].

However, issues of social importance are rarely short-lived. As cultural controversies linger or resurface, societies often turn to myths of the past. As mythic critic David Sutton (1997) explains, "In times of crisis people turn to their *mythos* for comfort and guidance. One must consider, however, that these narratives are not carved in metaphorical stone. They are malleable as the situation dictates" (p. 213). Given the tendency of societies to turn toward their cultural narratives, it is not surprising that the *Apes* mythology reappeared some thirty years later.

In 2001, director Tim Burton (*Batman, Edward Scissorhands, Batman Returns, Sleepy Hollow, Charlie and the Chocolate Factory, Sweeney Todd*) reimagined *Planet of the Apes,* but did not meet with as much success. In this dark, action-packed, technologically stunning film, U.S. Air Force astronaut and primate trainer Leo Davidson (Mark Wahlberg) is among the many aboard the space station Oberon. When an electromagnetic storm approaches, Pericles, a trained chimpanzee, is sent to pilot a space pod equipped with a probe into the storm. Communication with Pericles is lost and Davidson steals a pod to search for his friend. He survives the storm only to crash land into a swamp on a tropical new world 1,000 years in the future. As his ship sinks, he comes across a tribe of humans fleeing a squadron of military Apes. Most of the humans— including Davidson — are captured and taken back to the Ape's city to be sold. Ari (Helena Bonham Carter), a female chimpanzee, arrives at the auction house to protest the treatment of the humans and chooses to buy Davidson and Daena (Estella Warren) to work as "house humans," an assignment made possible since humans, in this version of the film, can speak. Determined to escape, Davidson breaks out of his cage and frees Daena and her family, who quickly decide to accompany him. Davidson also persuades Ari to help them find their way out of the city. However, General Thade (Tim Roth), who wants to marry Ari, witnesses the escape and sends his top Colonel, Attar (Michael Clarke Duncan), to rescue Ari and kill the humans. Believing that he has re-established contact with his home space station, the *Oberon,* Davidson leads the groups of fugitives to Calima, the supposed birthplace of the apes, only to discover that Calima is, in fact, the *Oberon*, which crashed 1,000 years earlier in pursuit of Davidson's lost pod. Old space logs reveal that the race of English-speaking apes on this strange planet are all descendents of Semos, a genetically enhanced ape onboard the Oberon who led a violent coup against the humans. As Attar approaches, hundreds of humans show up to fight against the apes. In the thick of the battle, a pod from the *Oberon* gracefully descends to the planet and opens to reveal Pericles, the trained chimpanzee whose mission to investigate a storm started Davidson's journey and the race of superior apes. Thade follows Davidson and Pericles into the *Oberon*, where Davidson traps him in the bulletproof command room. Leaving Pericles in Ari's capable hands, Davidson uses Pericles' pod to return to his home planet, Earth, in his own time, 2029. What he finds when he lands in Washington, D.C., however, is a monument of Thade in place of the Lincoln Memorial, and an advanced civilization of apes. The movie closes with a baffled Davidson struggling to make sense of this new twenty-first century Earth.

Burton's reimagining shared several characteristics with the 1968 film. In both movies, a masculine mythic hero fights his way through trials and tribulations to escape the domineering apes, who are intelligent, articulate and prejudiced creatures. In addition, many of the moral lessons at the heart of the stories remain largely unchanged. What was different, however, was the reaction of the public and critics. The 1968 version, as we have seen, met with popular (albeit not necessarily critical) success, and the 2001 film met with mild critical acclaim but was essentially a flop. Although the 2001 *Apes* won several industry accolades for make-up, costume and music, it also earned its share of Golden Raspberry Awards for Worst Remake or Sequel, Worst Supporting Actor (Charlton Heston), and Worst Supporting Actress (Estella Warren) (IMDB, n.d.). Critics noted that although "Burton's version is a gorgeous film that looks much better than the original in all sorts of ways," it is also "almost entirely lacking in the emotional power and political commentary of the original" (Booker, 2006, pp. 98–9).

This chapter explores why these similar myths generated such very different reactions. We advance two central arguments: First, although both versions of the myth relied on what American literary theorist and rhetoric scholar Kenneth Burke calls "perspective by incongruity," we contend that the 1968 version of *Planet of the Apes* was critically and commercially more successful than the 2001 film because the original text addressed a richer and wider variety of social and political tensions that were pertinent to the audiences of the time. Second, we illustrate how previous treatments of *Planet of the Apes* read the texts from one perspective, preventing a reading that addresses the polysemous, or multi-faceted, nature of the original movie.

We will begin by turning to Kenneth Burke's notions of "perspective by incongruity" and "piety" and Leah Ceccarelli's notion of polysemous texts to inform our analytical framework. By combining these concepts and using them to guide our analysis of the 1968 and 2001 films, we are able to offer insight into the successes and failures of the *Apes* movies as well as offer implications for mediated myths as a whole.

Perspective by Incongruity, Piety and Polysemy

We argue that the *Planet of the Apes* movies made use of what Kenneth Burke calls perspective by incongruity. According to Burke, each of us has an expectation — an orientation — of "how things were, how they are, and how they may be" (Burke, 1984, p. 14). When our expectations are violated through a juxtaposition of things that to do not fit together, an incongruity, our perspective on how things were, are, and will be, changes. Words and ideas that do not go together are brought together just as words and ideas that do go together are separated. Burke provides us with an example: "Were we finally to accommodate ourselves, for instance, to placing lion in the cat family, a poet might metaphorically enlighten us and startle us by speaking of 'that big dog, the lion' — or were we completely inured to thinking of man [sic] as an ape, we might get a sudden flash, a perspective, from a reference to man [sic] as the 'ape-God'" (Burke, 1984, p. 90). Both *Planet of the Apes* movies go so far as to suggest the sapien "ape-Gods" could be replaced by the simian "human-Gods." Perspective by incongruity serves as an "'opening wedge' that fractures our sense of how the world does and ought to function" (Whedbee, 2001, p. 48). When Taylor, encounters the "upside-down" world where apes dominate humans in the 1968 movie, audiences are invited to experience perspective by incongruity: by understanding how the simian society functions, audiences are better able to understand their own. The same can be said for Leo Davidson's discovery in the 2001 movie. Burke (1984) offers a rather lengthy and instructive passage that is surprisingly similar to what audiences experience in the *Apes* movies:

> Or let us even deliberately deprive ourselves of available knowledge in the search for new knowledge — as for instance: Imagine that you had long studied some busy and ingenious race of organisms, in the attempt to decide for yourself, from the observing of their ways, that inducements led them to act as they did; imagine next that, after long research with this race which you had thought speechless, you suddenly discovered that they had a vast communicative network, a remarkably complex arrangement of signs; imagine next learning all this race's motives and purposes as this race itself concerned them. Would you not be exultant? Would you not feel that your efforts had been rewarded to their fullest? Imagine, then, setting out to study mankind, with whose system of speech you are largely familiar. Imagine beginning your course of study *precisely by depriving yourself of this familiarity*, attempting to understand motives and purposes by avoiding as much as possible the clues handed you ready-made in the texture of the language itself. In this you will have deliberately discarded available data in the interests of a fresh point of view, the heuristic or perspective value of a planned incongruity [p. 121].

Although the *Apes* movies never ask viewers to completely discard information in the interest of a fresh point of view, audiences can, nonetheless, temporarily suspend their disbelief until they have absorbed the planned incongruity. However, to fully understand Burke's notion of perspective by incongruity, that is, how expectations can be violated to enact change, one must also explore what Burke means by "piety," the very perspective being challenged.

Inspired by Spanish poet and philosopher George Santayana, Burke (1984) sees piety as "*the sense of what properly goes with what*" (p. 74). Despite the religious connotation of the word "piety," for Burke, it is not limited to the religious sphere. Instead, "where you discern the symptoms of great devotion to any kind of endeavor, you are in the realm of piety" (p. 83). Perspective by incongruity, then, is impious "insofar as it attacks the kinds of linkage already established" (p. 87). This is precisely what makes perspective by incongruity such a potent rhetorical tool. According to Naomi R. Rockler (2002), "Perspective by incongruity is powerful because, if successful, it jars people into new perceptions about the way reality can be constructed and may encourage people to question their pieties" (p. 38). Pieties, then, are beliefs and values people have come to accept and expect in everyday life. Rockler offers an example of a carnivore confronted with a suggestion that her eating habits might be destroying the rain forest. The meat-eater's piety is that food sustains life — it does not destroy it — while the suggestion itself is the impious text.

That Burkean notions can be used to understand mediated myths seems fitting given the similarities between Burke's definition of piety and the function of myths. As Joseph Campbell told Bill Moyers, myths function by "supporting and validating a certain social order" (Campbell and Moyers, 1988, p. 31). Thus, myths can be pious or impious texts, depending on whether or not the perspective in question is already embedded in a given culture. According to Wayne McMullen (1996), "Central to the application of a mythic perspective to film is viewing the film as a dialectic between competing value systems" (p. 18). Indeed, a clash between pious and impious positions is necessary for a myth to survive, for as Stone (1993) explains, "Myths are thought to depend so fully on the tension between competing value systems that, without such tension, the essence of the narratives behind the myth dissolve" (p. 491). Myths teach us about what pieties we should cling to and which pieties we should abandon.

Burke's perspective by incongruity as a rhetorical strategy does not have to have a single piety as its target. The notion of polysemy can further guide our analysis of mediated myths. *Planet of the Apes* can be seen to function against multiple pieties. However, audiences in different historical positions will not weigh all of the perspectives in similar fashions. According to Doty (2000, p. 151),

...few mythic or ritualistic elements remain unchanged for very long, and the ways one "believes" in a myth element or ritual moment may vary considerably during one's lifetime or across a society's historical development. Even the ways mythic materials are recounted may vary according to what the raconteur surmises about the particular interests of the listeners, his or her socioeconomic position, or according to the particular storyteller's skills, politics, and affiliations (what folklorists refer to as compromising the text, texture, and context of the material).

In light of Doty's observation, we agree with Meyer (2003) that, "Polysemic interpretations of myth are essential to our understanding of complex narrative forms, particularly in mediated contexts through which narratives reach a global audience" (p. 527).

According to Leah Ceccarelli (1998), scholars have used the term polysemy in a least three ways: polysemy defined as resistive reading, strategic ambiguity, and hermeneutic depth. In the resistive reading camp, scholars have argued audiences bring their own interpretations to the text and actively deny the initial meaning intended by the message's sender. These interpretations offer room for resistance against the hegemonic coding given by a text's creator. However, a resistive reading does not necessarily claim the hegemonic coding is not present in the text; it could simply result in a reading that disagrees with the creator's coding. Strategic ambiguity is a polysemic strategy used by rhetors to intentionally destabilize meaning in a text, often resulting in differing parties accepting the text. Unlike resistive reading's grounding in the audience, this understanding of polysemy is rooted in the text. The text is ambiguous enough to contain multiple meanings. Finally, hermeneutic depth refers to how a text *should* be read. According to Ceccarelli, this view of polysemy asks audiences not to simply resist texts, or understand ambiguous texts from one of many potential perspectives, but instead, asks audiences to realize the range of possible interpretations simultaneously "to appreciate the text's deeper significance" (p. 408). The 1968 *Planet of the Apes* finds its significance in the way it constituted a text with hermeneutic depth. Following Ceccarelli, we argue the 1968 movie enjoyed success not just because of its use of perspective by incongruity, but also in the way the text contained such a range of possible interpretations. In other words, there were *perspectives* by incongruity, and no single perspective alone could explain the movie's lasting social influence. The movie addressed race relations, nuclear proliferation, class struggle, religious zealotry, *and* animal rights. By doing so, audiences encountered a rich, mediated myth with hermeneutic depth that offered lessons and advice about how the world was, is, and should be.

PIETIES AND PERSPECTIVES BY INCONGRUITY IN *PLANET OF THE APES* (1968)

Turning to previous analyses of the 1968 version of *Planet of the Apes*, we observe that scholarly attention circulates around two major pieties and a host of minor pieties that are challenged in the original movie. Some commentators have argued the success of the original *Planet of the Apes* could be explained because it "tapped a deep vein of symbolism in American national mythology: the symbolism of race difference and race conflict" (Slotkin, 1998, p. vii). According to these observers, the piety being fractured is a commitment to racial inequality. At first glance, there is compelling textual and historical evidence to support this interpretation: the simians take humans as "slaves" who can be used and disposed of, and the United States does have a long history of dominance over non-white groups and of comparing them to animals. Eric Greene's (1998) book *Planet of the Apes as American Myth: Race, Politics, and Popular Culture* is perhaps the most developed reading of the movie from a racial perspective. Others concur with Greene's assessment and see the movie as an "obvious allegory of interracial relations" (Rankin, 2007, p. 1019; McHugh, 2000). M. Keith Booker (2006) has even argued the shift in perspective that takes place in the movie is one of the key devices used in this racial opening wedge:

> The sudden shift in perspective that makes humans the object of race hatred on the part of animals (and, by extension, whites the despised Others of blacks) provides precisely the sort of cognitive jolt that provides all the best science fiction with its principal power. This jolt asks audiences to see racism with fresh eyes... [p. 99].

Given the movie's civil rights-era backdrop, it is easy to interpret the movie as a text that uses a perspective jolt to awaken American audiences from their racial slumber.

Other observers have attempted to explain the success of the 1968 *Planet of the Apes* by noting the way it challenges a different societal piety. Rather than seeing a racialized myth with lessons for proper conduct between blacks and whites, they have chosen to see the film as a statement against nuclear weapons. Jonathan Kirshner (2001) and Stephen O'Leary (1988) have made strong arguments in favor of this view. As with the racial reading, there are strong textual and historical reasons to adopt this interpretation. The movie opens with Taylor daydreaming about the world he has supposedly left behind: "I wonder if Man, that marvel of the universe, that glorious paradox who has sent me to the unknown ... still makes war against his brother and lets his neighbor's children starve." A late 1960s audience aware of the Cold War climate and conditions in Vietnam could have easily believed that man indeed still wages war. The movie's final scene of Taylor finding the Statue of Liberty and realizing that he was on a post-nuclear catastrophe Earth certainly strengthens the view that this movie offers lessons against war. In one of the most dramatic moments of the movie, and one of the most recognized movie endings in film history, Taylor drops to his knees and proclaims, "Oh my God. I'm back. I'm home. All the time, it was.... We finally really did it. You maniacs! You blew it up! Ah, damn you! God damn you all to hell." Heston's dramatic delivery on the beach punctuates the movie's anti-nuclear message. This is what Burke (1959) would call a kind of symbolic "atom cracking" (p. 308), wherein the films takes the atom or symbol (i.e., the Statue of Liberty) that typically has a specific cultural meaning (i.e., freedom, hope and possibility) and shatters it (i.e., forcing the Statue to represent slavery, hopelessness and nuclear annihilation).

Although we have touched on the two dominant readings, these are not, by far, the only two mentioned by those we have cited. The movie's anti-religious tones have also been observed in the way faith-protecting apes wished to stop the advancement of science (Booker, 2006; Kirschner, 2001). In one of the movie's more comical scenes that is representative of the 1925 Scopes Monkey trial, Dr. Zaius, as part of a three-orangutan tribunal, charges Taylor with heresy. As Cornelius and Zira attempt to reason with the tribunal using their scientific findings, the three orangutans pose with one covering his eyes, another covering his ears, and the final his mouth. Indeed, the text illustrates the dangers to be found in religious zealotry.

Scholars also hint at the problematized class relations between orangutans, chimps, and gorillas, respectively, as they are placed into a class hierarchy (Booker, 2006, p. 102; Rankin, 2007). This observation is not lost on Taylor:

Dr. Zaius: Tell me, why are all apes created equal?
Taylor: Some apes, it seems, are more equal than others.

Gorillas, as the invisible working class, have few lines in the original movie while orangutans clearly rule the society as protectors of the faith with chimps placed between the two groups. Although there is evidence the text also addresses class relations, this is usually treated as a minor theme by observers as the racial and anti-nuclear perspectives dominate the commentaries.

With the variety of pieties already mentioned, it seems as though scholars have offered a rather fractured reading of the movie with some scholars contending the movie's success can be attributed to the way, to use Burke's terms, perspective by incongruity is used to challenge a particular piety. However, we contend there is also an obvious, yet often overlooked animal rights perspective in the movie. References to vegetarians in the beginning of the movie, an active anti-vivisection society protesting the potential gelding of Taylor, human placement in zoos and human experimentation in place of animal experimentation clearly lends textual support to this reading. Landon, one of the astronauts who arrive with Taylor, is lobotomized in an animal experiment aimed at improving the surgical practices to be used on apes. The third astronaut who survives the crash, Dodge, is eventually stuffed and put on display in a museum. Although we can make the argument that previous treatments of the movie have been anthropocentric, or human-centered, our purpose is not to privilege and elevate a reading that features only one piety. We view *all* of the previously mentioned interpretations as necessary to a critical understanding of how *Planet of the Apes* functions as a mediated myth with pertinent lessons for today's society. In other words, the original *Planet of the Apes* movie is a mediated myth that benefits from the potential of polysemic readings.

PIETY AND PERSPECTIVE BY INCONGRUITY
IN *PLANET OF THE APES* (2001)

Although the 2001 version of *Planet of the Apes* is different from the first movie in some respects, it nonetheless stays committed to using the same rhetorical devices. Director Tim Burton, when asked whether or not he would take on the project, explained his attraction to the idea, claiming the "mythology has this circular kind of quality." He goes on by stating, "I started to think, well, this is what I like about movies: seeing life from a different angle. *Planet of the Apes* was like a reversal. You're seeing things, but it's reversed, so it throws you off a little bit and puts you into another place, looking at things from a different way" (Wartofsky, 2001, p. G01). The reversal Burton observed in the first movie, what Burke would call perspective by incongruity, is precisely what motivated him to shoot the second telling of the myth. Of course, Burton's version was updated for the era and adjusted to fit his particular, darker style.

Much like the 1968 film, Burton's vision offered an impious myth that stood against racial injustice. However, Burton's reimagining contained textual elements that made the statement much more obvious to audiences. For example, in the 2001 *Apes* movie, human slaves are used at the service of apes. In one scene where Davidson, Ari, and Gunnar attempt to flee the city, they encounter two human slaves who are the house servants of a powerful ape family. Gunnar immediately comments that they are "house humans" and expresses his hesitancy in taking them beyond the city walls. It is implied that the house humans could potentially foil the escape attempt. The allusion to America's history of slavery is unmistakable.

The 2001 version certainly emphasizes the racial point more than the original, but this did not lead to a successful critical reception of the text. According to the *New York Times* film critic Elvis Mitchell, "the picture states its social points so bluntly that it becomes slow-witted and condescending; it treats the audience as pets" (Mitchell, 2001, p. E1). During one scene, Limbo even parrots the words of Rodney King, "Can't we all just get along?" Jay Carr of the *Boston Globe* noted, "The new film equates the humans in their loincloths much too overtly to African-American slaves. The more lightweight 1968 version limned the antiracist theme more deftly" (Carr, 2001, p. D1). The 2001 *Apes* features house humans who can speak, while the 1968 version does not. The 1968 version even explains that humans could not be used as slaves because the apes believed humans could not be tamed. However, the point becomes complicated when taking some of Burton's other choices into consideration.

The racial equality element of the movie borders on being a performative contradiction. On the one hand, Burton was able to recreate many of the perceived tensions between house slaves and field slaves in his text. On the other hand, some choices weakened the audience's view of the apes as representative of dominant slave-owning whites and the humans as enslaved minorities. This is especially true for the ape side of the dynamic. For example, the apes in the 2001 film are clearly physically superior to the humans. They are stronger and capable of leaping great distances. In the 1968 film the apes are much closer in their appearance and movements to human beings. Although this change makes the newer *Apes* movie visually exciting, it detracts from what Burke (1969) would call the process of identification. Real audiences and the apes on screen are no longer symbolically similar in the more recent version. Who in the audience could leap the way the apes in the movie had? Although the racial equality reading of the 2001 text is certainly valid, how it is framed to work on audiences is complicated.

One key way the 2001 version differs from the 1968 film in terms of pieties has to do with the anti-nuclear element. The 2001 *Apes* removes the surprise ending of the first film. A nuclear holocaust is no longer responsible for the rise of the simians. Instead, genetic manipulation of space apes by humans is introduced as a causal factor. As Davidson and the escape party arrive at Calima, they discover that it was Davidson's ship and an escaped chimp named Semos that was responsible for the apes. However, despite the irony, genetic engineering itself is never seriously treated as a piety that needs to be seen from a different perspective. Audiences may have actually used support for genetic engineering to resist the text, one of the many possible responses to polysemy outlined by Ceccarelli. In addition, upon discovering his crashed mothership, Davidson does not react with the same level of passion as Taylor did when reacting to the Statue of Liberty in the first movie. The difference is striking. While the 1968 audience would have likely reacted to the idea of a nuclear holocaust with dread, the 2001 audience would not have had the same kind of visceral reaction to genetic engineering.

With the anti-nuclear element absent in the newer movie, a new ending was needed. Burton decided to turn to the original Pierre Boulle (1963) novel for his inspiration. After Pericles interrupts the final battle between humans and apes toward the end of the movie and Davidson cages Thade, Davidson takes Pericles' pod and begins his journey back to Earth. Upon arriving, Davidson finds that the Earth has been taken over by Apes; this is similar to Boulle's ending. However, critics and audience members were unforgiving in their assessment of the finale. Mitchell thought audiences would "be muttering, 'what happened'" (Mitchell, 2001, p. E1)? And he was right. In a *USA Today* poll of people who saw the 2001 movie, "48% admit they did not get the finale. And those claiming to understand it give various explanations of what it means" (Soiano, 2001, p. 6D). The final scene did not give a thorough sense of closure and explanation to the events of the film on nearly the same level as the 1968 original had done.

As for the minor pieties in the first text, they remained minor themes in the newer text. The movie's depictions of the dangers to be found in blind religious faith are clear throughout the movie. In an early scene, Attar acts as an enforcer of the faith when he commands attendees of a dinner to bow their heads to give thanks to Semos. Later, Attar questions his religious beliefs after seeing Pericles land the pod. Being exposed to a secular, scientific, and technological explanation for his species' origins, Attar sees the truth. Yet, all of these scenes are secondary to the explicit racial overtones of the movie.

Although the impious stance against religious dogma is still apparent, the second *Apes* movie encounters problems in its depiction of class struggle. The 2001 movie appears to contain a greater range of classes, but eliminates the element of class segregation between apes. General Thade and his father Zaius, played by Heston in a cameo appearance, are powerful and respected chimpanzees. This would not have been a logical decision in the first movie because chimpanzees were not in the ruling class and did not rise to positions of military or political power. The class divisions, although present to some degree in the newer text, are harder to observe.

The final minor piety addressed by the 2001 movie relates to the treatment of animals. This is still clearly present in the newer version. The animal psychologist from the first movie, Zira, is replaced as defender of the humans by the "human rights" activist Ari. Although one could see Ari as an abolitionist as much as an animal rights character, later scenes in the movie confirm the impious nature of the movie. For example, in one scene Thade takes his niece to buy a human child to take home as a pet. In other scenes humans replace animals as beasts of burden. However, just as the physical superiority of apes could cause identification problems for audience members in terms of racial inequality, the same problem exists for the animal rights issue. The apes are so different from the humans in the newer version that it becomes difficult to relate to the animals as though they are like human beings. The movie could be seen as a text that reinforces tendencies to see animals as unworthy of fair treatment. As with the racial inequality perspective, the animal rights dimension functions in a number of potentially contradictory ways.

When compared to its predecessor, the 2001 *Planet of the Apes* still functions as a polysemous myth that operates primarily through a use of perspective by incongruity. However, the text has lost a degree of its hermeneutic depth. Racial inequality was certainly addressed, but in such a forced fashion that some audience members and critics reacted negatively to its message. Some stylistic elements could even be viewed as a performative contradiction. The anti-nuclear discourse of the first movie is absent in the second and is never replaced by an impious stance toward genetic engineering. In terms of minor plots, only the stance against religious zealotry can be seen as unproblematic in its presentation. Burton's movie was visually stunning, but lacking in terms of depth. Perhaps this is why some critics have noticed that the 2001 *Apes* was "spectacular but empty" and, therefore, that "Burton and his screenwriters never capture the grand sense of myth that made the earlier film exciting" (Denby, 2001, p. 88).

Although our analysis has proceeded by noting what observations about pieties could be found in the scholarly literature and critical commentaries related to the two movies, Burke (1966) also reminds us that every selection is also a deflection. In this sense, we are left to speculate about what was not mentioned in the readings of the movies. What was being deflected? We find it odd that in discussions of race and class that gender did not receive more attention. Looking back at the texts, we conclude that most scholars and commentators not only suffered from a human-centered bias, but they also virtually ignored questions of gender inequality. As it turns out, the highly impious 1968 movie and the moderately impious 2001 movie were both pious texts in regards to unfair treatment of women. For example, in the 1968 movie the astronaut Stewart is sent along with the three male astronauts to act as a new Eve. As Taylor notes in the movie, she was to give birth to the new colony of humans with the "hot and eager help" of the three men. (Why there were *three* men and *one* woman to populate an entire new race of humans is not explained in the text.) In addition, Stewart, whom we can assume would have been the only intelligent, free-spirited woman on the new planet, is killed off before she utters her first word. Similarly, in the 2001 movie, Ari is an unemployed rabble rouser who escapes punishment for her heretical defense of humans because of her powerful father. Ari and Daena's roles are saturated with flirtatious attempts to win the affections of Davidson, who only seems motivated by a desire to abandon the two on the foreign planet. Of course, there is also the argument that Zira is an empowered doctor in the first movie. Our point is not that the text supports or resists patriarchy, but that gender has been ignored and that what appear to be largely impious texts in their selection are also pious texts in their deflection. Future analyses of the *Apes* myth should certainly offer a far more detailed reading of gender issues in these polysemous texts.

CONCLUSION

In this chapter, we have examined why the 1968 version of *Planet of the Apes* met with more critical and popular success than its later 2001 retelling. Drawing on Kenneth Burke's articulation of perspective by incongruity and piety, in combination with an understanding of polysemy, we conclude that the 1968 film achieved a level of hermeneutic depth that the second film did not. In terms of being an impious text, the 1968 original used perspective by incongruity to challenge contemporary pieties about racial inequality, nuclear war, religious dogma, class struggle, and animal rights. Although the 2001 version also used perspective by incongruity to challenge some of the same pieties, including racial inequality and religious zealotry, the text's style and content did not offer consistent messages for identification when addressing class issues and animal rights. When introducing a new origination explanation for the events in the film, genetic engineering, the movie actually transformed into a pious text that did little to challenge the technological storyline.

The later version also omitted commentary on nuclear war. For these reasons, the 1968 version of the *Planet of the Apes* was able to achieve a greater success than its 2001 counterpart.

Additionally, based on our reading of the *Apes* myth as it changed over time, we have attempted to advance an approach to criticism that combines the ideas of Burke and Ceccarelli to analyze mediated myths. Although we have only examined one myth, the approach we have adopted here can nonetheless be repeated in examinations of other mediated myths that also use juxtaposition and challenges to societal pieties. For, as Janice Hocker Rushing (1986) notes, "Every culture, then, has its supply of myths which defines its identity and dictates its moral vision" (p. 265). Of course, as critics we must be ever mindful of the multiple (im)pieties and perspectives that are constantly present in potent myths.

We wish to end this chapter with a few words from Slotkin (1998), who notes that "the images and myths we take for granted as part of the world of entertainment often have deep historical roots and evoke powerful, ideological traditions. Only by examining that history, and subjecting those myths to critical analysis, can we move beyond the moral and conceptual limitations of our mythic traditions" (p. ix). It is our hope that we can use this chapter as an opening wedge for new readings of old myths that are steeped in history and tradition. And it seems scholars will soon have another opportunity to examine the *Planet of the Apes* myths. Twentieth Century–Fox, the film studio that released both the 1968 and the 2001 movie, is developing a new film in the *Apes* tradition. As writer/director Scott Frank told CHUD.com, *Caesar* "will not feature talking monkeys, and it will not end with chimpanzees running wild in the streets" (Faraci, 2008). It also will not be a remake — not of the original and not of *Conquest of Planet of the Apes*, the 1972 film whose main character was named Caesar. What CHUD.com reports *Caesar* will have in common with its predecessors, however, is its exploration of multiple cultural pieties and impieties, and that means the next installment of the *Apes* myth will be fertile ground for scholars to examine how new myths are reappropriated in different cultural contexts (Faraci, 2008).

References

Adler, R. (1968a, February 25). The Apes, the Fox, and Charlie Bubbles. *The New York Times*, p. D1.

_____. (1968b, February 9). Screen: She reads Playboy, he reads Cosmopolitan. *The New York Times*, p. 55.

Berardinelli, J. (2001a). *Planet of the Apes (1968)* [Review of the film *Planet of the Apes*]. *Reelviews.net*. Retrieved November 1, 2008 from htttp://www.reelviews.net/movies/p/planet_apes68.html.

_____. (2001b). *Planet of the Apes (2001)* [Review of the film *Planet of the Apes*]. *Reelviews.net*. Retrieved July 30, 2008 from htttp://www.reelviews.net/movies/p/planet_apes01.html.

Booker, M.K. (2006). *Alternate Americas: Science fiction film and American culture.* Westport, CT: Praeger.

Boulle, P. (1963). *La planete des singes.* Paris: R. Julliard.

Burke, K. (1959). *Attitudes toward history* (2nd ed.). Los Altos, CA: Hermes Publications.

_____. (1966). *Language as symbolic action.* Berkeley, CA: University of California Press.

_____. (1969). *A rhetoric of motives.* Berkeley, CA: University of California Press.

_____. (1984). *Permanence and change* (3rd ed.). Berkeley: University of California Press.

Burton, T. (Director). (2001). *Planet of the Apes* [FILM]. Twentieth Century–Fox Film Corporation.

Campbell, J., and Moyers, B. (1988). *The power of myth.* New York: Doubleday.

Carr, J. (2001, July 27). When hairy met silly: Earthbound 'Planet of the Apes' misses the original film's wit. *The Boston Globe,* p. D1.

Ceccarelli, L. (1998). Polysemy: Multiple meanings in rhetorical criticism. *Quarterly Journal of Speech, 84,* 395–415.

Denby, D. (2001, August 6). Misanthropes; Apes and teens. *The New Yorker,* 88.

Doty, W.G. (2000). *Mythography: The study of myths and rituals* (2nd ed.). Tuscaloosa: University of Alabama Press.

Ebert, R. (1968, April 15). Planet of the Apes. [Review of the film *Planet of the Apes*]. *Rogerebert.com.* Retrieved November 1, 2008 from http://rogerebert.suntimes.com/apps/pbcs.dll/article?AID=/19680415/REVIEWS/804150301/1023.

Faraci, D. (2008, December 1). Scott Frank tells CHUD "I'm not remaking Conquest of The Planet of the Apes." CHUD.com. Retrieved January 30, 2009 from http://chud.com/articles/articles/17231/1/SCOTT-FRANK-TELLS-CHUD-quotl039M-NOT-REMAKING-CONQUEST-OF-THE-PLANET-OF-THE-APESquot/Page1.html.

Greene, E. (1998). *Planet of the Apes as American myth: Race, politics, and popular culture.* Middletown, CT: Wesleyan University Press.

Internet Movie Database. (n.d.). *Awards for Planet of the Apes (2001).* Retrieved July 30, 2001 from http://www.imdb.com/title/tt0133152/awards.

Kirschner, J. (2001). Subverting the Cold War in the 1960s: Dr. Strangelove, The Manchurian Candidate, and The Planet of the Apes. *Film and History, 31,* 40–44.

McGuire, M. (1977). Mythic rhetoric in *Mein Kampf:* A structuralist critique. *Quarterly Journal of Speech, 63,* 1–13.

McHugh, S.B. (2000). Horses in blackface: Visualizing race as species difference in "Planet of the Apes." *South Atlantic Review, 65,* 40–72.

McMullen, W.J. (1996). Mythic perspectives in film criticism. *Journal of the Northwest Communication Association, 24,* 17–30.

Mitchell, E. (2001, July 27). Film review: Get your hands off, ya big gorilla! *The New York Times,* p. E1.

Meyer, M.D.E. (2003). Utilizing mythic criticism in contemporary narrative culture: Examining the 'present-absence' of shadow archetypes in *Spider-Man. Communication Quarterly, 51,* 518–529.

O'Leary, S.D. (1988). *The Planet of the Apes:* The fable of the hundredth monkey in antinuclear discourse. *Argumentation and Advocacy, 25,* 20–30.

Planet of the Apes. (1968). [Review of the film *Planet of the Apes*]. *www.variety.com.* Retrieved November 1, 2008 from http://www.variety.com/review/VE1117794029.html?categoryid=31&cs=.

Rankin, S. (2007). Disalienation and the irrepressible revolutionary wish: Apes, Heston, ludics, home. *The Journal of Popular Culture, 40,* 1019–1031.

Rockler, N.R. (2002). Overcoming "It's just entertainment": Perspective by incongruity as strategy for media literacy. *Journal of Popular Film and Television, 30,* 16–22.

Rushing, J.H. (1986). Mythic evolution of "The New Frontier" in mass mediated rhetoric. *Critical Studies in Mass Communication, 3,* 265–296.

Schaffner, F.J. (Director). (1968). *Planet of the Apes* [DVD]. APJAC Productions.

Slotkin, R. (1998). Foreword. In E. Greene, *Planet of the Apes as American myth: Race, politics, and popular culture* (pp. vii–x). Middletown, CT: Wesleyan University Press.

Soriano, C.G. (2001, August 2). Damn murky 'Apes' end! *USA Today,* p. 6D.

Stone, J.F. (1993). A motivational/metaphysical model analysis of *Platoon. Western Journal of Communication, 57,* 478–493.

Sutton, D. (1997). On mythic criticism: A proposed compromise. *Communication Reports, 10,* 211–217.

Wartofsky, A. (2001, July 29). For Tim Burton, 'Apes' is enough: The offbeat filmmaker finds a primal attraction to remaking '68 classic. *The Washington Post,* p. G01.

Whedbee, K. (2001). Perspective by incongruity in Norman Thomas's "Some wrong roads to peace." *Western Journal of Communication, 65,* 45–64.

4

The Hero with the Thousand-and-First Face: Miyazaki's Girl Quester in Spirited Away and Campbell's Monomyth

DEE GOERTZ

What is the face of a hero? Joseph Campbell in his book *Hero with a Thousand Faces* (1968) argues that the character of the hero has appeared in story after story for thousands of years in mythologies around the world — a thousand different faces fit the character of the hero. However, parts of his monomyth or paradigm are so dependent on the maleness of the hero that it is hard to imagine him picturing a female hero.[1] Nevertheless, if Campbell had lived long enough, he surely would have recognized the young, needy, frightened, skinny, ten-year-old girl protagonist of Hayao Miyazaki's acclaimed animated film *Spirited Away* (2001) as a hero. Her name, Chihiro, which can be interpreted as meaning "looking deeply" or "inquiring after many things" (Boyd and Nishimura, 2004, ¶ 5), as well as her physical person, suggests that Miyazaki has created a new kind of hero.[2] Indeed, Miyazaki has said that he is fed up with the usual answers to the problems of the modern world, and so deliberately created a different kind of hero in his films. In an interview conducted three years before *Spirited Away* was made, he said, "The reason I present the hero as a girl is probably because society traditionally accords control to man, in Japan and in the rest of the world. We've reached a time when this male-oriented way of thinking is reaching a limit. The girl or woman has more flexibility. This is why a female point of view fits the current times" (Miyazaki, 1998, p. 129). It is not surprising then that his films abound in memorable female characters both major and minor, of all ages. Some of those with girls as main characters include *Nau-*

sicaä (1984), *Castle in the Sky* (1986), *My Neighbor Totoro* (1988), *Kiki's Delivery Service* (1989), *Princess Mononoke* (1997), and *Howl's Moving Castle* (2004).

In *Spirited Away*, Miyazaki has not only changed the gender, age, and personality of the hero but also the nature of the hero's deeds, explaining, "I would say that this film is an adventure story even though there is no brandishing of weapons or battles involving supernatural powers" (Miyazaki, 2004, p. 15). Chihiro would not be able to wield a sword or a lightsaber to save her life. Moreover, Miyazaki has changed the nature of the hero's foes. They are not villains that the hero needs to rid the world of; he asserts, "I know it's considered mainstream but I think it's rotten. This idea — that whenever something evil happens someone particular can be blamed and punished for it — is hopeless" (Holm, 2006, p. 62). Chihiro overcomes her challenges not through dominating or annihilating her foes but through empathy and compassion. Much of this seems a far cry from the usual hero story; certainly it is rare in contemporary films, animated or not. Girl protagonists abound in children's and young adult fiction aimed at girl consumers, but their presence on the big screen, especially as action heroes, is still rare enough to warrant celebration and a closer look.[3]

In this chapter, I apply the concepts of the literary hero formulated by Joseph Campbell to *Spirited Away*.[4] When I first started this project, I was sure that I would find his ideas too limited to a Western male's point of view to relate to a Japanese film about a girl. However, after a close rereading of *The Hero with a Thousand Faces*, I found that Campbell makes thorough use of scholarship on Hinduism and Buddhism and also includes the occasional female hero in his formulations. Although I do not completely agree with his assumption throughout that the gender and cultural context of the hero is irrelevant to the monomyth, his paradigm is quite relevant to Chihiro's story, probably because both Campbell and Miyazaki seem to be deeply influenced by Buddhism.[5] However, it is still useful to supplement and even counter his work at times by examining the Japanese context — Shintoism, Buddhism, the aesthetic concepts of *wabi sabi* and *mono no aware*, and Japanese folktales. Moreover, as Campbell's paradigm does not fit a female hero as well as one would wish, I have incorporated a feminist approach: I question Campbell's use of exclusive language, which ultimately limits his idea of the hero.[6] Lastly, a formalist close analysis of the film itself reveals the patterns in the imagery that might not be initially apparent. This combination of approaches will show how Miyazaki has created a new kind of hero, one who offers solutions to today's psychic, ecological, economic, and political problems. Chihiro might be a better role model than Buffy the Vampire Slayer, even. While Buffy is sexy, powerful, and violent, Chihiro draws on inner resources of perseverance and compassion that anyone might have and cultivate.

CAMPBELL'S MONOMYTH APPLIED
TO *SPIRITED AWAY*

Campbell conceives of the hero's journey as occurring in three phases: Departure, Initiation, and Return. In the first, the hero departs his ordinary world and "is drawn into a relationship with forces that are not rightly understood" (Campbell, 1968, p. 51). A supernatural being comes to his aid to help him cross the threshold, which is a "form of self-annihilation" (p. 91). In the Initiation phase ("a favorite phase of the myth-adventure" [p. 97]), are included all the familiar trials of the hero, culminating in a "supreme ordeal" which results in his gaining his reward (p. 246). In the last phase, Return, the hero then recrosses the threshold, leaving the transcendental powers behind, and returns to his own world. These three broad phases, as well as many of their particularities, can be readily found in Miyazaki's *Spirited Away*.

Departure

The film opens with a realistic contemporary situation that would be recognizable in developed countries worldwide: a father and a mother and their ten-year-old daughter are driving in an Audi to a new home in a suburban area. The impatient father misses his turn and decides to search for a short cut literally off-road. He gets lost and then leads his family through a mysterious tunnel, looking for a bit of safe adventure in what he thinks is an abandoned theme park. In Campbell's terms, the hero enters the "zone unknown" (Campbell, 1968, p. 58) (called a "liminal world" by Boyd and Nishimura [2004]) due to "A blunder — apparently the merest chance — [which] reveals an unsuspected world" (Campbell, 1968, p. 51). Chihiro's father is the one who blunders here, looking for a shortcut to their new home, driving at breakneck speed down an unpaved forest road, and insisting on walking through the tunnel that Chihiro senses is dangerous. During this phase, Chihiro shows that she is both more reluctant to take this journey and more ready for it than either of her parents. According to Campbell, reluctance is not uncommon to the hero, but readiness is all, as "the terrors [of the quest world] will recede before a genuine psychological readiness, [but] the overbold adventurer beyond his depth may be shamelessly undone" (Campbell, 1968, p. 84). This is exactly what happens in the film: her hubristic parents fail early on in the quest because of their gluttony and insensitivity to the spirit world, but as Chihiro grows through her experiences and develops her Buddhist and Shinto values, the spirit world loses its terrors for her.

At this point, Campbell's paradigm can be usefully supplemented by an examination of how Buddhism and Shintoism shape the hero's journey. In Shinto terms, *Spirited Away* can be seen as a parable of the individual's development of a sincere heart. As Boyd and Nishimura (2004) interpret the film, "This notion of learning to live with a sound, pure heart/mind is a central theme in Miyazaki's *Spirited Away,* as the story depicts Chihiro's journey from being a sulking child to that of a young person who acts with genuine sincerity toward others and the world" (¶ 12). From a Buddhist perspective, she must learn to relinquish selfish desire and develop compassion for all beings. The opening episode sets up these themes and also positions Chihiro as ready to learn these lessons. The very first image of the film is a frame-filling bouquet of pink flowers (a symbol of ephemerality in Japan) surrounding a card in girlish handwriting: "Good luck, Chihiro. We'll meet again."[7] This card becomes very important in the film because it reminds Chihiro of her real name just when she has forgotten it. She almost loses the card in the scene, suggesting that she does not understand its deeper meaning: the assurance of connectedness, a key Buddhist idea that the separateness of the ego is an illusion. Chihiro's grief at leaving her friends is grounded in this illusion.

In this scene, Chihiro's grief pulls her backward instead of forward, and she sulks against the ineluctable forward movement of the car. She curls up in a fetal position in the back seat (a position she will return to many times during the film), clutching the sign of her friends, the bouquet. The Second Noble Truth of Buddhism is underscored here: Suffering is caused by attachment. Chihiro suffers because she is attached to the past; she futilely clings to the very symbol of the inevitability of the passage of time. The simple exchange she has with her mother about her flowers reiterates these lessons though neither she nor her mother can recognize them:

> Chihiro: Mommy, my flowers died!
> Mother: No wonder, the way you clung to them. A little water when we get there and they'll perk right up.

Neither Chihiro nor her mother realizes that they are like the woman in the Buddhist Mustard Seed parable who carries around her dead child looking for someone to cure him. Only mindfulness of the present and acceptance of transience (the Third Noble Truth: to eliminate suffering you must eliminate attachment) will help them. The motif of clinging recurs when Chihiro walks through the tunnel with her mother: "You'll make me trip, Chihiro, clinging like that." The mother realizes that clinging is futile, but gives Chihiro false hope that the fading of her flowers can be reversed.

Her mother shows the same kind of half-knowledge when they pass the Shinto shrines by the side of the road shortly after the beginning of the film. She is able to identify them but shows no further interest. Significantly, though, Chihiro is the first to notice them, and she seeks knowledge of them. Her eyes widen signifying her readiness to "see" them. Miyazaki repeats this motif of Chihiro's eyes widening in these early scenes whenever a hint of the spirit world appears—a grinning statue in the woods, the wind pulling leaves into the tunnel—showing not only her fear but her preparedness to experience the spirit world in a way that her parents, with their hearts hardened to Shinto truths, cannot. At the beginning of the film, Chihiro appears to have no inner resources: she is all neediness and sullenness because she is fearful.

Chihiro and her parents walk through the tunnel and the sense of being in a new world increases. They cross a series of thresholds—the tunnel itself, an airy waiting room, a sunlit meadow, a rocky streambed. Suddenly the father sniffs the air like an animal—food is cooking somewhere and it is lunchtime. The parents hurry to find the source of this delicious aroma in a gaudy deserted village, which the father confidently, but erroneously, identifies as an abandoned theme park. They find a restaurant, the counter piled high with steaming foodstuffs, which the parents dig into despite Chihiro's protests. As they shovel the food in with both hands, grunting and moaning, Chihiro turns away in disgust to explore the village. She is drawn to a large colorful building with steam rising from it. (In the dubbed version, she murmurs, "It's a bathhouse," for the benefit of English-speaking audiences.) A boy appears (we later learn that his name is Haku) and warns her to flee this world before the sun sets, promising to distract the other inhabitants with a spell. As dusk descends alarmingly fast, Chihiro races back to her parents, passing dim ghost-like figures, but finds in their place only grotesque clothed pigs, squealing and spewing spittle as they are whipped away from the food. Chihiro has instinctively passed the first test of the hero by respecting the boundaries of the spirit world and shunning the food meant for them. With their hubris, greed, and insensitivity to the spirit world, the parents show themselves as they really are — pigs. Thus begins one of the key themes in the film — the dangers of overconsumption, not only of food but of all the resources of the natural world — that will be repeated in the stories of several characters. Chihiro's main trials are in saving each of these characters by helping them purge and purify themselves. These will be discussed in turn in the Initiation section.

The last section under the heading "Departure" in Campbell is "The Belly of the Whale" in which he explains that the undertaking of the hero's journey is a form of self-annihilation. *Spirited Away* includes this theme in a number of ways. Through their greed, her parents have essentially abandoned Chihiro, leaving her surrounded by an increasing number of spirits— some monstrous ones with tusks and claws, others that look like overgrown Easter chicks— who are arriving at nightfall to refresh themselves at the bathhouse. As it darkens, Chihiro literally starts to fade. Haku, the magic boy who has already tried to help her once, finds her and feeds her a bit of spirit food so she will not disappear, but her self-annihilation is continued symbolically. Haku tells her she must get a job in the spirit world in order to survive and save her parents. First, she descends into a sort of Underworld — the basement boiler room of the bathhouse — to ask work of the frightening looking boiler man, Kamaji, with his extendable spider legs. He sends her upstairs to the owner of the bathhouse, the witch Yubaba. Chihiro's persistence in demanding a job, despite Yubaba's frightening refusals, pays off. The witch then makes her sign a contract magically removing part of her name and leaving her a new identity —

Sen, the lowest employee in the rigid bathhouse hierarchy.[8] She also must give up her clothes for a work uniform, further erasing her old identity. During this scene she tries to protest and Yubaba magically zips her lip — symbolizing another kind of annihilation that researchers on girls have warned about — the loss of voice.[9] (Luckily, Yubaba must undo the spell soon after.) Like Jonah in the whale and Odysseus in the Underworld, the hero must die to her old identity and be reborn symbolically.

At this point, Chihiro has already overcome a number of obstacles, showing she is fit hero-material after all: she resists the temptation of the spirit's food, she braves a terrifying descent down a flight of open wooden steps, and she stands up to a number of scary figures— including Kamaji, the huge spider-like boiler man, and a sumo-wrestler-like white radish spirit — both of whom turn out to be gentle helpers. But the scariest figure of all is Yubaba — a greedy businesswoman who has the huge warty nose and long sharp nails of a Hansel and Gretel type witch or a Baba Yaga, the terrifying witch of Russian folklore who devours trespassing children. Like the Greek goddess Circe, Yubaba can turn humans into animals, or in the case of Chihiro's parents, make manifest the inner pig. Yubaba belittles Chihiro relentlessly and threatens to slice open her throat with her huge nails. Visually this image parallels one later in the film when Yubaba realizes her baby is gone. She flares up, breathing fire, hair flying like Medusa's snakes, and smoke leaking from the corners of her mouth like boar's tusks.[10] With her voracious greed and magic powers, Yubaba is a formidable opponent, indeed.

Initiation

The core of the hero's journey according to Campbell is the Initiation phase. In *Spirited Away*, Chihiro's trials reflect two interrelated patterns: (1) overconsumption and purgation, and (2) loss of identity and recognition. They interrelate because the loss of identity comes through overconsumption and the recognition through purgation. The task that Chihiro needs to perform is ultimately not that different from the greatest heroes in literature and sacred texts around the world. She needs to free up the life energy of her world by purging the land of forces that impede it. The impeding elements are the excess "stuff" that the contemporary world has produced and human greed for it. Chihiro is not only able to free her parents but a host of other characters as well because she has compassion for all. She is willing to put her quest for her parents' freedom on hold while she aids others. Her shield is her lack of greed and her weapon is compassion that sees past surface appearances so that she can treat each of these characters with respect.

The first major task — reminiscent of Hercules' cleaning of the Augean stables— is the cleansing of the Stink Spirit, a task that reflects Miyazaki's environmental interest. As the parents' gluttony reflects what is wrong with consumerism, the Stink Spirit's plight represents the pollution and destruction of the natural world. After Chihiro bathes him, the Stink Spirit appears in his true form as a River God that had been sodden with filth and crammed with the detritus of modern civilization — a bicycle, a mop, chunks of rusted machinery. Even the shrewd Yubaba had failed to recognize him at first and when she does recognize him, she appreciates only his money. Like Chihiro's mother, her knowledge and understanding is limited by her materialism. But Chihiro treats him with a sincere heart, not a greed-motivated one. The scene in which she purifies him and releases his energy is a tour-de-force of animation and shows Miyazaki at his best. A close look at this scene — its pacing and soundtrack as well as its imagery — will reveal something of Miyazaki's skill in conveying this theme cinematically.

First of all, how is it possible to stink on screen? Miyazaki makes the Stink Spirit stink by painting him with brown excrement-like goo oozing off him in oily globs. When he speaks, a yellow vapor seeps out of his mouth. Yubaba's and Chihiro's hair stands on end when he approaches. One of the lesser spirits faints. The Stink Spirit's money plops wetly in Chihiro's hand as her hair spikes out even further. The scene is comic, yet we see Chihiro's grit in handling the abjectness that no one else in the bathhouse can bear. She stiffly leads him to the big bath, which she and Lin, her mentor and only friend among the women workers, have just finished cleaning, another Herculean task. She also shows her pure heart by understanding his needs when no one else can.

This scene is key in Chihiro's journey because it involves her own cleansing and rebirth as well as the River God's. As she adds water to the tub, she slips in and ends up fully immersed and stuck upside down with her head in the mud. The god lifts her out of the mud and into the air, saving her from drowning. He holds her close to his side so she can see the bicycle handle sticking out of it. She tells Yubaba that he has a thorn in his side that is hurting him, and Yubaba and the whole bathhouse crew help pull it out, releasing a mass of junk and sludge much bigger than the Stink Spirit itself. For a moment — a long moment for an animated movie — there is silence except for a quiet dripping of water, until the workers notice the tiny gold nuggets that have sifted out of the junk. Tellingly, as the bathhouse staff yells "Gold!" the foreground is shown filled with junk, a subtle equation of gold with waste that Miyazaki makes more explicit later, in a scene in which Yubaba's gold turns to dirt resembling the excrement washed off the River God. The River God had been filled with the detritus of modern human consumption. Miyazaki shows that all our material preoccupations are ultimately excremental.

Chihiro has made great progress in this scene in her journey toward herohood. She has passed tests of physical exertion and courage, and the community loudly acclaims her deed. The bathhouse workers, and more importantly, the assembled spirit-customers, warmly applaud her work. The River God himself says "That's good" ("Well done" in the dubbed version) and leaves in her hand a grayish-green ball that turns out to be a gift of powerful medicine. Her respect for and ability to communicate with the River God even in his stinky form shows that her fearful curiosity in the spirit world has blossomed into a sincere heart. In Buddhist terms, she has compassion for the Buddha-nature beneath the excrement[11] as she has compassion for her parents beneath their swinish embodiments. Moreover, the imagery of her immersion in water carries powerful symbolic suggestions. The first one is of purification, an important part of Shintoism. Another is death and rebirth, which is yet another symbol of the self-annihilation that the hero must undergo, as well as an image of Christian baptism. A third symbol is of the sacred marriage between human and divine, body and spirit. But since this particular aspect of the scene closely relates to Chihiro's relationship to Haku, who turns out to be another river god, I will discuss it later.

The next character that Chihiro saves is No Face, perhaps the most interesting secondary character in the film. No Face is genderless, though I will refer to it as "he" since he speaks in a male voice after he swallows one of the bath house workers. He appears as a dark shape wearing a white mask with neutral, Noh-mask-like features.[12] The animators have done an exceptional job making subtle changes in the mask to express sadness or joy. No Face is the embodiment of loneliness and need. He hovers at the edge of the bath house until Chihiro welcomes him in — a compassionate act that nevertheless has dire consequences initially. No Face tries to do something for her in return and gives her the herb token she needs to clean the big tub for the Stink Spirit, who will arrive in the next scene. But his insatiable desire for her approval leads him to pursue her with many more bath tokens than she needs. Chihiro's sense of moderation makes her refuse the excess, and No Face retreats with a look of pain.

However, when No Face discovers that the bathhouse workers are excessively grateful for gold, he heaps it on them and consumes more and more platters of food, stuffing it in as a substitute for Chihiro's regard. "I'm starving!" he cries, even after consuming rooms full of food. The imagery links this to the parents' transformation scene; at first, the food, aesthetically arranged on colorful plates, is enticing and beautiful, but after the gorging begins, the food falls and jumbles together in a nauseating mess. The gorger becomes a drooling monster. No Face begins to devour the workers who serve him, and at last is contained in a room covered with huge images of demons. The Buddhist parable is plain — desire can never be fulfilled for long and attachment leads to a vicious cycle of satiation and deprivation.

In a more conventional film, this is where the hero would draw his ancient, storied sword and whack the head off the monster. Not in Miyazaki's film. Chihiro even does something counter to her self-interest — she feeds No Face the last half of the medicine gift from the River God instead of saving it for her own parents. At some level, she recognizes the Buddhist truth that treating her parents' problem as separate from or as more important than No Face's will not work. In a powerful scene of purgation, No Face vomits up all he has devoured, disgorging at last the workers he has swallowed. Chastened, he follows Chihiro and her entourage at a distance until she compassionately invites him to share her train tickets (there is just the right number) for the next leg of her hero's journey, to Yubaba's sister's house to return her gold seal and ask forgiveness for Haku.

Shortly before the No Face episode, Chihiro has purged Haku of the magic gold seal he had stolen from Zeniba, Yubaba's twin sister, and swallowed. Haku, who originally seemed to be simply a boy with magic powers, is slowly revealed to be more. Here, he is shown to have a dragon form, and in a dramatic and highly original chase scene he is pursued across the sky by what looks like a flock of white birds. He crashes into the bathhouse as Chihiro looks on with horror while blood splatters the room. She realizes that the birds are really flat pieces of paper that fly back across the sea, except for one that, hidden, attaches to Chihiro's back as she follows Haku up to Yubaba's quarters. The scene shows how much she has already grown as a hero; she resolutely climbs up a precarious ladder and across a treacherous pipe, whereas earlier she had been terrified to walk down a rickety flight of steps. Symbolically, too, having successfully negotiated her descent into the Underworld, she is rising to a higher plane, only to fall once more before rising again triumphantly with Haku near the end of the film.

In Yubaba's room, while Yubaba is downstairs trying to deal with No Face's rampage, Chihiro meets two more formidable opponents: a monstrous baby, who threatens to break her arm, and Yubaba's twin sister, Zeniba. At first, Zeniba seems as hostile as Yubaba. She threatens Chihiro—"I'll rip your mouth out," going for Chihiro's voice as Yubaba did — and claims that the curse she put on her seal will kill Haku, even though her flock of paper birds failed to do so. For mischief's sake, Zeniba turns Yubaba's human-faced bird flunky into an insect and her precious baby into a chubby mouse. In these transformed shapes, these characters redeem themselves by following Chihiro and aiding her. Chihiro grabs onto Haku still in his dragon form as he falls precipitously down a chute all the way to Kamaji's boiler room. In another display of courage and compassion, Chihiro then feeds Haku half of the River God's medicine by prying open his fanged jaws and shoving her arm down his throat while he thrashes violently, his tail shattering Kamaji's herb and root storage drawers. Haku coughs up the seal along with a slug-like curse and begins to recover. Chihiro's bravery and generosity in this scene show that she has indeed moved further along the hero's path by helping purge Haku of his evil deed. Comically, Miyazaki confirms Chihiro's status as hero the end of this scene. The mouse mimes her squashing of the slug with her bare toes to a crowd of admiring soot sprites; an epic about her deeds is already being composed.

To complete Haku's recovery, Chihiro decides to make a final journey to another place of potential annihilation — Swamp Bottom, right into the lair of Zeniba, who Kamaji warns is every bit as fearsome as she seemed to be. As a beautiful pacing device, Miyazaki prolongs Chihiro's train journey across a turquoise sea[13] to give the audience an emotional rest after the intensity of the No Face scene. Nothing happens to further the plot for minutes. The train stops at lonely stations where shadowy passengers disembark. At one point, we see a shadow girl at a stop who might represent what Chihiro would have become if she had faded at the beginning. This episode evokes the Japanese aesthetic value of *mono no aware*, which suggests that true beauty is achieved when the artist captures the sadness of its transience. It also expresses the Buddhist ideas of mindfulness of the moment and the relinquishing of desire.

Zeniba surprisingly turns out to be a kindly helper. "Call me granny," Zeniba says as she serves Chihiro, No Face, Baby Mouse, and Bug-Bird a pleasant but modest tea. Her home, as opposed to that of her "tacky" sister, is in a quiet rural location and is simply and rustically furnished. We see how No Face can act in this *wabi sabi*[14] environment: he eats quietly but satisfyingly with a fork and knife. It is only the greedy, materialistic surroundings of the bathhouse that bring out his monstrous side. "The boys," as Zeniba calls Chihiro's friends No Face, Baby Mouse, and Bug-Bird, work hard to spin and knit a magic protective hair tie for Chihiro ("threads your friends wove together"), symbolic counterpart to the flower card that reminds Chihiro of her name and her friends' love for her.

Even though Zeniba is fearsome at first, she emerges as the nurturing Good Mother. This intertwining of "good" and "evil" in a character is typical of Miyazaki's mature and complex treatment of this issue. Moreover, her twin sister Yubaba is more complex and interesting than a one-dimensional villainess: she is also a loving, if over-protective, mother. The downside of her over-protection is shown by the grotesque size of her baby whom she keeps confined in a luxurious, womb-like circular room. He cannot walk and he is afraid to leave. His arrested development grotesquely mirrors Chihiro's curling up in a fetal position when she is particularly fearful. Even though Yubaba persists in her opposition to Chihiro to the last, she seems more self-serving than evil. Yubaba and Chihiro's mother share the same failing—selfish attachment. Put together, Yubaba and Zeniba complete the portrait of the dual nature of the Universal Mother.

Haku arrives at Zeniba's house in his sinuous dragon form, and Chihiro climbs on his back for the flight to the bathhouse to complete her quest. Put together, Chihiro's purging of Haku and their flight together parallel Chihiro's purging and mystical union with the River God. To analyze this using Campbell's paradigm, however, requires a bit of linguistic acrobatics because of the gender bias of his language. Despite his own attempts to do so, reconciling his concepts of the "Meeting with the Goddess" and "Atonement with the Father" with a female hero is tricky. Campbell's solution is to reverse the genders of the characters, and this works to a point. So instead of the male hero's greatest triumph being the sexual union with the goddess, a ten-year-old girl hero's greatest triumph is the mystical communion with the god (in this case, two). Symbolically, the sexual element is there, but much muted—nothing like St. Teresa's erotically charged encounter with the archangel, for example. Significantly, both gods are river gods, reversing a common association in both eastern and western traditions of water with the female.[15] Visually, Haku and the River God each show three sides: first they each appear as male humans (though the River God's human form is as a Noh mask); second, as phallic dragons (the Eastern dragon is much more snake-like than the typical dinosaur-like Western dragon); and third, as womb-like bodies of water. As such, they fulfill Campbell's description of the divine being as androgynous.

One message of the hero's journey is that duality is an illusion; what was thought to be separate and opposing is part of a unit: god/goddess, good mother /bad mother, father/ogre, nirvana/samsara, yang/yin. This union of opposites in the sacred marriage of divine/human is "the source-moment that generates and regenerates the world and man" (Campbell, 1968, p. 251). Campbell interprets a Holy Saturday ritual in the Catholic Church this way. As the priest dips the phallic candle of the Holy Spirit into the womb of the baptismal font, the "water of transformation" (p. 251), the worshippers are "plunge[d] into the mythological realm; to break the surface is to cross the threshold into the night-sea" (p. 251). In both scenes in the film, Chihiro plunges into the mythological realm of water and Miyazaki shows us close-up images of her face: wide-eyed, attentive, suspended in time. In the first, Chihiro is engulfed in the womb-like body of the River God, and her wide-eyed gaze is juxtaposed in montage with an image of his human aspect — the Noh old man mask — rising in the steam intoning "That's good." The intimacy of this quiet, literally breathless moment and their mutual salvation (he has pulled her from the sludge and she has released his clogged energy) suggests a mystic union.

Even more like a sacred marriage is the parallel scene with Haku: his human aspect is a boy near her own size and age and he is presented throughout the film as a love interest. She straddles him and holds onto his horns as they fly. She remembers a childhood incident in which she fell into a river and almost drowned. We see the image of this memory as the womb-like body of the river surrounds her. She suddenly speaks its name: the Kohaku River. Haku's dragon scales fall away dramatically, and the two of them plunge downward. As he revives, now as a human, he remembers his true form — a river that had been blocked up by human development and, wandering without an identity, had fallen prey to Yubaba's exploitation. His eyes have changed: they are rounder and full of anime "shines" (reflections of light), and they match Chihiro's soft expression and joyful tears. They fly side by side now, hand in hand, as equals. Though it may not make logical sense that his "true" identity is represented by a human boy, it makes emotional and mythic sense.

From this point to the end of the film, Haku appears no longer as a mysterious Other but as an equal partner to Chihiro. We see them several more times; holding hands and standing side by side, about the same height with similar androgynous features, even similar unisex clothes. Their similarity points to an important passage in Campbell (1968) about the hero's apotheosis (or transcendence):

> This is the meaning of the image of the bisexual god…. Therewith the two apparently opposite mythological adventures come together: the Meeting with the Goddess and the Atonement with the Father. For in the first the initiate learns that male and female are … "two halves of a split pea"; whereas in the second, the Father is found to be antecedent to the division of sex: the pronoun "He" was a manner of speech, the myth of Sonship a guiding line to be erased. And in both cases it is found (or rather, recollected) that the hero himself is that which he had come to find [p. 163].

In this, Campbell tries to escape boundaries of gender and almost succeeds, though elsewhere his androcentrism betrays him more obviously[16]. And this in turn points to the true genius of Miyazaki's choice of heroes: by making Chihiro the center of consciousness of this film, the one we viewers identify with, Miyazaki adds a new and different face to the thousands of heroes that have come before, most of them male heroes (or females "mastering" their enemies like the males do) that allows the vision of unity in Campbell's paradigm to come to life.

Return

As Chihiro has two mystic unions (the "ultimate adventure" of the hero according to Campbell, 1968, p. 109), she also gets more than one prize ("boon") to take back to her own world. Campbell asserts that the boon is "scaled to [the hero's] stature and to the nature of his dominate desire" (p. 189). One prize Chihiro takes back with her is her restored parents, the fulfillment of her initial goal. As one last test, Yubaba has made her identify her parents from among a dozen identical pigs. Chihiro answers correctly that none of them are her parents, and Yubaba's contract binding her name disappears magically in a puff of smoke. Again, Chihiro's pure heart allows her to see the deeper truth under the surface illusion. She also returns with a second prize: something she acquired in the spirit world—a woven hair tie, the token of her friendship with the Baby Mouse, the Bug-bird, and No Face.

Chihiro and her parents recross the threshold, walking through the tunnel in a scene identical to the one at the beginning of the film, saying the same things and even walking in the same direction across the frame. At first it seems that there will be no evidence of their experience in the spirit world. In the Japanese version, not even Chihiro indicates that she remembers anything about her adventure. Then we see the hair tie glinting in the sun. As a token of connectedness, it embodies the same theme as the card that Chihiro brought into the spirit world. Since both tokens pass the boundary of the two worlds unscathed, it suggests the transcendence of that connectedness, a Buddhist truth that Chihiro has learned. When she and Haku part, he assures her that they will see each other again but warns her not to look back as she crosses the meadow toward the tunnel. She is tempted, but with a look of resolution, she keeps looking forward, and thereby passes a test that more than one hero has failed. The ending evokes the sense of *mono no aware* as well: Chihiro is free, she has won, she is running across a sunny meadow, but she is leaving her true love behind. The sadness completes the beauty of the image. Mindful Chihiro appreciates the moment even as she allows it to slip away. What a change from the fearful girl at the beginning who clings to her fading flowers instead of trusting in the message of connectedness on the flowers' card: We'll meet again.

The ending of the film has been altered significantly in its Disney-distributed dubbed version — and no wonder; the possibility that Chihiro does not remember her adventure would be intolerable to many American viewers. In both versions the family walks through the tunnel and the mother complains again about Chihiro's clinging (a trait we had thought she had grown out of). The father is dismayed to see his Audi covered with dust and leaves, the only clue that more time has passed than they would guess since they walked into the tunnel. But then in the American version (in a voice-over conversation absent from the Japanese version), the father assures Chihiro that going to a new school will not be so bad. A newly confident Chihiro replies, "I think I can handle it," a remark that sends an invisible wink to the viewer, who mentally grins and nods in reply, "Yeah, Dad, you would not believe what Chihiro can handle." The American viewer would leave the theater assured that the experience has changed Chihiro's life for the better — an unambiguous happy ending to make tolerable the unfamiliar ambiguities of the rest of the film.

The Japanese version leaves it completely open as to the effects, if any, that this adventure will have on Chihiro. Japanese culture in general values ambiguity more than American culture does (Davies and Ikeno, 2002). But a more philosophical basis for this ending can be found in Hayao Kawai's Japanese-Jungian interpretation of fairy tales, *The Japanese Psyche*. He analyzes one of the most popular fairy tales in Japan, "The Bush Warbler's Home" — a story illustrating the forbidden chamber motif found in fairy tales worldwide. Unlike Western versions of this story ("Bluebeard's Castle," for example), "The Bush Warbler's Home" ends with the same image it started with — the farmer standing in the middle of a field, the beautiful spirit woman and her mansion disappeared: "namely, nothing has happened" (Kawai, 1996, p. 21). But far from interpreting this negatively, Kawai shows that the story is now seen to illustrate the ineffable Buddhist concept that Emptiness is also Fullness: the story encompasses "Nothing and, at the same time, Being" (p. 20). Japanese audiences embrace the Nothingness that this story illustrates as well as the Nothingness of *Spirited Away*'s ending,[17] but American audiences demand a definite ending to their films, preferably a happy one.

To put a karmic spin on the ending, evidence within the film suggests that Chihiro's experience will have an effect on her life even if she does not consciously remember it. Even though neither Haku nor Chihiro had conscious memories of their earlier meeting until late in the film, the connection they had made when she fell in his river remained to create their bond in the present. Again, the message is that separateness is illusion; connections transcend time and space.

CONCLUSION

At the return threshold the transcendental powers must remain behind; the hero re-emerges from the kingdom of dread (return, resurrection). The boon that he brings restores the world... [Campbell, 1968, p. 246].

The boon that Chihiro brings— the assurance of connectedness— has the potential to restore our world. This new hero, in her vulnerability and inexperience, shows us that we can solve our problems without egocentrism or violence — even if we cannot imagine that we are capable of solving them. Certainly many of the problems of the contemporary world — war, economic injustice, consumerist excess, environmental degradation — would lessen if people felt and acted on their interconnectedness with all beings. On a psychic and spiritual level, the sense of lack that drives people to over consume, exploit, and even kill would lessen. Ultimately, the film itself, along with others created at Studio Ghibli that carry this message like *Nausicaä* and *Princess Mononoke,* is the boon that the hero, Miyazaki, brings back from his journey into the imagination. Although Campbell's paradigm gives us valuable insights into the meaning of the hero's quest, it is up to Miyazaki to provide the kinds of characters, male and female, who allow us to see again the subtlety and inclusiveness of Campbell's vision. Chihiro helps her friends *and* enemies find their best selves, as Susan Napier (2006) says, "It is finally up to Chihiro to create presence out of absence, not only to recover her own vanishing self but also to help others recover their own genuine subjectivities" (p. 308). One of the consequences of these surprising choices is that Miyazaki allows us "to become estranged from what we take for granted and to open up to new possibilities of what the world could be" (Napier, 2005, p. 156). We, too, are spirited away.

NOTES

I would like to thank James Roberson, Rick Bennett, and the editors of this volume for their helpful comments on earlier versions of this chapter.

1. For example, his description of the symbolism of the hero's marriage is particularly gendered: "The mystical marriage with the queen goddess of the world represents the hero's total mastery of life; for the woman is life, the hero its knower and master" (p. 120).

2. This is not to say that Chihiro is entirely unique as a girl hero. Almost all of Miyazaki's protagonists are girls between the ages of ten and twenty, and Japanese anime in general

has an abundance of girl protagonists and girl heroes. Chihiro is different, though, in several ways: she is nonviolent, she is not sexy or cute, and she is quite unpromising as a hero initially.

3. Recent popular books that feature girl protagonists include the Katie Kazoo, Junie B. Jones, and Babysitter Club series. Reference works like *Once Upon a Heroine* (1998) and *Great Books for Girls* (2002) list hundreds of books with girls as main characters. Moreover, there are more and more films being made based on popular girl's books, *Twilight, The Princess Diaries, The Sisterhood of the Traveling Pants, Nim's Island, Nancy Drew*, and *Kit Kittredge*, to name a few. None of these films have the quality or worldwide acclaim of *Spirited Away*, however. *The Golden Compass* is a special case, arguably being a better film and book than most of the above.

4. I'm not trying to argue that Miyazaki deliberately used Campbell's monomyth or any particular hero quests to structure his story. In fact, Campbell's theory assumes that this story is so widespread in world culture that it would not matter whether or not Miyazaki had direct knowledge of Campbell's book. It is worth noting, though, that in his early days, Miyazaki worked on anime featuring a number of famous girl protagonists from the Western tradition: Heidi, Anne of Green Gables, and Pippi Longstocking, as Helen McCarthy (1999) reports.

5. Although they don't focus on *Spirited Away*, Loy and Goodhew (2004) have extensively documented the Buddhist theme of non-violence in Miyazaki's films *Nausicaä* and *Princess Mononoke*.

6. In this, my task is similar to that of Cochran and Edwards (2008) who show how *Buffy the Vampire Slayer* "reshapes" Campbell's idea of the hero.

7. I have tried to be consistent in quoting the English subtitles to the Japanese version rather than the dubbed English version. Since dubbed versions have to match the mouth movements of the characters, they tend to be less literal than the directly translated subtitles.

8. James Robeson points out that "sen" can refer to a small amount of money (ten sen equal one yen). Yubaba's renaming attempts to diminish Chihiro's value in an almost literal way (personal communication, October 21, 2008).

9. *The Little Mermaid*, both the original story and the Disney movie, illustrates this theme when the Sea Witch extracts the Mermaid's voice as payment for legs.

10. Here she resembles closely Barbara Creed's (1993) description of the *vagina dentata* in *The Monstrous-Feminine* (p. 111). Also, Yubaba's familiar, the human-headed "Yu-bird," resembles the siren of classical myth.

11. Susan Napier (2006) notes a relevant mythological parallel: "Finally, on a mythic level, the episode's structure of misidentification followed by revelation, while typical of many archetypal myths concerning a disguised god, is also evocative of a specific Japanese miracle story in which the Empress Komyo bathed a thousand lepers to discover that the final one was the Buddha in disguise" (p. 303).

12. My colleague in Psychology, Dr. Michelle Mamberg, pointed out to me that he looks like the figure in Edvard Munch's painting "The Scream," a resemblance enhanced by the fact that No Face first appears on a bridge. As Munch's figure represents the angst caused by modern living, so does No Face.

13. The strangeness of a train traveling on water (the tracks have been shallowly submerged by the previous night's rainstorm) adds to the poignancy of the episode.

14. Silence and simplicity. See Davies and Ikeno (2002).

15. On the other hand, Ovid's *Metamorphoses* recounts several stories of river gods who have or attempt sexual encounters with human women, but in those encounters the god is a sexual predator. In Miyazaki's version, Chihiro accidently plunges in and is gently extracted by each god.

16. See note 1.

17. Proof of this is in the film's earnings. *Spirited Away* holds the box office record in Japan (Schilling 2008).

REFERENCES

Boyd, J. W., and Nishimura T. (2004). Shinto Perspectives in Miyazaki's Anime Film "Spirited Away." *Journal of Religion and Film, 8* (2). Retrieved April 8, 2000, from http.//www. unomaha.edu/jrf/Vol8No2/boydShinto.htm

Campbell, J. (1968). *The Hero with a Thousand Faces*. (2nd ed.). Princeton, N.J.: Princeton University Press.

Cochran, T. R., and Edwards, J. A. (2008). *Buffy the Vampire Slayer* and the Quest Story: Revising the Hero, Reshaping the Myth. In D. Whitt and J. Perlich, *Sith, Slayers, Stargates, and Cyborgs: Modern Mythology in the New Millennium*. New York: Peter Lang.

Creed, B. (1993). *The Monstrous-Feminine: Film, feminism, psychoanalysis*. New York: Routledge.

Davies, R. J., and Ikeno, O. (2002). *The Japanese Mind: Understanding Contemporary Japanese Culture*. Tokyo: Tuttle Publishing.

Holm, L. (2006). *Spirited Away*. In *Anime: The Ultimate Guide Book to Japanimation*. (pp. 60–62). London: SFX Collection.

Kawai, H. (1988). *The Japanese Psyche: Major Motifs in the Fairy Tales of Japan*. (H. Kawai and S. Reece, Trans.). Dallas, TX: Spring Publishing.

Loy, D. R., and Goodhew, L. (2004). *The Dharma of Dragons and Daemons: Buddhist Themes in Modern Fantasy*. Boston, MA: Wisdom.

Miyazaki, H. (1998). Hayao Miyazaki: Floating Worlds, Floating Signifiers. In P. Wells (Ed.), *Art and Animation* (pp. 22–25). London: Academy Group.

_____. (1999). *Hayao Miyazaki: Master of Japanese Animation*. Berkeley, CA: Stone Bridge Press.

_____. (2004). Chihiro's Mysterious Town: The Aim of this Film. In *The Art of Miyazaki's Spirited Away* (pp. 15–16). San Francisco: VIZ.

_____. (Director). (2001). *Spirited Away*. [Film]. Japan: Studio Ghibli.

Napier, S. (2005). *Anime from Akira to Howl's Moving Castle*. (2nd ed.) New York: Palgrave MacMillan.

_____. (2006). Matter Out of Place: Carnival, Containment, and Cultural Recovery in Miyazaki's *Spirited Away*. *Journal of Japanese Studies*, 32(2), 287–310.

Reider, N. T. (2005). *Spirited Away*: Film of the Fantastic and Evolving Japanese Folk Symbols. [Electronic version]. *Film Criticism, 29* (3), 4–27.

Schilling, M. (2008). "Ponyo" opening leaves room for debate. *Variety Asia Online*. Retrieved July 25, 2008, fromhttp://www.varietyasiaonline.com//content/view/6515/1/.htm.

5

The Odyssey of Madame Souza: A Heroine's Quest in The Triplets of Belleville

DAVID WHITT

In the 1985 Academy Award-winning Ron Howard film *Cocoon* three retirement community senior citizens, Arthur (Don Ameche), Ben (Wilford Brimley), and Joe (Hume Cronyn), looking for some excitement in their lives, have been routinely breaking into a neighbor's indoor pool for an uninvited swim. However, one day before diving in, the three are surprised to see several large organic pods submerged on the pool floor, but decide to ignore whatever risk of these mysterious objects may pose. During their dip each begins to feel revitalized, stronger, acting more energetic than they have in years. Unbeknownst to the trio their renewed energy is the result of absorbing the life force from the pods, which are actually protective shells or cocoons retrieved from the ocean floor housing ancient extraterrestrial beings called the Antereans. Much of the film's humor and conflict centers around how these elderly men react to their newfound youthful vigor, eventually sharing their secret with some, while others are more skeptical about this fountain of youth. What makes *Cocoon* an unusual and memorable adventure story is not just watching Arthur, Ben, and Joe rediscovering their athletic abilities or sexual prowess, but also their bravery and determination in helping return the cocoons to the ocean to save the dying Antereans inside, and then assisting their alien comrades in getting back home.

In the realm of science fiction-fantasy *Cocoon* is something of an anomaly. Consider popular science fiction-fantasy films with characters that through their bravery, strength, cunning, or intelligence are deemed heroes. The original *Star Wars* has Luke Skywalker, Han Solo, Chewbacca, and Princess Leia; *The Matrix*: Neo, Morpheus, and Trinity; *The Lord of the Rings*: Aragorn,

Legolas, Gimli, Gandalf, and the Hobbits. From the ability to use the mystical Force to help overthrow a galactic Empire, to using swords and magic to fight dragons and orcs, to utilizing computer technology to free humanity from control of an artificial intelligence, the heroic behavior exhibited by these individuals has entertained and inspired millions of moviegoers, generating billions at the box office, and created a lucrative, though volatile, market for action figures. However, the same cannot be said about *Cocoon*'s geriatric group of heroes. Arthur, Ben, and Joe are not warriors, soldiers, or wizards equipped with superior weaponry, demonstrating exceptional strength, or magical abilities. They are three average guys feeling the natural effects of aging, spending their time playing shuffleboard and ballroom dancing; certainly not the typical lifestyle or behavior of a "hero."

The critical and commercial success of *Cocoon,* with its genial and courageous elderly male heroes, begs the question; where is the female equivalent of Arthur, Ben, and Joe in contemporary popular culture? In other words, a grandfather can be a hero, but what about a grandmother or older woman? From the Bionic Woman and Wonder Woman in the 1970s to Elizabeth Swan (*Pirates of the Caribbean*) and Kara "Starbuck" Thrace (*Battlestar Galactica*) today, female heroes in film and television are typically young, attractive, strong, and brash. The importance of image in our society, and its impact upon box office receipts and television viewership, does not leave much room for a fictional character, especially a female, who may not reflect the ever changing and constantly demanding standards of youth and beauty.

An example of a female character who breaks the traditional mold of the hero is from the 2003 animated French film *The Triplets of Belleville* (*Les Triplettes de Belleville*). *Triplets* incorporates elements from Homer's classic 2,500-year-old poem *The Odyssey,* but with a unique spin on the hero's journey. Like *The Odyssey, Triplets* is an epic adventure tale of an individual's struggle against great odds and personal sacrifices to return home and reunite a family. However, the hero of this journey is not a sword-wielding soldier, but rather a short, elderly grandmother with a wicked right foot. Written and directed by Sylvain Chomet *Triplets* tells the story of a Madame Souza, a grandmother who searches for her cyclist grandson, Champion, kidnapped by the French mafia during the Tour de France. Champion has been transported to the city of Belleville and forced to compete in torturous simulation of the Tour. Souza, along with her oversized but faithful dog Bruno, weathers ferocious seas, navigates busy street intersections, and fights hunger-pangs to find Champion in the sprawling metropolis of Belleville. During their quest they meet a variety of memorable characters including a rodent-faced mechanic, a restaurant maitre d' who literally bends over backwards for his customers, and, of course, the Triplets of Belleville, a once famous song and dance trio in the 1930s who now perform like a geriatric version of Stomp with a newspaper, refrigerator, and vacuum cleaner. They also use grenades to blow frogs out of the water for their dinner.

With its vibrant and exaggerated animation, virtually dialogue free script, and dark narrative, *Triplets* received critical (if not commercial) acclaim on both sides of the Atlantic, winning the French Lumiere Award for Best Film, the Jury Special Prize at the Copenhagen International Film Festival, and Academy Award nominations for Best Animated Feature and Original Song. *Chicago Sun Times* film critic Roger Ebert (2003) called *Triplets,* "creepy, eccentric, eerie, flaky, freaky, funky, grotesque, inscrutable, kinky, kooky, magical, oddball, spooky, uncanny, uncouth, and unearthly" (p. 1); while Richard Neupert of *Film Quarterly* (2005) states, "Chomet creates a rich and coherent world that moves at a delirious pace, while his visual world owes a great deal to specifically French contexts, including 1930s music, Jacques Tati [French comedic filmmaker], the Tour de France, poster art, and comic books" (p. 38). Additionally, *Triplets* has received praise for its use of 3-D computer animation combined with more traditional 2-D drawing (Robertson, 2004; Fauvel, 2005).

However, while the artistic and technical aspects of *Triplets* have garnered the most attention, the story itself also deserves consideration, especially in terms of its mythic structure and themes. Chomet draws heavily from Joseph Campbell's discussion of the monomyth and borrows elements from Homer's *The Odyssey* to create a striking visual collage of characters, locales, and conflict. The purpose of this chapter is to examine how Chomet uses these myths to construct his affecting tale, and in the process creates an atypical heroine for the new millennium — a diminutive elderly grandmother with glasses, and severe leg length discrepancy (i.e. her right leg is several inches shorter than her left). However, before this can be done it is first necessary to briefly discuss Joseph Campbell's monomyth and its significance to hero mythology.

THE HERO(INE)'S ADVENTURE

According to Robert A. Segal in his book *Theorizing About Myth* (1999), "The study of hero myths goes back at least to 1871, when the English anthropologist Edward Tylor argued that many of them follow a uniform plot, or pattern: the hero is exposed at birth, is saved by other humans or animals, and grows up to be a national hero" (p. 117). Other scholars, such as Austrian Johann Georg von Han (1876) and Russian folklorist Vladimir Propp (1928), also discovered similar or repetitive narrative elements in their analysis of Aryan and Russian fairy tales, respectively. Segal argues that one of the most influential scholars of hero patterns was the American mythographer Joseph Campbell (1904–1987). Campbell's impressive body of work is incredibly diverse, cutting across countless cultures and historical eras. From the ancient Greeks and Egyptians to Australian aborigines and Native Americans, Campbell is a wellspring of knowledge regarding their heroes and gods, rites and rituals. In *The Hero with a Thousand Faces*, originally published in 1949, he outlines the components or formula of the monomyth, defined as the "standard path of the mythological adventure of the hero ... represented in the rites and passage: *separation—initiation—return* [italics added]" (2004, p. 28). Campbell describes, in great detail, the various stages of the hero's mythic journey, beginning with the call to adventure, moving through the road of trials, to eventually returning, forever transformed by their experience. In between there are many thresholds to be crossed, beasts to be defeated, and friends to provide aid. Campbell tells journalist Bill Moyers in *The Power of Myth* (1991) that the typical hero adventure

> begins with someone from whom something has been taken, or who feels there's something lacking in the normal experiences available or permitted to the members of his society. This person then takes off on a series of adventures beyond the ordinary, either to recover what has been lost or to discover some life-giving elixir. It's usually a cycle, a going and returning [p. 152].

Based on this admittedly brief summary the monomyth could be interpreted as a basic blueprint or paint-by-numbers guide to mythic storytelling. However, what makes the monomyth vital is how its narratives teach morals, values, and life lessons. Leeming (1998, p. 6) argues that the monomyth "is an expression of the journey of the hero figure, or our own journey through physical and psychic life, and of the evolutionary path of humanity and full consciousness ... the hero does what we would all like to do; he literally 'finds himself.'" Similarly, Henderson (1997) contends that, "At the heart of these stories there often lies a central conflict between some pair of opposites: good versus evil, light versus dark, even male versus female. As we watch this conflict unfold, we find the germ of meaning that can help us make sense of our own lives" (p. 18).

Arguably, the more celebrated and familiar stories that reflect the monomyth have been those about heroic men. Indeed, names such as Gilgamesh, Achilles, Jason, Hercules, Beowulf, and King Arthur have been part of the cultural, religious, and academic dialogue for centuries. Consequently, the stories of mythic women are far less renowned or, at their worst, infamous by their treachery or malevolence. Knapp (1997) argues, "In mythical or in empirical experience, the status of women throughout the ages, with few exceptions, has not been an enviable one" (p. xi). For example, Cahill (1995) describes how female characters in Greek myths were typically mothers, wives, or virgins defined in terms of their relationship to men, with many engaging in morally questionable behavior such as Medea who kills her children, Clytemnestra who commits adultery and murder, or Jocasta who marries her son. Because of their emphasis on adventure, fighting, and conflict Greek myths, Cahill explains, "are men's stories.... Their substance is the stuff of men's lives and fantasies—victory in war, glorious death on the battlefield, heroic enterprise, the slaying of monsters, the fathering of sons. None of this has much to do with women" (p. 7).

While women have been generally overlooked or disregarded in mythology, this is not to say their stories are not worthy of attention. Bill Moyers addresses this very point in his interview with Joseph Campbell (1991), asking the mythic scholar,

Then heroes are not all men?
Campbell: Oh, no. The male usually has the more conspicuous role, just because of the conditions of life. He is out there in the world, and the woman is in the home. But among the Aztecs, for example, who had a number of heavens to which people's souls would be assigned according to the conditions of their death, the heaven for warriors killed in battle was the same for mothers who died in childbirth. Giving birth is definitely a heroic deed, in that it is the giving over of oneself to the life of another.
Moyers: Don't you think we've lost that truth in this society of ours, where it's deemed more heroic to go out into the world and make a lot of money than it is to raise children?
Campbell: Making money gets more advertisement. You know the old saying: if a dog bites a man, that's not a story, but if a man bites a dog, you've got a story there. So the thing that happens and happens and happens, no matter how heroic it may be, is not news. Motherhood has lost its novelty, you might say.
Moyers: That's a wonderful image, though — the mother as hero.
Campbell: It has always seemed so to me. That's something I learned from reading these myths [p. 153].

Campbell's image of mother as hero is intriguing since it does not fit within the traditional structure of the monomyth. However, it does support his contention that there is "a kind of secondary hero to revitalize the tradition [the hero's adventure]. This hero reinterprets the tradition and makes it valid as a living experience today instead of a lot of outdated clichés. This has to be done with all traditions" (p. 173). In other words, the hero myth is dynamic, evolving to reflect the social and cultural attitudes, values, and beliefs of a time. Sainato (2004) examines this notion of the revised or modernized hero through her analysis of the films *Robin Hood: Prince of Thieves* (1991), *A Knight's Tale* (2002), *Shrek* (2001), and the television series *Buffy the Vampire Slayer* (1997–2003). She contends that the changing portrayals of knights and heroes "show us on-screen defenders who rarely fit the picture of traditional medieval knights and thus challenge our definitions of what constitutes a knight or hero" (p. 133).

One contemporary reinterpretation of the hero's adventure is that of Madame Souza in *The Triplets of Belleville*. The story itself is a variation on Homer's *Odyssey* that tells of the hero Odysseus and his ten-year journey back home to Ithaca after the Trojan War. Along the way he meets goddesses, fantastic creatures, and even visits the underworld, until finally reunited with his wife Penelope. There is also another story within *The Odyssey*, that of Odysseus's son Telemachus leaving Ithaca in search of his father. *Triplets* taps into both narrative threads as Madame Souza searches for her grandson Champion, much like Telemachus searching for Odysseus, and during her quest travels across stormy seas, meets strange characters, and visits a dark underworld like Homer's hero.

Triplets is not the first time *The Odyssey* has been used as source material in fiction, and it certainly will not be the last. French poet and novelist Raymond Queneau (1903–1976) argues, "It doesn't seem to me that anyone has discovered much that's new since the *Iliad* or the *Odyssey*." Various forms of popular culture over the past several decades would seem to support Queneau's contention. From James Joyce's classic novel *Ulysses* (1922) to the Broadway musical *The Golden Apple* (1954) to the ABC television series *Lost* (2004 — present) *The Odyssey* has been interpreted and adapted in a variety of different forms. However, perhaps the most popular *Odyssey* inspired stories are those created for big screen. When writing the screenplay for the 1979 Francis Ford Coppola film *Apocalypse Now* John Milius stated, "It [*Apocalypse Now*] was a combination of not just [author Joseph Conrad's] *Heart of Darkness* but like [sic] *The Odyssey*. [Colonel] Kilgore was like the Cyclops, he was something that had to be overcome, you know, had to be tricked, and the Playboy Bunnies were like the Sirens." In 2001, Joel and Ethan Coen loosely based their film *O Brother, Where Art Thou?* (2000) on *The Odyssey*, and received an Academy Award nomination for Best Adapted Screenplay. Even the children's animated *The SpongeBob SquarePants Movie* (2004) has several *Odyssey* references, including a bag of wind and a diver who looks like a cyclops. More recently, The Internet Movie Database of October 17, 2008 reported that actor Brad Pitt is tentatively scheduled to star in a version of *The Odyssey* set in outer space. Such diversity across print, television, and film mediums would seem to support Raymond Queneau's other belief that "One can easily classify all works of fiction either as descendants of *The Iliad* or of *The Odyssey*."

(GRAND)MOTHER AS HERO: MADAME SOUZA

As an 80-minute virtually dialogue free animated feature *Triplets* is certainly not as multifarious a tale as *The Odyssey*, but it does contain several of its themes, motifs, and symbols, while also reinterpreting Campbell's monomyth. The film begins in late-1940s France, in the home of Madame Souza, a short, stout, bespectacled woman who wears a high-heeled shoe on her right foot since her right leg is several inches shorter than the left. Souza is also guardian of her young, wide-eyed, and slightly overweight grandson Champion (what happened to his parents is never explained). According to Perlich (2009) Souza's unknown and ambiguous lineage is an inversion of the monomyth since typically the hero's origins are known. In an attempt to raise the boy's spirits Souza tries first, unsuccessfully, to get him interested in playing the piano, and then buys him a puppy, which is named Bruno. However, despite his new canine friend Champion is still melancholy. One day, while making Champion's bed, Souza discovers a scrapbook of newspaper pictures, all images of bicycle riders. The next day Champion comes home from school and is surprised to find a new tricycle inside the front door. The scene ends with Champion enthusiastically tearing around the front yard, much to the pleasure of his grandmother.

When we next see Madame Souza and Champion, several years have passed. Bruno is now a full-grown dog, with skinny legs carrying the weight of an oversized body. Champion has grown as well, and is now a muscular and toned cyclist, with skinny arms, narrow waist, and huge thighs and calves. He has been training for the rigorous annual Tour de France bicycle race using a rather unorthodox exercise and dietary regimen of his coach, Madame Souza. For example, she follows behind Champion in his old tricycle, pushing him via a whistle to peddle up an incredibly steep hill, massages his muscles with a push lawnmower and vacuum cleaner, adjusts the spokes on his bicycle tires with a tuning fork, and then finally carries an exhausted Champion upstairs to bed.

The Call to Adventure

The opening twenty minutes of *Triplets* establishes the close relationship between grandmother and grandson. Although Madame Souza is not Champion's biological mother, it is clear she wants to please and take care of him just as any mother, or for that matter, parent would. She certainly goes out of her way to try and make Champion happy, becoming intensely involved in his desire to become a Tour cyclist. It is her commitment to family and love of her grandson that provides Souza with the courage and motivation needed for the dangerous journey that soon lies ahead. In terms of Campbell's monomyth Madame Souza is ready to answer the call to adventure. Again, Perlich (2009) argues Souza's actions are an inversion of the monomyth since she is motivated by the uncertainty of her future (i.e. Champion's safety) instead of the past, which typically motivates mythic protagonists.

The scene then shifts to the Tour de France. Madame Souza, Bruno, and a cigarette-rolling mechanic are following Champion in a relief truck, while people of various shapes and sizes line the road to cheer on the cyclists. During a steep mountain climb Champion begins to fall behind the pack, allowing a large square-shouldered man dressed in a black suit and tie to throw several sharp tacks in the road, puncturing a relief truck tire. The mysterious man then gets into a truck that looks identical to the one transporting Madame Souza, and drives past her with another large square-backed man dressed in an identical black suit and tie.

While Madame Souza's mechanic attempts to unsuccessfully fix the tire on their vehicle, the men in the duplicate truck catch up with Champion and two other cyclists who have quit their climb because of exhaustion. The three are placed in the back of the truck and their bicycles left on the side of the road. Meanwhile, Madame Souza develops a creative solution to their tire problem; she gives Bruno a piece of gum, places another on the wheel well, effectively bonding the dog's mouth to the vehicle. With Bruno as the fourth wheel they try and catch up with Champion, but instead find his abandoned bike. Soon after Souza notices the fake relief truck in an alley completely empty except for Champion's hat. She places the hate in front of Bruno's nose and the dog begins to track his master's scent. Bruno quickly follows Champion's smell to a dock where a large cargo ship holding Champion and the two other cyclists is just beginning to leave port. Desperate for any mode of immediate marine transportation Madame Souza pays her last Franc to rent a paddleboat, and she and Bruno begin the grueling task of trying to catch up with the freighter.

As discussed earlier the first step in the monomyth, according to Campbell, "begins with someone from whom something has been taken" (p. 152). Clearly, for Madame Souza this something is a person, her grandson Champion. Henderson (1997) explains, "The hero's journey actually begins with the call to adventure, the first occurrence in a chain of events that will separate the hero from home and family" (p. 22). In *The Hero with a Thousand Faces* Campbell writes that during this stage of the monomyth, "destiny has summoned the hero…. The hero can go forth of his own volition to accomplish the adventure … or he may be carried or sent abroad by some benign or malignant agent" (p. 53). For Madame Souza she does not refuse the call to adventure, which is the next stage in the monomyth, but rather immediately puts her life, and Bruno's, at risk by renting a rickety metal paddleboat to navigate the open sea without food and water or even knowing where they are going.

The Crossing of the First Threshold

In terms of the monomyth, Madame Souza has removed herself from the safety of her home and natural surroundings, crossing what Campbell defines as the first threshold. He explains, "With the personifications of his destiny to guide and aid him, the hero goes forward in his adventure until he comes to the 'threshold guardian' at the entrance to the zone of magnified power…. Beyond them is the darkness, the unknown, and danger" (p. 71). Campbell describes various threshold guardians in folk mythology such as African tribal ogres and half-men, and Russian "Wild Women" and water shape shifters. While not as protective or perilous a figure as Campbell's examples, the paddleboat owner could be considered a threshold guardian. Although he does not prevent Madame Souza from beginning her quest, she must still pay this guardian for transportation to begin her journey into the unknown. That night Souza and Bruno experience great peril during their ocean voyage, as a vicious storm with powerful waves and hard rains pummel their vessel. This event is similar to a scene in Book Five of *The Odyssey* as a vicious storm created by the god Poseidon destroys the raft carrying Odysseus on his way to an island in the Mediterranean. However, unlike Odysseus's fragile vessel Madame Souza and Bruno's paddleboat miraculously survives the storm, and follows the freighter into the port of Belleville.

The Labyrinth

As the smoke from the freighter ascends into the sky, night suddenly becomes day. The ship exhaust once emanating from twin smokestacks is now coming from a single chimney on top of an impossibly tall building. The camera slowly moves down to reveal the dramatic skyline of Belleville, a sprawling and congested metropolis of architectural wonders, blimps, and an obese version of the Statue of Liberty holding what appears to be an ice cream cone in her right hand and a hamburger on a tray in her left. The city of Belleville with its densely populated neighborhoods, winding streets, and towering skyscrapers reflects the mythical symbol of the labyrinth. According to Henderson (1997) in classical mythology, "the labyrinth has always represented a difficult journey into the unknown. It is really a metaphor for our experience of life, which often seems, while we are in the midst of, to be a twisting, winding road with no sense to its digressions; only in the end, if we're lucky, does a pattern appear that seems to have been in place all along" (p. 47). Jaskolski (1997) explains how cities such as Troy, Constantinople, Jerico, and Jerusalem were "symbolic cities, conceived of as labyrinths—the city as protected sacred precinct and as representation of the world" (p. 31). In the film's official press kit (Les Armateurs, 2003) Sylvain Chomet explains his inspiration for the city of Belleville,

> The first image of Belleville in my film shows the Chateau de Frontenac in Quebec. We used many details from Quebec and Montreal in trying to show how these cities might have turned into New Yorks.... The bridge in my film is the Jacques Cartier Bridge, shown surrounded by typical Quebec architecture. There is a passing reference to the Statue of Liberty which relates to the American way of life and also to the incredible number of fat people one sees in US cities. I've always been struck by that [p. 6–7].

With its French, Canadian, and American influences Belleville may not be representative of the entire world. However, Chomet's city is certainly an impressive architectural wonder, a multi-cultural labyrinth inspired by the symbols, commercialism, and fast food lifestyle of Western culture.

Madame Souza and Bruno disembark from their paddleboat into the metropolitan labyrinth of Belleville just in time to see Champion in the back of a carrier being driven off by the square-backed black-suited men. Champion and the other bikers are being transported to the French Wine Center, a building that serves as a legitimate front for the French mafia's illegal activities. In the Wine Center's basement a large-eared rodent-faced mechanic has mounted three bicycles on a platform. He demonstrates to the mafia boss how by turning the pedals a movie projector is powered, showing images of the French countryside. The faster the cyclist peddles the faster his marker moves up a mechanical incline. In short, the mafia is sponsoring its own torturous version of the Tour de France for the purposes of gambling. To control the three cyclists each is connected to an IV drip pumping into their bodies a drug that creates a strange hypnotic state. Each cyclist focuses only on the virtual countryside images projected on the movie screen, while continuing to peddle on their stationary bikes.

Hero Partners

Meanwhile, Madame Souza and Bruno wander the streets of Belleville all day not knowing where to go or who to talk to in their search for Champion. That evening they make camp under a bridge by a river and Souza entertains herself by playing an abandoned bicycle tire rim. Suddenly, out of the shadows, three tall, elderly women, the Triplets of Belleville appear and begin to snap their fingers and begin singing and dancing to the Souza's beat. Soon after the Triplets take Souza and Bruno home to their rundown, unsanitary, and cockroach infested apartment building. The Triplets apartment is filled with musical instruments, and on the wall there is a poster of the sisters during their heyday in 1930s. Souza is then treated to a rather unappetizing three-course meal, with soup and entrée created from frogs blown out of the water by a grenade, and dried tadpoles for dessert. Wanting to return the Triplets hospitality Souza attempts to clean up around the apartment. However, when she attempts to put leftovers in the refrigerator, use a vacuum cleaner on the rug, or even read a newspaper, a different Triplet intercedes, treating their respective objects with great care and affection.

The Triplets can be interpreted in different ways. First, they are clearly hero partners, described by Henderson (1997) as individuals who assist the hero on their journey. The sisters are not only helpful and kind, but as will be described later, are resourceful, surprisingly strong, and risk their lives to help rescue Champion. They are also akin to the Sirens in *The Odyssey*, though not the seductive creatures described in Book Twelve of Homer's tale as women "crying beauty to bewitch men coasting by" who will "sing his mind away on their sweet meadow lolling" (p. 210). Instead the Triplets are Sirens of a different kind, whose purpose for decades has been entertainment rather than the demise of men.

Months pass by, Christmas is celebrated, and winter quickly transforms into spring. The next time the Triplets, Madame Souza, and Bruno are seen they are at a cabaret. The Triplets are the evening's headline entertainment, an act using a newspaper, refrigerator, and vacuum cleaner, with Madame Souza joining in on a bicycle rim, to create a unique musical rhythm. Unbeknownst to the Triplets and Souza, the mafia boss responsible for capturing Champion is at the cabaret. Lying on the floor next to the mafia boss Bruno smells Champion's scent on his handkerchief, pulls it out of his pocket, and brings it to Madame Souza. She then notices the headlines in the newspaper held by one of the Triplets regarding the French mafia's involvement in the Tour de France and sees a picture on the front page of the boss in the cabaret. She begins to suspect that this man may be responsible for Champion's capture. Later, Souza begins a stakeout of the Wine Center and becomes interested in the rodent-faced mechanic who is leaving the building. Disguising herself as a blind woman, with Bruno as her guide dog, Souza follows the mechanic's every move. Souza's use of a disguise here, and then later as the mechanic, is also a motif in *The Odyssey*. In the poem Odysseus not only fools the Cyclops by withholding his name, but also towards the end of the story dresses as a beggar to gain access to his home to plot against his wife's suitors. With Bruno's assistance, Souza follows the mechanic to a barbershop where he sits outside waiting for a shave. To protect his rather large ears the mechanic wears a set of oversized metallic earmuffs, which Souza manages to steal, along with his jacket, while he has a hot towel around his face. Upon returning to the Triplets apartment Souza removes the contents from the mechanic's jacket and finds a blueprint for the bicycle machine built for the mafia.

The Belly of the Beast

The scene next shifts to outside the Wine Center. One-by-one cars are stopping at the front door as mafia bosses, along with their square-backed muscle, are going inside the building to a large theatre where Champion and the two other cyclists are peddling feverishly. In the balcony dozens of men are yelling, shaking wads of money, and making wagers, while underneath the bicycle machine the rodent-faced mechanic is lubricating the gears with an oil can. Suddenly, cyclist Number Two can no longer keep up the frenetic pace and collapses on the floor, his body writhing in pain and panting for air. The room grows silent as the head odds maker walks over to the fallen cyclist, pulls out a pistol from his jacket, and shoots him dead while Champion and cyclist Number Three continue peddling, seemingly unaware that their comrade has been murdered.

Meanwhile, The Triplets, Madame Souza, and Bruno have infiltrated backstage of the theatre dressed as a square-backed henchman, even managing to knock the rodent-faced mechanic unconscious. Madame Souza quickly disguises herself as the mechanic, putting on his clothes and placing on her head the metal earmuffs stolen from him earlier. She manages to fool the head odds maker into believing she is the mechanic and goes underneath the bicycle machine, but not before taking a moment to sadly stare at what has become of her beloved grandson. Once inside the bicycle machine Souza removes several nuts and bolts, causing the device to begin shaking loudly, and quieting the boisterous crowd. The head odds maker again pulls his pistol, looks inside the machine, but then sees the Triplets behind the curtain. After a brief struggle the odds maker is knocked unconscious after being head butted by a Triplet. Their cover blown, the Triplets try distraction and begin to dance as several men in the crowd begin singing "Swinging Belleville Rendez-Vous," the song made famous by the Triplets decades before. Suddenly, the bicycle machine begins to slowly move forward, tearing up the floorboards. The head mafia boss snaps his fingers and each man in the crowd pulls out a gun and points it at the stage. Madame Souza then blows a whistle and turns off the lights as gunfire fills the theatre. Fortunately, one of the Triplets has brought along two grenades, the first of which she throws into the crowd, causing everyone to disperse, the other blows open a hole in the wall for the slow moving bicycle machine to escape.

The Wine Center theatre filled with bosses and minions of the French underworld is similar to Campbell's description of the Belly of the Whale where the hero is "swallowed into the unknown" (Campbell, 2004, p. 83). He describes several myths in which the hero is eaten by a monster and escapes by cutting his way out of the creature's stomach. In *Triplets* the belly of the beast is more metaphorical symbolizing darkness reflected in both appearance and purpose. Because of the theatre's secret location within the Wine Center, and its dark and smoky environment and menacing criminal clientele, this is the place of greatest danger to Madame Souza and her hero partners. They manage to escape by cutting their way, or more specifically, blowing their way out of this sinister and shady belly of underworld using high explosives. The Triplets, Madame Souza, and Bruno are now close to completing their epic journey, but one last obstacle remains.

Crossing the Return Threshold

Once outside the Wine Center the bicycle machine, still powered by Champion, cyclist Number Three, and now one of the Triplets, begins to quickly move away from the building while the mafia boss and several members of his criminal entourage begin their pursuit. After a thrilling car chase through the winding and steep streets of Belleville, each automobile crashes or meets some other tragic fate. Now on a bridge connecting Belleville to the countryside The Triplets, Madame Souza, and Bruno believe they are finally in the clear when the mafia boss and two of his henchmen come speeding out of the darkness. Lacking hand grenades or any other weapons Madame Souza, with a look of determination, climbs off the bicycle machine onto the bridge. As the mafia boss's car bears down upon her, the car's headlights becoming brighter, Souza sticks out her right leg, and with her elevated shoe trips the car on its side, sending it over the bridge and into a smokestack of a ship passing underneath. As the bicycle machine rides into the countryside it passes a sign that reads: "BELLEVILLE ~ THANK YOU FOR YOUR VISIT ~ COME AGAIN!"

The unusual band of heroines has now crossed what Campbell would refer to as the Return Threshold. He writes, "The hero adventures out of the land we know into darkness; there he accomplishes his adventure, or again is simply lost to us, imprisoned, or in danger; and his return is described as a coming back out of that yonder zone" (Campbell, 2004, p. 201). Madame Souza, Champion, and Bruno are a family once again, a grandmother's quest to find her grandson now complete, much like Telemachus and Penelope reuniting with Odysseus. The final scene of the film moves forward several years to the home of Madame Souza. A woman's voice is heard to say "Is that it then? Is it over do you think? What have you got to say to Grandma eh?" As the image pulls back a gray-haired Champion is seen sitting at a table watching television and replies "Yes, I think that's probably it. It's over Grandma." Finis.

IMPLICATIONS

In the Official Sony Pictures Press Kit for *Triplets* (Les Armateurs, 2003), writer and director Sylvain Chomet was asked how he would like people to react to his film. He replied, "I'd like them to make it their own and match it to their own memories. One gentleman came and told me that the film had moved him because Madame Souza reminded him of his own Greek grandmother. I liked that" (p. 8). This connection between motion picture character(s) and audience has always been essential to the medium, imprinting upon the viewer a uniquely personal, and at times, emotional experience. While not everyone will have the same reaction to Madame Souza as the gentleman Sylvain mentions, she is arguably a unique and memorable character in terms of her physical appearance, motivation, and courageous exploits. Consequently, the analysis of this diminutive grandmother's adventures has implications in terms of our attitudes toward age, the study of gender, and the revision of Campbell's monomyth.

Age

On May 22, 2008, after a nineteen-year hiatus, archeologist, adventurer, and part-time college professor Indiana Jones was once again back in action on the big screen, cracking his whip and cracking wise in *Indiana Jones and the Kingdom of the Crystal Skull*. After almost two decades between Indiana Jones films what seemed to generate the most media discussion was not Indy's mysterious object of historical importance, treacherous nemesis, or love interest, but whether actor Harrison Ford, at age 65, could still perform the film's trademark harrowing stunts. Several newspaper editorial cartoons even made light of Ford's, or more specifically, Dr. Jones's age. Jeff Stahler's May 21, 2008, cartoon published in the *Columbus Dispatch* has a couple outside a movie theater looking at a marquee that reads "Indiana Jones and the search for his Reading Glasses." Dan Piraro's *Bizarro* strip of June 12, 2008, titled "Indiana Jones and the Search for the Lost AARP," shows Indy packing his clothes in a suitcase saying out loud, "What'd I do with that darn discount card? I'm not paying full price for this trip!" Even one of the film's main characters, the tough young Marlon Brando wannabe Mutt Williams (Shia LaBeouf) tells Indy, "You know, for an old man you ain't bad in a fight. What are you, like 80?" and even calls him "Gramps." In response to the concern over Harrison Ford's age film critic Richard Corliss of *Time* magazine wrote, "Ford looks just fine, his chest tanned to a rich, Corinthian leather; he is still lithe on his feet.... Indeed he seems sprightlier than much of the movie" (p. 58).

While Madame Souza is not as well known internationally as Indiana Jones (the four Indy films have generated close to $2 billion worldwide compared to only $14 million for *Triplets*) this does not mean she is not just as heroic or as worthy of analysis as the more popular Fedora-wearing Ph. D. Despite their differences they share one important characteristic — age. However, whatever limitations Indy or Madame Souza may have because of age does not prevent them from answering the call to adventure or risking their lives for a loved one. If anything, their age has provided each with a greater appreciation of family, and wisdom only gained through years of experience. In other words, they are atypical role models, not to be criticized or ignored because of their maturity, but rather embraced as productive and gifted individuals. Perhaps it is too idealistic to suggest that the adventures of Indy and Madame Souza can provide an initial small step influencing attitudes toward ageism, or even generate social dialogue regarding this issue. It is probably more realistic to believe that their exploits will, at the very least, teach us an important life lesson of how we should not be defined or limited by our years lived, but only by our desire, will, and imagination. *Triplets* commentary on ageism reflects Hart's (1990) contention that "myth and rhetoric have a symbiotic relationship. Myth gives rhetoric something to say and rhetoric gives myth impact in everyday life" (p. 321). Perhaps through the success of films like *Triplets*, *Indy IV*, and the Disney-Pixar animated motion picture *Up* (2009), with its 78-year old adventurer Carl Fredricksen, will open the door for more films that highlight the older generation, further expanding the image and abilities of the mythic hero.

Gender

Cheris Kramarae's Muted Group Theory agues that language is a man-made construction as women's words and thoughts are devalued in our society. In her book *Women and Men Speaking: Frameworks for Analysis* (1981) she argues, "Women's words are, in general, ignored by historians, linguists, anthropologists, compilers of important speeches, news reporters, and businessmen, among others" (p. xiii). Women thus become a muted group because "the values and assumptions encoded in our language are primarily those of males" (p. 29). Griffin (2009) explains how historically female modes of expression have been ignored or ridiculed as the cultural establishment "excludes women's art, poetry, plays, film scripts, public address, and scholarly essays from society's mass media" (p. 457). Griffin also cites British social anthropologist Edwin Ardener's observation about women's absence in anthropological research, and author Virginia Woolf's protests of women's nonplace in recorded history. This marginalization has allowed men's stories, i.e. hero myths, to be celebrated over time, while those myths about women are often ignored or forgotten. Most scholarship of women and myth examines their influence in ancient cultures such as Greece or Rome (Pearson and Pope, 1981; Cahill, 1995; Agha-Jaffar, 2004; Lefkowitz, 2007). While this historical exploration is certainly worthy of analysis, scholars should also examine how more contemporary female characters and stories draw upon myth. For example, the popularity of the television series *Buffy the Vampire Slayer* has generated a great deal of interest among fans and academics, generating several books, journal articles, the Online International Journal of Buffy Studies (http://slayageonline.com), as well as *Buffy*-centric conferences the United Kingdom, Australia, and the United States. While *Buffy* is a unique popular culture phenomenon, there are undoubtedly other interesting female characters in television and film that also deserve attention and analysis from a mythic perspective.

The Monomyth

In *Sith, Slayers, Stargates, and Cyborgs: Modern Mythology in the New Millennium* (2008), Tanya Cochran and Jason Edwards encouraged additional research into how Campbell's notion of the hero's journey is being recast in film and television. Certainly the examination of Madame Souza in *The Triplets of Belleville* is one response to Cochran and Edwards' call. Not surprisingly, a quick investigation of the online research databases Article First, Academic Search Premiere, and eLibrary found limited scholarship on the monomyth, especially any involving heroines. One journal article from Palumbo (2008) analyzed Sarah Connor from *The Terminator* (1984) as a monomythic heroine. Another by Maines (2005) titled "The Female Hero's Quest for Love and Power" examines fantasy author Patricia McKillip's *Riddle-Master Trilogy*. However, in her discussion of the hero quest Maines argues,

> It is certainly possible to use Campbell's monomyth as a critical framework for analyzing the quest of the female hero of fantasy.... However adaptable Campbell's monomyth might be, a narrative pattern induced from examples overwhelmingly male-centered is not necessarily the best tool to use in critical examination of works in which the hero is female and inhabiting a world similar enough to our own for her to be bound by social conventions that limit her freedom of decision and action [¶ 2–3].

She cites Pearson and Pope's *The Female Hero in American and British Literature* (1981) who argue, "Our understanding of the basic spiritual and psychological archetype of human life has been limited, however, by the assumption that the hero and central character of the myth is male" (p. 4). They propose a new paradigm from which to examine the female hero, outlining the various stages of her journey from slaying the inner dragons of patriarchal society, to her return where she discovers or creates community and describes her experience. Pearson and Pope believe that "recognition of female heroism is important, not only as a way of reclaiming women's heritage, but also as a corrective to the male bias implicit in traditional discussions of the hero" (p. 5). Perhaps instead of analyzing female heroes based exclusively on Campbell's male-dominated monomyth, scholars should also consider Pearson and Pope's formula for a more gender inclusive analysis of women and myth.

Conclusion

In her discussion of on-screen medieval heroes such as King Arthur, Lancelot, and Robin Hood, Sainto (2004) writes,

> We may not expect our heroes to have perfect lineages or to behave ideally all the time; we do, however, expect nobility of heart, complete with a willingness to risk everything for a greater cause. Perhaps this accepted fallibility in our modern heroes indicates an understanding of the human nature in all of us. Yet we still search for heroes —for people who enrich our lives through their abilities, their virtues, or their sacrifices [p. 135].

In *The Triplets of Belleville* writer and director Sylvain Chomet's provides his elderly female protagonist Madame Souza with such nobility of heart, willingness to risk everything for a greater cause, virtue, and sacrifice. Souza is an unusual heroine for the new millennium, a grandmother who lacks size, wears glasses, and has one leg shorter than the other. However, when her grandson Champion is kidnapped she does not hesitate for a moment to try and save his life; surviving stormy seas, fighting the nefarious French mafia, and even tolerates eating frogs. Her small stature, quiet dignity, and inner strength is reminiscent of another mythic film hero, the 900-year-old Jedi master Yoda who tells Luke Skywalker in *The Empire Strike Back,* "Size matters not."

References

Agha-Jaffar, T. (2004). *Women and goddesses in myth and sacred text.* UK: Longman.

Brunner, D., and Cadieux, P. (Producers), Chomet, S. (Director). (2004). *The Triplets of Belleville* [Film]. Sony Pictures Classics.

Cahill, J. (1995). *Her kind: Stories of women from Greek mythology.* Orchard Park, NY: Broadview Press

Campbell, J., and Moyers, B. (1991). *The power of myth.* New York: Anchor Books.

_____. (2004). *The hero with a thousand faces.* New Jersey: Princeton University Press.

Cochran, T. R., and Edwards, J. A. (2008). Buffy the vampire slayer and the quest story: Revising the hero, reshaping the myth. In D. Whitt and J. Perlich (Eds.), *Sith, slayers, stargates, and cyborgs: Modern mythology in the new millennium* (pp.145–169). New York: Peter Lang.

Corliss, R. (2008, June 2). Indy fatigable. *Time, 171* (22), 57–58.

Cousineau, P. (2001). *Once and future myths: The power of ancient stories in our lives.* Boston, MA: Conari Press.

Ebert, R. (2003, December 26). *The Triplets of Belleville.* Rogerebert.com. Retrieved April 29, 2008, from http://rogerebert.suntimes.com

Fauvel, M. (2005). Nostalgia and digital technology: The Gleaners and I (Varda, 2000) and *The Triplets of Belleville* (Chomet, 2003) as reflective genres. *Studies in French Cinema, 5* (3), 219–229.

Griffin, E. (2009). *A first look at communication theory* (7th ed.). New York: McGraw Hill.

Hart, R. P. (1990). *Modern rhetorical criticism.* New York: Harper Collins.

Henderson, M. (1997). *Star wars: The magic of myth.* New York: Bantam Books. Homer. (1963). *The odyssey* (R. Fitzgerald, Trans.). New York: Doubleday.

Knapp, B. L. (1997). *Women in myth.* New York: State University of New York Press.

Kramarae, C. (1981). *Women and men speaking: Frameworks for analysis.* MA: Newbury House Publishers.

Lefkowitz, M. R. (2007). *Women in greek myth.* MD: Johns Hopkins University Press.

Leeming, D. (1976). *Mythology.* New York: Newsweek books.

Leeming, D. A. (1998). *Mythology: The voyage of the hero.* New York: Oxford University Press.

Les Armateurs (2003). *The Triplets of Belleville.* France: Vivi Film. http://www.sonyclassics.com/triplets/triplets_presskit.pdf

Maines, C. (2005). Having it all: The female hero's quest for love and power in Patricia McKillip's Riddle-Master Trilogy. *Extrapolation, 46* (1), 23. http://elibrary.bigchalk.com

Neupert, R. (2005). *The Triplets of Belleville. Film Quarterly, 58* (3), 38–42.

Palumbo, D. (2008). The monomyth in James Cameron's The Terminator: Sarah as monomythic heroine. *The Journal of Popular Culture, 41* (3), 413–427.

Pearson, P., and Pope, K. (1981). *The female hero in American and British literature.* New York: R.R. Bowker Co.

Perlich, J. (2009). Correspondence with author. January 5, 2009.

Pitt to star in 'outer space odyssey' (2008, October 17). IMDB.com, Retrieved October 17, 2008, from http://www.imdb.com/news/ns0000002/ ?date=2008–10–17

Robertson, B. (2004). Illusions of grandeur. *Computer Graphics World, 27* (2), 18–23.

Sainto, S.B. (2004). Not your typical knight: The emerging on-screen defender. In M.W. Driver and S. Ray (Eds.), *The medieval hero on screen* (pp. 133–150). Jefferson, NC: McFarland.

Segal, R.A. (1999). *Theorizing about myth.* Amherst, MA: University of Massachusetts Press.

6

Rethinking the Monomyth: Pan's Labyrinth *and the* Face of a New Hero(ine)

JOHN PERLICH

> Children are the world's most valuable resource and its best hope
> for the future.
> — John Fitzgerald Kennedy

I have survived many challenges during my lifetime but parenting is undoubtedly the most daunting task to present itself. While parenting is the uncontested joy of my life, navigating the waters of child-rearing is reminiscent of Odysseus's (or Jason's, or Aeneas's) attempt to successfully pass Scylla and Charybdis. The reward for parents is profound — in this sentiment I agree with the opening quotation from President Kennedy. Indeed, the future will be determined by the next generation; and parents are charged with their instruction, safety, and upbringing. It requires very little imagination to arrive at the antithesis of Kennedy's quote — children who are raised poorly can become the world's most costly consequence and its worst dread for the future. Anyone familiar with Erik Erikson's theories regarding psychosocial development would recognize the role that parents play as children spread their roots (or atrophy) as a result of their earliest encounters (1950, 1963). It is the relationship between Kennedy's thesis and the logical antithesis that causes any parent to tremble. Albeit it is the most rewarding of all possible endeavors, parenting also provides abundant opportunity for worry.

Like other authors in this volume (most notably Klosa [in Edwards & Klosa, 2010]), I have spent considerable time during the last few years contemplating the role that 'culture' will play in the development of my daughters. In the beginning I was a naïve parent and assumed that *cartoons are just cartoons* and that if I had watched a program when growing up it should be completely acceptable for my children. My cavalier attitude was quickly supplanted with a more mindful standpoint developed during graduate school and informed by a wide array of rhetorical, feminist, and media theorists (e.g., George Gerbner) who have proven both anecdotally and empirically that Marshall McLuhan's premises regarding the content of media (subordinated to media channels) should be cautiously reappraised from a more dialectical perspective.[1] As a result of both my training and standpoint as the new parent I became both cautious and skeptical of children's programming.

Admittedly, the old stand-by programs are still available and deserve our adulation (translation: thank goodness for *Sesame Street*). However, I found myself critically appraising both contemporary popular culture and classical mythology regarding its worthiness for exposure to my children. Viewing these *texts* from a more critical perspective causes me to lament the role of women in mythology, literature, and popular culture. Women in myth are often equated with trophies/conquests (e.g., Alcestis, Britomartis, Helen), depicted as witch/deceiver/weak-willed/seductress (e.g., Badb, Cassandra, Circe, Clytemnestra, Hecate, Morgan Le Fay, Pasiphae), or find their value only when they aspire to be like men or accomplish deeds considered worthy for men (e.g., Atlanta, Cloelia). Without men to define them they are at a loss (e.g., Dido). Female protagonists who might be represented by grand or master narratives in the annals of history are often invisible or forgotten. There are notable and visible exceptions (e.g., Gaia), however, these archetypes are often recognized as Earth-Mothers, Givers-of-Life, and known for nurturing qualities.

Compare for example the roles of Olwen and Culwch in classic Welsh mythology. In the tale of Culwch, Olwen simply waits for the male protagonist to accomplish great deeds while she, in turn, is courted, admired, and sought for as a bride. Culwch, on the other hand, had to overcome insurmountable tasks (thrown in his path by a wicked stepmother and a powerful giant, Yspaddaden) in order to prove himself worthy of Olwen. Cotterell and Storm (1999) described the tasks facing Culwch, which included:

> Among other things, Culwch had to uproot a forest, burn the wood for fertilizer and plough the cleared land in one day; force Amaethon, the god of agriculture to nourish its crops; make the smith god Govannon forge tools for the work; bring four strong oxen to help; obtain magic seed; provide honey nine times sweeter than that of a virgin swarm; get a magic cup and a hamper of delicious meat; borrow the drinking horn of the underwater king Gwyddbwyll and the magic harp belonging to Teirtu (an instrument that played itself); capture the birds of Rhiannon, whose song could wake the dead and lull the living to sleep; provide a magic cauldron; a boar's tusk for the giant to shave with and shaving cream made from a witch's blood; steal a magic dog, leash and collar; hire as a huntsman Mabon, son of Modron, who had first to be released from prison; find a wonderful steed and swift hounds; steal a comb, scissors, and razor from between the ears of a fierce boar; and persuade a number of unlikely guests to come to Yspaddaden's stronghold [p. 160].

Culwch, in the role of the classic protagonist, is given dozens of charges that seem impossible (the extreme nature of his quest is both laughable and exemplary). Olwen, on the other hand, is given one task — she must wait. She waits, as an object or possession, pining to be claimed.

The role of women in popular culture has not been much brighter. Modern film, fiction, and television often include women as "friends to provide aid" (Whitt, 2010) rather than heroes with stories of their own (e.g., Princess Leia in *Star Wars*; Trinity in *The Matrix*; Hermione Jean Granger in the *Harry Potter* series; Eowyn in *The Lord of the Rings*). While there are notable exceptions (e.g., Bella in *Twilight*), even these treatments are not without critics. Indeed it has been difficult, as a parent, to provide my daughters with worthy tales from contemporary and classic myth, fiction, and popular culture. I do not want them to grow up in a vacuum; however, my desire to provide them with admirable models that expand horizons (rather than limit) has been equal to Cloelia's swim across the Tiber in Roman myth. Obviously, good parenting (and storytelling) can make a grim situation more negotiable — and yet, our goal as parents often involves introducing voices to the voids that exist around us. Rare is the tale of a female who travels the path of the protagonist and heeds "the call to adventure, moving through the road of trials," and "eventually returning, forever transformed by their experience. Other authors in this volume (Goertz, 2010) have articulated the mutedness of women, calling for a "new face" or the 1,001st face_, representing the need for a new chapter in the collective study of the monomyth.

With this challenge in mind I stumbled upon a new hero. Though few would find the cinematic tale of this heroine as appropriate viewing for children, the story provides a window into the type of narrative that warrants our consideration. Her tale is parallel to well-known heroines from childhood tales (e.g.: Alice, Dorothy) with a potentially grim conclusion. Set in the post–Civil War Spanish Countryside, Guillermo del Toro's *Pan's Labyrinth* (*El laberinto del fauno*) relates the tale of a most unusual heroine, Ofelia (a.k.a. Moanna, Princess of the Underground Realm) (Navarro, Cuaron, Torres-blanco, Augustin, & del Toro, 2006). Smith (2007) describes the war torn proscenium that provides context for most of the film:

> ... it is Spain in 1944 and guerrillas are holding out in the woods against the triumphant Franco regime.... The screen flares up to white and the camera swoops over bombed buildings. A wide shot of a ruined bell tower shows the famously devastated village of Belchite, a drawing of which appeared on the cover of the Francoist magazine *Reconstrucción* as early as 1940. (The village, an uncanny tourist attraction, remains ruinous even today) [p. 4].

The remarkable manifestation of the heroine in *Pan's Labyrinth* was important for the filmmakers because del Toro believes that children embody the ideal essence — and their spirit is tarnished as a result of basic interactions with adults during the socialization process (Navarro, et. al., 2006). In del Toro's words, the film is about choice and disobedience; it is about the definition of self, more specifically it is about a girl achieving transcendence and coming to realize and actualize her ideal self (Navarro, et. al., 2006). Using intentional juxtaposition of tensions—the violence of our mundane world with the magic and tranquility of fantasy—*Pan's Labyrinth* both follows and rejects/redefines the master narrative of the hero's tale.

The purpose of this essay is to deconstruct the hero-myth, or monomyth, which typically epitomizes fantasy and science fiction texts by comparing and contrasting this archetype with Ofelia (a.k.a. Princess Moanna) in *El laberinto del fauno*. In order to understand the cultural implications of this feminist utopian tale it is first necessary to understand the lengths that del Toro took to define and identify Ofelia as the simultaneously conventional yet unorthodox protagonist in this film (and therefore contrast Ofelia with the masculine-eye that typically characterizes the narrative of monomyth). Contrarily, it is also possible to view Ofelia's adventures as prototypical of the monomyth. As a result of a thorough reading of this film it is also feasible to identify divergences and new contributions to comparative mythology, particularly with regard to the heroine's journey, and the implications for modern mythology.

DEFINING THE HERO(INE)

> It is easier for a father to have children than for children to have a
> real father.
> —Pope John XXIII

Dark liquid drips down a hole. As the camera searches for the origin of the viscous drops it lands upon a red-stained hand. The hand, at first motionless, moves slightly as the camera continues following the source of blood. We watch as the stream moves backward in time going into the nose of a young girl—as the fluid returns to her she trembles and quivers. Indeed, it seems we are watching life itself reborn within the child. Del Toro (Navarro, et. al., 2006) explains in the director commentary segments which accompany the DVD release version of *Pan's Labyrinth* that this image, the blood returning to Ofelia, and the opening scene of the film, was the most difficult segment to craft during the process of writing his screenplay; del Toro literally had writer's block for months until he imagined the moment when the blood would reverse direction and enter her nose. Del Toro's epiphany resulted from his visualization of the scene and the rest of the story fell into place. At the moment that time reverses, and we see life return to the little girl, a prologue begins— at first the words seem unrelated to the plight of the child, but on subsequent viewings the meaning of these words becomes clearer:

A long time ago, in the Underground Realm, where there are no lies or pain, there lived a princess who dreamt of the human world. She dreamt of blue skies, soft breeze and sunshine. One day, eluding her keepers, the princess escaped. Once outside, the bright sun blinded her and erased her memory. She forgot who she was and where she came from. Her body suffered cold, sickness and pain. And eventually she died. However, her father, the king, always knew that the Princess" soul would return, perhaps in another body, in another place, at another time. And he would wait for her, until he drew his last breath, until the world stopped turning....

As the prologue unfolds, the viewer is taken to a subterranean city filled with delicate spires and ornate buildings. We watch as the child darts through massive gates and dashes up a spiral staircase toward the mortal world above. Immediately following the prologue we see the young girl who was bleeding in the opening scene; curiously, she is now healthy and alive, sitting in a car that travels through remote woodland — almost as though she were reborn.

This is how we are introduced to Ofelia. In del Toro's (Navarro, et. al., 2006) words she is a metaphor for many things, including magic, innocence, fantasy, peace, and choice. In order to establish her as both heroine and protagonist, Ofelia is quickly juxtaposed with her opposites— banality, corruption, violence, and the mundane — embodied in modest terms within the material world presented to us by del Toro, and captured dramatically in stark terms by Captain Vidal, Ofelia's Fascist step-father, whom del Toro dubs the ultimate antagonist and villain (Navarro, et. al., 2006).

From the perspective of feminist film studies, a character like Ofelia is likely to be viewed in one of several conventional frames *unless* the filmmaker takes great lengths to redefine her essence and standpoint. When women appear in a film they are often viewed through a masculine gaze that assumes the viewer (and literally in this case the director) are male (Mulvey, 1975). Consequently, the male gaze is often a viewpoint that objectifies the woman or subjugates the character as a possession (e.g., Bella in *Twilight*). This occurs particularly if the male characters in the film are meant to be framed as beneficent and potent. The resulting translation causes the female character to be seen as object of love for the male characters or as a possession of the male characters (in this case a villain named Vidal). As Mulvey (1975) explains,

> The psychoanalytic background [...] is relevant to the pleasure and unpleasure offered by traditional narrative film. The scopophilic instinct (pleasure in looking at another person as an erotic object), and, in contradistinction, ego libido (forming identification processes) act as formations, mechanisms, which this cinema has played on. The image of woman as (passive) raw material for the (active) gaze of man takes the argument a step further into the structure of representation, adding a further layer demanded by the ideology of the patriarchal order as it is worked out in its favorite cinematic form — illusionistic narrative film [p. 16].

Clearly Mulvey contends that female characters (in film and often literature via the mind's eye) are predominantly eroticized or subjugated through the lens of modern cinema. Too often women in film are denied the active role of protagonist (in this case the right to complete the cycle of the monomyth) and this tendency, Mulvey believes, is largely the result of a dynamic interplay between the type of media and subtle social forces.

The argument returns again to the psychoanalytic background in that woman as representation signifies castration, inducing voyeuristic or fetishistic mechanisms to circumvent her threat. None of these interacting layers is intrinsic to film, but it is only in the film form that they can reach a perfect and beautiful contradiction, thanks to the possibility in the cinema of shifting the emphasis of the look. It is the place of the look that defines cinema, the possibility of varying it and exposing it. This is what makes cinema quite different in its voyeuristic potential from, say, strip-tease, theatre, shows, etc. Going far beyond highlighting a woman's to-be-looked-at-ness, cinema builds the way she is to be looked at into the spectacle itself. Playing on the tension between film as controlling the dimension of time (editing, narrative) and film as controlling the dimension of space (changes in distance, editing), cinematic codes create a gaze, a world, and an object, thereby producing an illusion cut to the measure of desire. It is these cinematic codes and their relationship to formative external structures that must be broken down before mainstream film and the pleasure it provides can be challenged [Mulvey, 1975, p. 16].

Del Toro, as a male director, faces a tremendous challenge if he is to create an active protagonist for the feminist utopian tale. Unless del Toro is able to create stark contrast between the protagonist and male antagonist (Vidal), Ofelia will be subjected to a secondary role (as possession or object) with the antagonist becoming the focus of the film. In simplest terms, we will wait for the female character to redeem or save the male character, transforming him into the true protagonist, consequently subverting the power of the female character — that is, unless a dramatic contrast is established and the male character seems incapable of transcendence or unwilling to transform.

In this matter del Toro is genius, creating through imagery one of the most wicked and monstrous villains in the history of cinema; a truly stunning accomplishment considering that Vidal at first seems handsome and typical if not completely meticulous. His immaculate appearance, however, is an intentional device meant to craft the antagonist — as del Toro explains, the Captain's attention to minutia underscores his inability to see the big picture. Consequently, he is unable to maintain a balanced or rational perspective in his relationships with people (Navarro, et. al., 2006). The essence of the Captain is in the mundane, as del Toro notes, he is defined by his watch. He will not tolerate Ofelia's interest in the fantastic, and his banality extends even to military strategies. However, the true corruption and violence represented by this sociopath known as the Captain is captured by del Toro in a scene that reflects the director's experience with the horror genre. Immediately following a tranquil and touching scene in which Ofelia lay upon her mother's bosom and whispers a fairy-tale to her unborn brother, we are thrust into a scene that rivals the most gruesome and disconcerting moments in film. As the Captain repairs his watch, two officers rush into his command center to announce that a pair of suspected guerrilla fighters has been captured. Vidal follows his captains outside where he confronts a father and son who justify their firearms by explaining that they were hunting rabbits. As the Captain rummages through their belongings he finds nothing to incriminate the two peasants— nothing that cannot be explained rationally as innocent and innocuous. When the young man vehemently defends his father's honesty regarding their motive, Vidal calmly steps toward the young man and begins to crush his face with the blunt end of a wine bottle that was retrieved from their bags. After the Captain obliterates the skull of the younger man, the father unleashes his rage by screaming at the villain who cold-heartedly murdered his son and Vidal shoots the infuriated father's skull without remorse. In the wake of this massacre, Vidal ruffles through a bag belonging to the peasants that has been left unopened and discovers a pair of hares. Numb to the discovery, the Captain stares down his officer and snarls, "Maybe you'll learn to search these assholes properly before you come bothering me." The gruesome slaughter of an innocent father and son was manufactured by Vidal in order to facilitate a lesson for his troops.

The villainy of Vidal serves to displace the default gaze of the filmmaker; Ofelia will no longer be seen as a passive object or possession of Vidal. His villainy is complete and becomes a crucial catalyst. Ofelia cannot embrace the Captain without joining the ranks of the antagonist. The actions of Vidal crystallize Ofelia as antithetical to him (the Captain is the primary male character in the film) and establishes her alone as the protagonist of this story. It is from this point that we follow the path of our heroine as it unfolds in the archetypical trajectory of the monomyth. Clearly, del Toro succeeds in setting the stage for a most unusual hero within the first few minutes of the film. We now travel the film witnessing the world through, and adopting the gaze of, a young girl.

OFELIA'S JOURNEY

Parents can only give good advice or put them on the right paths, but the final forming of a person's character lies in their own hands.
— Anne Frank

While Ofelia is clearly meant to stand out as an unusual and unorthodox protagonist, contrarily, it is also possible to view Ofelia's adventures as prototypical of the monomyth and the stages of separation, initiation, and return (Campbell, 1968). It is interesting to note that the first two scenes in this film set up the duality of Ofelia/Moanna (both her death and her life) and instigate a compelling storyline. Del Toro is in fact telling us the story of two characters (or facets of a single character)—Moanna, Princess of the Underground Realm, and Ofelia, the daughter of Carmen and step-daughter of Captain Vidal. Therefore, we are actually witnessing two heroine journeys that come to fruition with the ending of the film. Moanna, the Princess, has fled from her homeland to explore the surface world, her memory erased by the blinding sun, and she travels along the road of trials in a material incarnation known as Ofelia. At the end of the film, Moanna/Ofelia will cross the return threshold and rejoin her father and mother in the Underground

Realm. We witness Ofelia begin her heroine journey a few minutes into the film.

The movie starts, literally, at a crossroads for Ofelia as her significance becomes manifest in two worlds—the fantasy world and the world of reality. Ofelia of the material world, however, does not begin her path down the road of the heroine's journey until the second scene in the film. We are reintroduced to Ofelia (after watching her die in the first scene) as she sits in the back seat of a car, reading a book of fairy tales, and sitting next to her mother, Carmen. The vehicle travels through a sunlit forest. As pollen floats along the breeze and shadows dance upon the leaves, the scene has a magic and mystical quality.

Sitting in the back seat of the vehicle, Ofelia is being gently lectured by her mother regarding the folly in reading children's stories, explaining that Ofelia is too old for fairy tales (del Toro, 2006, p. 4). In this scene, Ofelia and her mother are being loosely drawn as opposites of one another. It is slightly humorous to note that immediately after Carmen scolds Ofelia for her belief in magic, Carmen is car-sick and forces the driver to stop the vehicle in the middle of the woods (as if the forces of magic were seeking retribution?). It is implied at this point that Carmen's car sickness is the result of a difficult pregnancy, which in addition to setting up the first stage in the heroine quest, establishes a budding brother-battle between Ofelia and her unborn sibling.

SEPARATION

The Call: Although the call to adventure officially begins for the protagonist while she is Moanna, Princess of the Underground Realm, Ofelia's heroine journey through the material world begins shortly after her mother, Carmen, stops the vehicle in order to deal with the nausea caused by a troubled pregnancy. During her mother's rest in the woods, Ofelia begins to wander about—much like any bored young girl might do—and happens upon a Celtic-looking obeliskoid pillar of stone. The stone has been carved to resemble a face, albeit the visage is in disrepair. The open mouth of the statue mimics a pained expression and pleads with Ofelia for assistance. On the ground Ofelia notices a stone carved with an eye on the surface. The chunk of stone seems to fit the crevice on the face of this monolith. As she returns the eye to the statue, a clicking sound can be heard and a diminutive mantis-like insect crawls from the mouth of this ancient green-man.

The *eye* of the statue is an important symbol as it represents attention, diligence, watchfulness, and ultimately action as implied by the director (del Toro, 2006). In fact, later in the film the *lack* of ocular receptors and/or blindness is symbolic for the fascist regime that surrounds Ofelia and, according to del Toro (2006), the mindless and thoughtless disregard that often explains atrocities committed by groups, organized bodies, and institutions. The simple act of placing the eye back onto the face of the statue is one that establishes a theme of volition. Therefore, the call to adventure is also a moment that will foreshadow the great boon that Ofelia shall not only procure but share with the material world.

It is clear when Ofelia repairs the Celtic statue that the insect, which will eventually transform into a more anthropomorphic shape, wants her to follow. The mantis-creature leaps from the pillar and takes flight. Ofelia begins to follow. Her journey, however, is cut short as she is called by her mother when the caravan prepares to continue along the road through the forest.

Refusal: Moments after the mantis-fairy appears to Ofelia, she is called away from the summons and continues with her mother, Carmen, along the wooded road to an old mill in the Spanish countryside. Here she first meets Captain Vidal who establishes himself as the antagonist in Ofelia's tale. When Ofelia greets him with the wrong hand (an allusion to Charles Dickens's *David Copperfield*) the Captain squeezes her hand tightly as punishment until she grimaces.

The old mill, a remote outpost used by the Fascists in their battle with guerrillas, is the main set of the film and the new "home" for Ofelia and Carmen. Smith (2007) describes the scene:

> Elderly women, overseen by steely housekeeper Mercedes, chop root vegetables or gut rabbits. It is a scene and an aesthetic reminiscent of Velásquez (for example, *Old Woman Cooking Eggs* in the National Gallery of Scotland), which is frequently reproduced in Spanish period pictures [p. 6].

The mill becomes a stage for domesticity and the mundane world — a setting that contrasts with the world of Ofelia's fairy tales. On the way toward the mill, Ofelia spots the mantis-fairy perched atop a sack of rations and she approaches the creature. This time, when the fairy takes flight, Ofelia follows the insect along a path through the woods and ultimately to an archway that symbolizes the first threshold on her heroine's journey. Engraved at the top of the arch is a face, similar to the one on the obeliskoid shape, with curved horns that might be found on a bull or satyr. As Ofelia follows the mantis-fairy it seems likely that she will descend into a labyrinth (the one that the Princess of the Underground Realm escaped in the opening scene) but she is interrupted by Mercedes, the mistress and keeper of the mill. Mercedes contrasts deeply with Carmen in that she does not quell Ofelia's love of fantasy. Instead, she stokes the flames of imagination eventually disclosing to her a (quasi)belief in fauns, or woodland place-spirits[3].

This is the second time that the mantis-fairy has attempted to solicit assistance from Ofelia — it is clear that the creature wants her to follow. Again, Ofelia is not allowed to heed the call due to interactions with adults in the material world. The interference of Mercedes seems accidental[4] considering her eventual role as a powerful symbol for women, in general, and for the female protagonist in particular; however, such analysis is forthcoming. Suffice it to say that only after the third visit from the mantis-fairy does Ofelia cross the first threshold and truly begin her journey toward fulfilling the mono-myth.

The First Threshold: It is evening when the mantis-fairy appears for the third time to Ofelia. As the little girl sleeps in her mother's bed, in her new home, with her mother, she is startled by an unexpected sound. Something is fluttering through the room. Ofelia reacts to the noise with pleas for her mother to wake but she does not stir. The mantis-fairy circles the room until it lands upon her quilt. Confronted by the now familiar creature, Ofelia calmly asks the winged being if it followed her to the Mill and if the creature would iden-tify itself as a fairy? The stick-insect is clearly confused by the question, and Ofelia is required to open a page from her fairytale book to explain her query. At this point in the story the stick-insect transforms into an anthropomor-phic shape and resembles a diminutive human with wings. The newly born fairy flies toward the window and points outside. Ofelia asks the creature if it wants her to follow and, if so, where she should go. She follows the fairy into the night.

When describing the scene where Ofelia chases down the green fairy, it is obvious that our heroine has begun the first stages of a hero's journey. Ofe-lia carefully pursues the green fairy who suddenly arrives at the ruins that sur-round the labyrinth. The scene is dark, and del Toro's choice of lighting emphasizes the absence of daylight. The primary color in the scene is blue. Everything is cast blue with shades of black. Del Toro has acknowledged that his choice of color demarks the distinction between the fantasy world and mundane reality; the line between these two worlds blurs in the second and third acts of the film, a fact that is reflected by del Toro's intentional use of color (Navarro, et, al., 2006). The use of color to distinguish a dileneation between fantasy and reality has been used successfully in other films (Boggs & Petrie, 2000, p. 201); this technique provides the viewer with an under-standing of Ofelia's experiences.

Making her way along the path through the maze, stepping cautiously over gnarled roots and other obstructions, Ofelia arrives at a stone staircase that descends into the darkness below her feet. The stairway is circular, resem-bling Celtic standing stones, and appears to be both ancient and forgotten. Slowly stepping down the spiraling stairs, Ofelia calls out with trepidation to find out if she is alone, repeating two words: "Hello" and "Echo." She seems at once both timid and curious. The atmosphere is portentous, yet she clearly seems intrigued by the old ruin. At the bottom of the stairwell, Ofelia stops as the green fairy lands upon an ancient monolith at the center of the cham-ber. The monolith, like the stairwell, is peppered with Celtic symbols, designs, and letters. While Ofelia explores her surroundings, the fairy flutters over to what appears to be another stone monolith — as the fairy lands on its surface the object undulates, growls, and comes to life. The stairwell is filled by the rumblings of a deep voice, the sound of hooves on stones, and the breath of a large creature. Turning toward Ofelia, a big horned biped exclaims, "It's you." The satyr-like creature asks Ofelia to be calm, and smiles as he pulls a wicker basket from the shadows. At this point in the heroine's journey she has crossed the threshold by entering the labyrinth. It is here that she becomes acquainted with her partners, the Faun and the Fairies.

The Labyrinth and Heroine Partners: Upon seeing Ofelia, the Faun, who is part-humanoid (torso, arms, chest, head) and part-ungulate (waist, legs, hooves), clearly recognizes our protagonist as he shouts with delight, saying something about her return. He tells her to not be afraid as she backs away from him (del Toro, 2006, p. 23). In the film, the Faun notices that Ofelia has been studying a monolisk at the threshold of the pool — on the monolisk is an engraved image of a small girl, embraced by a woman, embraced by a man-faun. The man-faun resembles the King of the Underground Realm (who we see in the third act of the film) with faun-like horns. The Faun interprets the monolisk by identifying the man as him, and the girl as Ofelia, gesturing to the child. In this way the Faun has subtly implicated himself as an altered manifestation of both Ofelia's true father and the king of the Underground Realm. However, since Ofelia has not been exposed to the prologue of the film (but the viewer has) she is unaware of the significance in the Faun's disclosure — the audience for the film can quickly assemble the pieces to the puzzle and discern the omnipresent and omnipotent nature of the Faun.

Other readers of the film and/or screenplay might disagree with an interpretation of the Faun as manifestation of, or symbolic of, the King of the Underground Realm. However, it should be noted that even del Toro (2006) argues for the intentionality of ambiguity regarding the Faun. When Ofelia expresses her curiosity toward the Faun, asking about his identity, the conversation takes an interesting turn. The Faun explains that his names are innumerable; they are old and only able to be pronounced by the fundamental elements of air and flora; his essence is earth, stone, and forest; yet he arrives at a final statement regarding his identity when he declares, I am faun. In his introduction to Ofelia he addresses her as "your highness," and this formal title is denounced by Ofelia. The Faun quickly corrects her, offering the statement that she is, indeed, Princess Moanna, daughter of the King of the Underground Realm. When she objects and offers that her father was a tailor, the Faun corrects her, explaining that she was not born as a human but instead from the essence of moon. He offers evidence to support his argument telling her that a mark on her left shoulder proves that her real identity as daughter of the King. The Faun's exuberance at the sight of Ofelia is finally summed up at the conclusion of their introduction when he informs her that the King has been searching for her, opening portals throughout the mortal world in order to find her, but the portal before her is the last. If she wishes to return to the Underground Realm she must prove her essence has not been lost (i.e. that she is not a mortal) by completing three tasks prior to the full moon. Thus, in this scene we are introduced to the Faun, the Labyrinth, and Ofelia (a.k.a. Princess Moanna) (del Toro, 2006, p. 24). In this moment we come to understand the Faun as embodiment of many things. His essence is complex; equally complex is the identity of Ofelia. At the end of this scene the Faun presents Ofelia with the leather-bound *Book of Crossroads*. If she chooses to open the book in solitude it will show her the future and what must be done to accomplish the three tasks. After she opens the book, which is empty, Ofelia begins to question the Faun only to find that he has disappeared from sight.

In del Toro's (2006) words, the Faun is the personification of nature, which is neutral — like nature the Faun should be seen as both benevolent and malicious; capricious and trustworthy; wicked and benign. Thus, the Faun is an embodiment of the tension between energies that occupy unified opposites or dialectical forces[5]. In hindsight it is clear that the Faun serves as guide, partner, friend, and father; however, at the conclusion of each test or trial faced by Ofelia, the Faun remains a potential nemesis— this continues through the first two acts of the film. Consequently, while the Faun is Ofelia's heroine partner, the reader/audience is left to wonder if the Faun might also serve as antagonist or antithesis for the protagonist. The tension between Ofelia and the Faun is intentional (Navarro, et. al., 2006).

From the beginning of the film we are introduced to other heroine partners for Ofelia. These partners live in the fantasy realm (the fairies) and the material world (Mercedes). The mantis-fairies (green, blue, & red), in particular, represent another type of supernatural aid for our protagonist. Del Toro's screenplay introduces the three fairies after Ofelia follows the green-fairy into the labyrinth — when the Faun opens a small wicker basket a blue and red fairy join their sister (del Toro, 2006. p. 23). Mercedes also embodies the spirit of resistance necessary to become a partner to our heroine. At one point in the screenplay (del Toro, 2006, p. 10), Mercedes tells Ofelia that her father requires her help to which Ofelia denies Vidal as being her father. She informs Mercedes that her real father was a tailor and died in the war. Her denunciation of the Captain as her father is explicit and somewhat spiteful. Mercedes smiles at the girl's insolence and the two walk away together at the end of a scene meant to define the partners of this heroine quest. It is clear that Mercedes shares Ofelia's disdain for her step-father.

While there are many heroine partners, undoubtedly, the most significant hero companion is the Faun. At the end of their introductory scene the Faun presents Ofelia with the *Book of Crossroads*. Del Toro explains that this tome is significant for all characters in the film because everyone exists at a crossroads. Admittedly, Ofelia is the protagonist and therefore her crossroads is more salient. After Ofelia is presented with the *Book of Crossroads* by the Faun she asks about the nature of the text only to find that the Faun has disappeared. In fact, after being presented with the manuscript, Ofelia is abandoned to discern the meaning of this tome on her own.

On the eve of a banquet that is *vitally* important to Captain Vidal, Ofelia consults the newly acquired *Book of Crossroads* during her bath time. Trying to connect with her daughter, Carmen interrupts the bath by offering an exquisite green silk dress lined with ivory netting. Attempting to respect her mother, Ofelia considers the dress, yet her distaste for the garment is plain. Again, out of fondness for her mother she attempts a weak smile, notes del Toro (2006, p. 28). As Ofelia disrobes, her belief in a supernatural world is confirmed when she discovers a moon-symbol on her shoulder. Following the realization of her nobility, Ofelia denies her mother's dress, and instead opens the magical book (p. 28). The choice to postpone getting ready and instead peruse the tome is rebellious, intentional, and signifies that Ofelia has embraced her new companion, the Faun. At first, the page in the *Book of Crossroads* is blank, but a curious image begins to take shape. It is a picture of Ofelia, along with chestnuts (or stones in the film); squatting at her side under a huge tree is a massive toad. A knock on the door interrupts Ofelia, and Carmen asks her daughter to hurry with the dress, excited to see her little Princess. Ofelia studies the birthmark on her right shoulder, a birthmark in the form of a crescent moon, exactly as described by the Faun. She smiles as she repeats both the Faun's and Carmen's line, "a Princess" (p. 28).

After her bath, Ofelia descends from the upstairs and into the kitchen of the mill where she meets up with Mercedes. The matron of the mill offers Ofelia some milk with honey and together they exit the kitchen and walk to the stables. Mercedes begins to milk a cow when Ofelia asks if she believes in fairies, to which Mercedes responds that she did, when she was a little girl. Ofelia then confides in Mercedes regarding her encounter with the fairies and faun (who she describes as ancient, large, and smelling of earth)—Mercedes wryly tells Ofelia that her mother always warned her to be wary of fauns (del Toro, 2006, p. 31). In this scene, Mercedes establishes herself as a trusted confidant for Ofelia—unlike her mother, Mercedes playfully accepts Ofelia's interest in a fantasy world, even going so far as to admit an interest when she was a child. Mercedes becomes a companion in the material world. After their conversation, Ofelia seems even more fixated with the Underground Realm.

As a result of both the conversation with Mercedes and the compelling image of a gnarled fig-tree in the *Book of Crossroads*, Ofelia must take action. She chooses to skip Vidal's banquet and instead explore the dense woods surrounding the mill. Her quest is described in the screenplay by a voiceover from Ofelia:

> When the forest was young, it was home to creatures who were full of magic and wonder.... At the heart of this forest stood a fig tree. The Forest Folk slept in its shadow. But now, the tree is dying. Its branches are dry, its trunk old and twisted. A monstrous toad has settled in its roots and won't let the tree thrive. You must put the three magic rocks in its mouth and retrieve a magic key from its insides. Only then will the fig tree flourish again [del Toro, 2006, p. 34].

In a gesture that symbolizes her desire to balance the fairy and material world, del Toro signifies the newfound volition of the protagonist through her actions in the film. Standing outside the fig tree she removes her green silk dress and delicately drapes the garment, including her hair ribbons, on the branches of a nearby tree. Donned in only a cotton slip and shoes she prepares to enter the hollow trunk. Her caution with the beautiful gown and hair ribbons is irrelevant because a storm is brewing — the breeze increases and a strong gust of wind flings her dress and hair-tie into the forest (del Toro, 2006, p. 34). At this point in the heroine tale, Ofelia struggles to balance the forces that vie for her attention from the material world and the fantasy world.

Belly of the Whale: In an attempt to reconcile the irreconcilable tension between fantasy and reality, Ofelia enters the gash at the base of the mammoth fig tree. At this point in the story Ofelia is torn between her desire to experience a fantastic adventure and the advice of her mother to *grow up*. Ofelia assumes as she enters the tree that her findings will be inconsequential. While she has no desire to part with the material world, it is clear that she hopes to confirm the realm of fantasy.

According to Campbell (1968), one of the most common rights-of-passage in the monomyth occurs when the protagonist becomes isolated from their familiar world and they are reborn (literally and/or figuratively) with the knowledge of a new world. While Campbell refers to this benchmark in the hero's journey as "The Belly of the Whale," del Toro captures this turning point in the odyssey of Ofelia with a poignantly feminine symbol — the womb. Del Toro asserts that the shape of the fig tree is intentional, resembling both the horns of the faun and the fallopian tubes of a woman (Navarro, et. al., 2006). The shape of the ancient fig tree establishes a referent meant to symbolize the womb, femininity, and transformation. Ofelia will literally be reborn when she emerges from the hole in the trunk of the tree.

Del Toro notes in the screenplay that Ofelia cautiously crawls through the fig tree; the opening is so small it can only be described as claustrophobic (del Toro, 2006, p. 34). The warrens under the tree are moist and organic, like the lining of an artery wall or intestines. Color choices are warm hues; brown, yellow, orange, and red accent the darkness around Ofelia. The colors suggest a blurring between the fantasy realm and the real world — the viewer is left to speculate if the scene is real or magical, as blue-tinged light was previously used to illuminate the fantastical. Determined to resolve the tension between fantasy and reality, Ofelia continues through the roots of the ancient fig tree carrying the three magical stones — tokens bestowed to her by the Faun — until she comes upon an incredible scene. As the passage branches in multiple directions, Ofelia wonders which way to turn. A soggy, slurping sound causes her to look left — the heroine is now eye to eye with a gigantic slime-covered toad. Horn-like protrusions above blinking eyes give the beast a menacing appearance. Ofelia greets the toad, but the creature seems disinterested.

Ofelia bravely announces that she is Princess Moanna and is unafraid of the monster; she chastises the amphibian for its parasitic behavior, shaming the creature for gorging on the pill bugs that surround them while the fig tree dies. As if in response, the toad lashes out with a putrid tongue at

Ofelia's head — it is clear, however, that the toad simply wanted to eat the pill bug stuck to her face. Satisfied with its meal, the toad lets out a deafening belch; the strength of its expulsion forces Ofelia's hair back and eyes closed. Her face is covered with a gelatinous sludge. Ofelia is disgusted by the gluttony represented in the toad. It is worth noting that while Ofelia confronts the beast, her step-father gorges above at a feast in the mill as peasants starve in Francisco Franco's Spain. The parallel between the beast and the Captain is clear.

Undaunted by the toad, Ofelia completes her quest. She picks up the three magical stones that have fallen in the ooze and also palms a large pill bug. Realizing the opportunity before her, she displays the insect for the toad and tantalizes the beast with this irresistible morsel. When the toad perks up in reaction to its next meal, Ofelia places the bug in the same hand as the three stones. Suddenly, the toad wraps its tongue around Ofelia's wrist and the appendage grasps the pill bug and stones. When the tongue retracts, the creature begins to quiver and belch as a result of the magical stones that were consumed. A bubble emerges from the mouth of the amphibian, and within seconds a quivering mound of innards plops to the ground. A sack of skin that was the toad lay shriveled on the cavern floor. Secured to the slimy mound of guts is a golden key, which Ofelia procures from the sticky mass. She emerges from the fig tree, covered in primordial slime, grasping the object of her quest. Dirty and tired, she walks toward the branch where the silk dress had been hanging — it is not there. Several feet away she finds the dress and hair ribbons on the ground, covered in mud. At the conclusion of this scene, Ofelia's flight from the womb signifies a rebirth. The worlds of fantasy and reality begin to influence each other and she is the catalyst for all events that unfold following her confrontation with the toad. The protagonist has begun a journey down the road of trials.

Initiation

According to del Toro (Navarro, et. al., 2006), the second act of *Pan's Labyrinth* begins after Ofelia has emerged from the roots of the fig tree. She has been reborn and the world will never be the same for her. It is in the second act of this film, explains del Toro, that the line between fantasy world and real world continues to blur (Navarro, et. al., 2006). In fact, at this point in the film the two worlds literally affect each other.

Road of Trials: Following her confrontation with the giant toad, Ofelia is covered with filth, her dress is soiled, and her hair is drenched with rain. Although she procured the magical key, the effort has sullied her from head to toe. As a result, the viewer is left to assume that Ofelia missed the important dinner — a banquet — held by her step father. The bounty of the banquet is lush and contrasts with the poverty suffered by most common-folk during post World War II in Francisco Franco's Spain. The gluttony of the banquet will be mirrored during the second test for Ofelia. The fact that she fasted during the feast is a significant character development.

Additionally, it is clear from Carmen's consternation that Ofelia's appearance and/or absence from the banquet has caused her embarrassment. Carmen scolds Ofelia, noting that she has hurt and disappointed both her and her new father, the Captain. In fact, Carmen is quick to note that Vidal seems to be the one who is most upset. This news produces a slight trace of satisfaction on Ofelia's face. She is pleased to have disappointed the Captain. Unlike the hero's journey, where the male protagonist often must confront a father figure and reconcile the father and son relationship (Campbell, 1968), Ofelia recognizes the illegitimacy of the patriarchal figure represented by Captain Vidal. Such a theme is salient when contrasting the journey of the hero with the journey of the heroine and deconstructing the monomyth. At the conclusion of this scene, a fairy enters Ofelia's room — she speaks to it with hushed tones, informing the fairy that she has found the key and requesting that the diminutive being take her to the labyrinth (del Toro, 2006, p. 44).

The crossing of the threshold embodied by the ancient fig tree initiates the start of an odyssey for Ofelia as she now travels what Campbell (1968) calls the road of trials. At the labyrinth, Ofelia meets the Faun who tells her that she should keep the key. He informs her that while she has succeeded, there are two more tasks to be completed before the moon is full. The Faun hands Ofelia a piece of chalk needed for the next test. The ambiguity of the Faun is reestablished by del Toro (2006, p. 45) in this scene as he ponders their future together, treasuring the possibility that they will soon be strolling through the palace gardens. Ofelia questions the Faun, asking how she can know that he is speaking the truth in these matters; the Faun responds with a wicked grin and a question rather than a statement, asking her what possible motive he would have for lying. The ambiguous and capricious essence of the Faun is intentional and will set the stage for a confrontation required to fulfill the journey of a heroine. It is the Faun (a fantasy figure), not Captain Vidal (the step-father), who will serve as the father-figure that is often confronted in the final stages of a monomyth. The Faun establishes himself as a catalyst for the eventual apotheosis, or divine transcendence, of the protagonist.

When morning arrives, Ofelia has gone without supper and should be famished, but the need to satiate her hunger for the fantasy world is more powerful. Her first action — a choice, per se — is to secret herself in the bathroom and pull the book from behind a radiator. She opens the book and a new image begins to appear on the pages. The image is equally magical, mundane, and feminine. The book bleeds with a crimson ink and the emerging shape resembles fallopian tubes (Navarro, et. al., 2006). The *Book of Crossroads* has filled with blood, an image that is startling and feminine. In fear, Ofelia drops the book and runs to her mother. Carmen looks up at Ofelia and extends a bloody hand toward the girl as she cries out for help (del Toro, 2006, p. 47).

It is clear that Carmen is in the midst of a potential miscarriage and is in danger of losing her own life. This moment establishes the next theme in the journey of a heroine, but one that takes on new meaning when deconstructing the monomyth of the female protagonist.

Brother-Battle: According to Campbell (1968), the classic archetypical journey of the hero often involves a brother battle, and Ofelia finds her road of trials blocked by the actions of a yet unborn brother. At the beginning of the film, Carmen attributes her motion sickness during the car ride to Ofelia's unborn brother, explaining that her sibling is not doing well (del Toro, 2006, p. 5). Even though he is still within the womb, Ofelia must fight her brother for the attention of her mother and the battle escalates as Ofelia travels the road of trials.

In an attempt to resolve the brother-battle, Ofelia must reconcile the fantasy realm with reality. She promises her brother a gift if he will calm down and be nice to Carmen. Laying next to her mother, Ofelia whispers that things are bad outside and that their mother is very sick; she promises to take him with her to the Underground Realm and make him a prince if he will stop hurting Carmen. Ofelia weeps as she pleads with her unborn sibling. It is meaningful that Ofelia's brother calms down after both her promise to him and as a result of help from the Faun.

The evening of the near-miscarriage, Ofelia is visited by the Faun who demands to know why she has not continued to read the *Book of Crossroads* or fulfilled her second task. When she explains that her mother is not well and her brother has been acting up, the Faun harshly criticizes her slow progress but also offers magical aid to Ofelia as he presents her with a mandrake root — a plant that he describes as yearning to be human. He instructs Ofelia to put the mandrake root under her mother's bed in a bowl of milk and feed the plant two drops of blood each day (del Toro, 2006, p. 51). After offering aid and council, the Faun urges Ofelia to begin the second task with the help of his magical fairies. During the second test we arrive with Ofelia at a new intersection in the road of trials.

Woman as Temptress: In the archetypical monomyth, a male protagonist is often enticed to stray from the path of the hero by a female temptress (Campbell, 1968). When the protagonist is a heroine, Campbell's articulation of the monomyth seems, at first glace, inapplicable. However, if the etymology of *temptress* is massaged, it is possible to arrive at a reading that is consistent with both Campbell (1968) and the historic identity of women. Billinghurst (2003, p. 13) deconstructs the image of temptress from Lilith to Cleopatra to Marilyn Monroe — the result of her analysis is that "temptress" constitutes a "composite of fact and fancy." The temptress often upsets the balance of power between men and women; the temptress is naughty; the temptress takes control and is often empowered. If we use the etymology of this word — rather than the hyper-sexualized common definition — to analyze the heroine's journey, it seems indeed that Ofelia becomes empowered as the result of disobedience, independent choice, and volition. In fact, both Mercedes and Ofelia use their free-will and disobedience to disrupt the machinations of Captain Vidal.

In order to prepare Ofelia for the second test, the Faun speaks to her in a patriarchal tone. He instructs her on the task and implies that success will be plausible only if she listens and follows his orders, when the opposite is true. In fact, for Ofelia to succeed she must disobey and make choices on her own. The Faun urges her complete subordination as he warns her about the next challenge. She will enter an ominous banquet hall that serves as the lair for a deadly slumbering guardian. The Faun commands her to touch nothing — no matter how tempting the fare and how placid the guardian — she must not disturb the place. She should pay particular care to avoid eating or drinking anything from the sumptuous buffet. Indeed, while Ofelia should not consume the food (again, her fasting is an important symbol that escalates her position as antithesis to Vidal), she only succeeds in procuring the second item required for her ascension by *disobeying* the fairies.

Using the piece of chalk provided by the Faun, Ofelia draws a door in her room and opens the portal into a long hallway of pillars shaped like fanning trees. She enters the hallway, circled by fairies, and approaches a banquet hall. At the head of the table sits the Pale Man, an ogre-like creature with no discernable eyes or nose. On the Pale Man's hands are stigmata. Resting on a plate in front of the ogre are two eyeballs. The Pale Man sits still at the head of the table which is filled with a feast of delicious foods. On the walls are murals and paintings that resemble Goya's, *Saturn Devouring His Son* (Navarro, et. al., 2006) — the images are violent depictions of the Pale Man consuming children. In the corner of the room is a pile of children's shoes.

At the sight of food, Ofelia's stomach growls. She went to bed without supper the night before and has not yet broken her fast. On one wall in the room are three niches, in each niche is a door, and on the doors are identical locks. The fairies swarm around the center door but Ofelia disobeys and insists that the correct door is on her left. She inserts the key, much to the frustration of the fairies, but her choice is correct. From the door she pulls forth a beautiful and ornamented dagger, it looks ceremonial and significant. Ofelia has succeeded by disobeying the fairies, but her defiance will also cost her. As she turns to exit the room her eyes rest upon a plate of ripe grapes. Unable to resist the temptation, she steals a grape and pulls it toward her mouth. The fairies castigate Ofelia but she does not heed their cries of warning. As she eats the grape, the ogre inserts the eyeballs from his plate into his stigmata and rises to his feet. He menacingly approaches Ofelia and the fairies attack him. Two fairies are consumed and the Pale Man nearly catches Ofelia as she flees the room via a new door that she draws on the ceiling with her chalk.

At the same time that Ofelia overcomes the challenge of the ogre in the fantasy realm, Mercedes disobeys the Captain in the material world by providing assistance to a group of guerrillas who continue the battle against Franco's troops. She presents the leader of the guerrillas with a key to the storeroom at the mill. The disobedience of Mercedes (and the key) echoes the rebelliousness of Ofelia. With the key to the storeroom, the guerrillas are able to prolong the fight against the fascists in their country. Mercedes has risked her life, like Ofelia risked hers, with volition. These parallel scenes introduce the ultimate boon that Campbell (1968) asserts is the pinnacle of the hero-myth.

Great Boon & Female Goddess: At the end of her road of trials, Ofelia procures a ceremonial dagger. This weapon will serve as a final catalyst in the coming apotheosis; however, the dagger is not the ultimate boon that defines this heroine journey. Ofelia, like Mercedes, has discovered the gift of volition. For centuries, women have been defined as subjects, subordinated as lesser citizens, denied the rights and privileges that should be accorded to all citizens. The only means to affect change in the power hierarchies that disenfranchise individuals is through ardent disobedience. Ofelia has completed the second stage of her heroine's quest by finding her own voice. She has learned to laugh at the possibility that she can hurt and offend Captain Vidal. Her actions in the lair of the Pale Man were disobedient — not without consequences— but the choices made were her own. Her belief in magic saved her mother, placated her brother, brought her closer to a real father, and ultimately will guide her toward apotheosis and inheritance. It is Ofelia who becomes the goddess by finding her voice. Unfortunately, the steep cost and consequences of volition will be revealed to Ofelia as the second act closes and the final stage of the monomyth comes to fruition.

The great boon discovered by Ofelia is choice, voice, and volition. As a testament to the value of this gift, other characters speak on the subject at several points in the film. One of the most powerful moments occurs after Dr. Ferreiro, the physician supervising Carmen during the pregnancy and hired by Vidal, disobeys the Captain by euthanizing a guerrilla who has been tortured by Vidal and is on the verge of giving away information. The guerrilla begs the doctor to end his life, which Ferreiro does. When Vidal learns of the betrayal he asks the doctor about his decision to be disobedient when he could have simply followed orders. The doctor's response captures the thesis of del Toro's film, "To obey — just like that — for the sake of obeying, without questioning ... that's something only people like you can do, Captain" (Navarro, et. al., 2006). As Ofelia finds her voice through the second act, her newfound freedom becomes contagious, spreading like fire through the mill and the Spanish countryside. Her gift is a boon for all.

Atonement with the mother: At the closing of the second act, Ofelia has completed the second task assigned to her by the Faun, she is filled with volition, and her mother is doing well thanks to the supernatural aid that has been provided by heroine partners. However, the path of the protagonist will soon take a turn for the worst. While Ofelia clearly forgives her mother, Carmen, for not being able to see, accept, or understand the fantasy world that surrounds them, atonement comes through tragedy when Carmen passes from the material world and rejoins Ofelia's father in the Underground Realm.

Using the supernatural aid provided by the Faun, Ofelia has essentially nursed her mother back to health. Even as Carmen denies the existence of magic, the power of the mandrake root has saved her life. It is Vidal, the antithesis of Ofelia, unbeliever and antagonist, who instigates a confrontation between Carmen and the heroine. Ofelia is checking on the mandrake root when Vidal finds her under the bed and confronts her, demanding to know what she is doing beneath her mother's bed (del Toro, 2006, p. 74). He rips the foul smelling mandrake root out of its bowl and is about to strike Ofelia when Carmen intercedes, asking him to leave them so that she might talk with her daughter (del Toro, 2006, p. 75). Ofelia attempts to explain her actions, disclosing to Carmen that the Faun had orchestrated her recovery and that his recommendations cured her poor condition. Carmen ignores Ofelia's pleas to flee the mill and Vidal, admonishing her child for an irrational belief in fairies and stories. Carmen's last words are a nihilistic attempt to return Ofelia to reality — a world that she simultaneously describes as cruel and complex. Carmen throws the root into the fire, screaming that magic does not exist. As the mandrake curls up in the fire we watch Carmen, overwhelmed with pain, fall to the floor. Though Ofelia cannot convince her mother that the fairy world is real, it is clear that she loves her mother and forgives her for the tragedy that prevents Carmen from understanding Ofelia's world. Carmen's death (as a result of ignorance) brings closure to the second act in del Toro's story.

The Return

As previously noted, *Pan's Labyrinth* follows the journey of two heroines— though it can easily be argued that they are facets of the same essence — Moanna, Princess of the Underground Realm, and Ofelia. As a result of the dual-essence of the protagonist, the final stages of the heroine's journey are complex and in some ways reject clear chronology. For this reason, it is possible to point at several distinct yet nonsequential moments within the film that qualify as meeting Campbell's (1968) monomyth.

Refusal of return: When Ofelia failed to heed the advice of the Faun while confronting the challenge of the Pale Man, it could be argued that she wanted to stay in the fairy world. The abundance of the banquet provided ample temptation for Ofelia to remain in this magical room and deny her material world. It was the wrath and menace of the Pale Man that forced her to flee and ultimately return to the mill. That evening, after partially succeeding in her second task, Ofelia is confronted by the Faun who is visibly angered when he learns of her transgression. The Faun renounces his belief in Ofelia and forecasts her doom. He exclaims that she has failed; he has made a mistake; she will never return to the Underground Realm; she will die as a human — living among them and growing old; her spirit will remain lost, her memory shall fade from the Kingdom, and she will never see her true home again. With these words, the Faun backs into the darkest corner of the attic and disappears. It is clear from both her actions in the ogre's room and following the confrontation with the Faun that Ofelia is desperate to escape the grim circumstances that surround her in the material world. Although she has been denied, her boon of volition begins to change circumstances in both the material world and the fantasy world.

Magic flight and return: Following the death of her mother, the Faun chooses to allow Ofelia a second chance. Like before, the Faun demands obedience; once again, Ofelia will ultimately only succeed if she disobeys. As the moment of apotheosis draws near, Ofelia must challenge the Captain, disregard the Faun, and ultimately make the ultimate sacrifice. There is a sense of urgency in the third act of del Toro's script. It is clear that Ofelia's/Moanna's window of opportunity for return to the Underground Realm is closing. While she is mourning for her mother, the Faun approaches Ofelia and declares that he will be giving her a second chance — this time she must listen and obey his instructions. She must take her infant brother from the command center of Vidal and bring him to the labyrinth. Ofelia wants to know why the Faun would want her brother but he suspiciously refuses to answer her query. When she explains that the door to her brother's room (also Vidal's office) is locked, the Faun prompts Ofelia to make her own door. The Faun presents Ofelia with another piece of chalk. The symbolism in the chalk is compelling, and the line, "create your own door," echoes del Toro's thesis regarding volition, choice, and action. She is determined to make the most of her second opportunity and uses the chalk to create a portal into her brother's nursery, which is also Vidal's headquarters. In this scene, Vidal is bloody and monstrous, having lost in a confrontation with Mercedes over her involvement with the guerrillas. Mercedes has maimed him, lacerating his face, chest and back. Undaunted by the hideous Vidal, Ofelia drugs his glass of Orujo, bundles her brother, and runs for the door. An explosion outside the mill causes Vidal to turn toward the exit just in time to see Ofelia fleeing with his newborn son. Vidal chases his step-daughter through the battle that has been unleashed upon his forces by the guerrillas. It is the moment of undoing for the antagonist. He has indirectly brought about the death of his wife, the guerrillas are rebelling against fascism, and his son is being spirited away thanks to the supernatural aid provided by heroine partners. Ofelia runs into the nearby labyrinth presumably to meet up with the Faun.

Crossing the Return Threshold. When she arrives at the labyrinth, the Faun appears to her, the site is what Campbell (1968) would call the return threshold. Ofelia will now face the third and final test from the Faun, and ultimately choose to offer her life. Demanding the infant boy from Ofelia, the Faun holds a golden dagger in his bestial hands. As the film progresses, the moon waxes, and the opportunity to open a portal into the Underground Realm approaches

—at the same time, the Faun has become younger with each passing scene. This reversal of the aging process serves to make the Faun seem more passionate, energetic, and fervent. The power manifest in a youthful and virile faun underscores the foreboding tone of this scene as he urgently appeals for the infant. The viewer cannot help but worry for the safety of Ofelia's sibling. Yet, Ofelia's brother unwittingly claimed the life of their mother. Ofelia is torn. Her opportunity for return to the Underground Realm is waning. Crying out that he cannot remain in the mortal realm any longer, the Faun is stunned when Ofelia refuses to hand over her brother. Articulating his disbelief, the Faun asks if Ofelia would sacrifice her sacred birth-right for a half-brother she hardly knows? Ofelia affirms her desire to protect the infant. Desperate, the Faun reminds Ofelia of the misery caused by this child; for him she will sacrifice her throne and the rightful place next to the King? Her two word response, "I will," is the last statement uttered by Ofelia. Vidal enters the threshold at the end of Ofelia's conversation with the Faun. The Captain can only see Ofelia. He places his hand on her shoulder, turns her toward him, and gently takes the baby from her arms. The Captain takes a few steps away from Ofelia, raises his pistol, and shoots her in the chest. The girl sinks to the ground and falls to rest near the entrance of the portal. Blood trickles from her nose and drips down into the heart of the labyrinth.

It is Ofelia's blood that ultimately opens the portal mentioned by the Faun. Ofelia's decision to protect the boy and sacrifice herself gains her access to the Underground Realm. Though her pupils dilate and her life pours into the pool at the bottom of the labyrinth, Ofelia hears a regal voice command her to rise. This is the moment of apotheosis.

Mistress of Two Worlds and Apotheosis. In death and transcendence, Ofelia has become what Campbell (1968) might call the Mistress of Two Worlds, she is the spirit who inspires the guerrillas at the conclusion of the film and she simultaneously returns as Princess of the Underground Realm. Vidal exits the maze only to be confronted by Mercedes and the victorious guerrilla troops. As Mercedes takes the newborn from Vidal, his last request is for Mercedes to tell his son about the time that he died; Vidal's obsession with time and the meticulous care for his watch was predicated by the death of his father, General Vidal (the pocket watch Vidal is seen fixing earlier in the film belonged to the General and had stopped running precisely at the time of his death). Mercedes coldly denies his request and informs Vidal that the child will not even know his name (del Toro, 2006, p. 95). With volition, Mercedes puts a note of finality on Vidal's reign of terror—the cycle of cruelty, begun by Vidal's father, has come to an end. As Mercedes utters his doom, the guerrillas shoot Vidal at the threshold to the labyrinth.

Having returned to the Underground Realm, Princess Moanna learns from her father that the sacrifice of self was the third test. She protected her innocent brother and gave of herself for others—a choice with profound implication. The film concludes with a voiceover from the narrator,

And it is said that the Princess went back to her father's kingdom — and that she reigned with justice and a kind heart for many centuries. And that she was loved by all her subjects.... And, like most of us, she left behind small traces of her time on earth. Visible only to those that know where to look ... [del Toro, 2006, p. 97].

As the film comes to an end, the last image we see is of the fig tree. On one of the branches, a flower begins to bloom. The ancient plant is growing once more. The words of Anne Frank, found at the beginning of this section, resonate with the viewer at the conclusion of this film. Indeed, Ofelia has endured the road of trials and experienced a moment of transcendence as a result of choice — her path is similar to other archetypical heroes, like Prometheus, Buddha, Moses, Elijah, Jonah, and Jesus[6].

IMPLICATIONS

Making the decision to have a child — it's momentous. It is to decide forever to have your heart go walking outside your body.
— Elizabeth Stone

At the beginning of this chapter the fundamental thesis of del Toro's film was explained using his words (Navarro, et. al., 2006): the film is about choice and disobedience; it is about the definition of self. Using intentional juxtaposition of tensions, the violence of our mundane world with the magic and tranquility of fantasy, *Pan's Labyrinth* both follows and redefines hero-myth. Undoubtedly, del Toro succeeds in explicating his thesis.

There is, however, a curious tension that results after viewing the film; as a reader of this text I am struck by the fact that the film provides a strong exemplar of the heroine's journey, and yet, I lament the fact that my daughters will not view this film until late young-adulthood. Del Toro profoundly succeeds in his juxtaposition of violence with tranquility. In fact, his use of brutality to establish contrast between Vidal and Ofelia is brilliant (and necessary as established in Mulvey's [1975] explication of gaze); however, it is the violent nature of this film that may prevent many from wholeheartedly engaging with del Toro's tale. The carnage in the film is disturbing; from Vidal's slaughter of the peasants; to Mercede's retribution against the Captain; to the violent death of Ofelia. Simply put, the film is not meant for kids. However, if the viewer can stomach the brutal acts depicted in this film, it is possible to appreciate del Toro's contribution to comparative mythology and his construction/deconstruction of myth. A careful reading of scholarship in the areas of comparative mythology and the hero's journey provides themes that are unique to the heroine's quest and are useful for explaining the implications of Ofelia's odyssey.

The Exit and the Heroine's Journey

It has been argued elsewhere in this book that the archetypal monomyth does not serve all groups equally well (Goertz, 2010; Whitt, 2010) — diverse populations are often muted as a result of tradition and historical precedence embedded within the monomyth. Campbell himself recognized that the archetypical hero-myth often explicates a male-oriented journey and that the heroine may indeed follow a different path and/or experience different trials (Campbell & Moyers, 1988). However, Campbell did not believe that gender would preclude a heroine from actualizing the stages of monomyth. In this matter I agree with Goertz (2010) who believes that Campbell's paradigm does not completely fit the journey of a female protagonist. At the same time, it is possible to recognize aspects of the hero-myth within Ofelia's quest. Perhaps the most salient theme to emerge from a deconstruction of del Toro's film is that women are visible in the composite archetypical champion that Campbell (1968) refers to as the hero with a thousand faces.

There is no reason to exclude women from the amalgam of characters who comprise the archetypical essence of a hero. Although their journey is different when compared with the path of a male protagonist, heroines encounter trials and ultimately achieve transcendence through apotheosis. When naming the unique journey of the female protagonist, Pearson and Pope (1981, p. 68) describe the stage of separation in the monomyth as "the exit from the garden." During the exit from the garden, Pearson and Pope contend that the heroine must come to recognize that the people upon whom she depends are actually captors; she must leave the garden of dependency on these captors, assume the role of spiritual orphan, and procure the treasure of freedom and unlimited possibility (1981, p. 68). The taken for granted independence of the male protagonist is challenged when the hero is female. Her first steps on the road of trials must lead toward separation from dependency.

In this matter, Ofelia exemplifies the path of a heroine. Her severance from Vidal is almost instantly achieved in the earliest moments of the film, and Ofelia's emancipation from Carmen occurs as a result of the rift in their perspective on fantasy and magic. The introduction of another potential mother-figure in Mercedes completes the divide that sunders the dependency Ofelia might feel toward Carmen. Eventually, in the film, traditional relationships are inverted when Carmen becomes dependent on Ofelia for her very life — a life that has been saved as a result of Ofelia's insurgence. Separation clearly occurs the moment that Ofelia is reborn from the womb of an ancient fig tree. She has soiled her mother's dress, entertained the fantasies of imagination, and upset the Captain. She is a spiritual orphan almost precisely at the moment that Ofelia begins to read the *Book of Crossroads*. Leaving the mill behind her and entering the woods symbolizes a partition between Ofelia and those charged with her care and upbringing.

Recognition of the Male

As previously noted, challenging the legitimacy of male authority figures is a crucial step along the road of trials faced by the heroine. Unlike the male protagonist, who must often atone and reconcile with a father figure (e.g., Luke Skywalker and Darth Vader), Ofelia must see the weakness in male figures before she can realize her own strength. Both Vidal and the Faun are flawed figures who must be challenged by Ofelia before she can complete her odyssey. Vidal's violent nature and "control freak" personality (Navarro, 2006) provide an Achilles heel that undermines his status with Ofelia. She delights in the opportunity to anger him, and this is evident immediately after her rebirth from the womb of the fig tree. Pearson and Pope (1981. p. 68) describe this moment in the quest of a heroine as recognizing "the emperor's new clothes"; this occurs as the protagonist sees things for what they really are. Vidal is not powerful, he is weak; as a Captain and officer he is not honorable, he is corrupt; Ofelia must see through the ruse of meticulous hygiene and aggressive outbursts and recognize his true nature.

The Faun is intentional in his illegitimacy, demanding obedience from Ofelia as a test. She must disobey the Faun and his fairies if she is to succeed throughout the odyssey. His demands for compliance are a challenge to her independence, and she must face the test of the Faun with determination in order to secure the second prize as articulated by Pearson and Pope (1981, p. 68) — the treasure of wholeness and autonomy. Here, again, Ofelia successfully navigates her road of trials. When confronted by three doors in the Pale Man's banquet hall she disobeys the fairies and succeeds to acquire the ceremonial dagger; on the eve of the full moon she refuses to shed the blood of an innocent and is willing to deny her inheritance. Each test is predicated on her ability to exercise independence and choice.

The only legitimately virtuous male figure in the film seems to be Dr. Ferreiro, however, his influence on Ofelia is muted as a result of their lack of interaction. Only Dr. Ferreiro seems to advocate del Toro's thesis regarding volition and choice. His disobedience of Vidal is rewarded with death, and Ferreiro's poorly timed murder precipitates Carmen's demise. After Vidal shoots Ferreiro, only an ill-equipped troop paramedic is left to assist Carmen in the premature delivery of Ofelia's brother; as a result, Carmen dies. Even in disobedience, Ferreiro seems to further the image of men in del Toro's myth as powerless, inept, and/or tarnished.

Celebration of the Goddess

Pearson and Pope (1981, p. 68) contend that the third stage of the heroines journey is complete when "the hero either literally or symbolically journeys to her ancestral home in search of her father, and discovers instead that it is her mother with whom she seeks to be rejoined." The treasure discovered at this stage in the quest is the realization that she is "a hero in the tradition of female heroes" — it is the prerequisite for the reward of community. At the end of *El laberinto del fauno*, Ofelia stands in a majestic courtyard in the

Underground Realm. Ofelia, now incarnate as Princess Moanna, has come home. Del Toro describes Princess Moanna's homecoming in his screenplay,

> This is an immense hall, in a dark, sumptuous castle. A swarm of fairies floats around her head. Before her, on a golden throne sits the King of the Underworld. At his side, an almost unrecognizable Carmen — radiant and gilded, she has transformed into a fairy queen. Between them, there is another throne, empty, waiting [del Toro, 2006, p. 96].

It is fitting that the last person to speak in the throne room is Carmen, who requests that she sit by her Father's side (del Toro, 2006, p. 96). Ofelia's final action in the material world is to smile. She has completed the heroine's journey and arrived at apotheosis.

As Pearson and Pope (1981, p. 68) suggest, the journey to self-fulfillment is complete when Ofelia realizes at this stage that "a woman is her mother." In this moment, "a rescue figure aids the hero in freeing herself from the myth of female inferiority and in identifying a viable female tradition" (p. 68). In many ways, the female protagonist provides an ideal opportunity to realize Campbell's (1968) union labeled the "master of two worlds." Pearson and Pope (1981) explain,

> The reconciliation with the mother allows the hero to develop within herself human qualities such as nurturance, intuition, and compassion, which the culture denigrates[7] as female. By extension, she is able to develop positive, sympathetic affiliations with other women. The hero comes to understand that neither "male" nor "female" qualities are positive when isolated from their compliments. For example, self-interest and compassion are positive only when combined. Thus, she not only develops both her male and female qualities, but redefines their meaning. A fully integrated human being, she is in a position to understand that the distinction between male and female qualities is created by the inequitable power relationship between men and women. This integrated selfhood, which the hero achieves in the process of her journey, precludes her assuming the role of dominating matriarch, the equivalent of the male conqueror-ruler. Because, to her, all humans are candidates for full heroism, no one is to be mastered or master [p. 177].

Related to the celebration of the goddess is the thematic development of "two mothers." Along the road of trials, the heroine learns to sort out the "conflicting models and messages to determine for herself which ones provide guidance and which lead to further captivity" (Pearson & Pope, 1981, p. 192). At the end of the film, Ofelia has become a synthesis of Mercedes and Carmen — she celebrates their strengths and chooses not to embrace their flaws; this is particularly evident in Ofelia's stalwart refusal to denounce magic and the fairy realm.

By the conclusion of the film, Ofelia embodies a dialectical essence — she is both strong and fragile; naïve and sophisticated; childish and mature. Her character represents wholeness. "At the end of her quest," explain Pearson and Pope (1981, p. 260), "the female hero returns to a new community with herself, with the natural and spiritual worlds, and with other people ... she also embodies the power necessary to revitalize the entire kingdom — to rid it of dragons...." The transfigured kingdom is a feminist utopia, "an ideal society in which the values of the female hero are the norm" (Pearson & Pope, 1981, p. 260). The dénouement of *Pan's Labyrinth* contrasts starkly with the dystopian elements of values often found in the modern world, the "powerful, dominating, oppressive, egotistical, and destructive qualities that pervade society" (Pearson & Pope, 1981, p. 261). In this way, feminist utopias like *El laberinto del fauno* provide a "corrective"; hope for a "utopian alternative" (Pearson & Pope, 1981, p. 263).

CONCLUSION

> There have been great societies that did not use the wheel, but there have been no societies that did not tell stories.
> — Ursula K. LeGuin

In a volume similar to the one you are now reading, we argued that the "appeal of myth" is that stories are "not only culturally significant but also rhetorically meaningful" (Perlich & Whitt, 2008, p. 3). The relationship between myth and rhetoric is subtle yet profound; as Hart (1990) explains, "Myth and rhetoric have a symbiotic relationship. Myth gives rhetoric something to say and rhetoric gives myth impact in everyday life" (p. 321). I believe that the implications of del Toro's work are profound. *El laberinto del fauno* is filled with rhetorical significance, particularly with regard to the constructs of identity, age, sex, and gender.

The quotations throughout this chapter have intentionally provided the reader with an understanding of my standpoint as a father. My actions, stories, and deeds are profoundly meaningful for my daughters—my daughters, in turn, shape me with every interaction. As they grow from children, to teenagers, to adults, they will undoubtedly struggle to find voice and direction in the world. They will disobey (both to my chagrin and delight) and such decisions will impact father, daughter, and our relationship. Their choices will be filled with implication; poor choices will be judged in hindsight, yet provide opportunities to learn, virtuous choices will be celebrated and treasured. As a parent, I will provide counsel and support—it is my duty to introduce my daughters to stories, models, and experiences that will reinforce a strong identity. I look forward to the opportunity of eventually viewing del Toro's film with my daughters—engaging in dialogue about choices, will, and volition; to celebrate that which is both strong and feminine. For now, I will treasure the opportunity to watch, each day, as my daughters embark on their own heroine quest, and to hear them share their tales with others.

NOTES

1. Although McLuhan (1964) famously declared that the "medium is the message," his remarks cannot be interpreted in a framework that allows for the complete disregard of content. Instead of putting priviledge on either the medium OR the content (which is a dualist tendency) these two interrelated influences would be best understood from a dialectical perspective (the media AND content are equally salient).

2. Goertz is, of course, referring to Joseph Campbell's (1968) epic book *The hero with a thousand faces*—a notworthy tome that reveals (in Campbell's own words) a tendency for the monomyth to priviledge and/or highlight male protagonsist (see Baker in this volume).

3. Place-spirits are common mythic creatures in a variety of cultures, and a fitting descriptor for the faun.

4. The guerrillas who oppose Franco's Spain are intentionally linked with the woodlands and fairy realm via the imagery and semiotic implications articulated by the director (del Toro, 2006). Thus, it seems that Mercedes' role as a foil when the fairy appears for a second time is happenstance.

5. I have used the work of several philosophers, scholars, and theorists to reference a dialectical tradition (see Altman, Vinsel, & Brown, 1981; Bakhtin, 1990; Bakhtin, 1994; Baxter, 1994a; Baxter, 1994b; Leinenweber, 1977; Maines, 1989; Montgomery, 1993; Rawlins, 1989; Rawlins, 1992; Rychlak, 1976; Werner & Baxter, 1994).

6. All of these archetypical heros are male and adults. It is rare to find such a splended rendering and redefinition of the heroine tale that both confirms and challenges the monomyth.

7. Pearson and Pope (1981) are not suggesting that these values are without merit; instead, they contend that such traits and abilities are subordinated as being of lesser value when compared with consolidating power, demonstrating might, and satiating the ego—all characteristics of dystopian feminist tales.

REFERENCES

Altman, I., Vinsel, A., & Brown, B. (1981). Dialectic conceptualizations in social psychology: An application to social penetration theory and privacy regulation. In L. Berkowitz (Ed.), *Advances in experimental psychology* (Vol. 14. pp. 107–160). New York: Academic Press.

Bakhtin, M. (1990). *Art and answerability.* Austin, TX: University of Texas Press.

_____. (1994). *The dialogic imagination* (9th ed). Austin, TX: University of Texas Press.

Baxter, L. (1994a). A dialogic approach to relationship maintenance. In D. J. Canary & L. Stafford (Eds.), *Communication and relational maintenance* (pp. 233–254). San Diego, CA: Academic Press, Inc.

_____. (1994b). Thinking dialogically about relationships. In R. L. Conville (Ed.), *Uses of structure in communication studies* (pp. 23–37). Westport, CT: Praeger Publishers.

Billinghurst, J. (2003). *Temptress: From the original bad girls to women on top.* Vancouver: Greystone Books.

Boggs, J., & Petrie, D. (2000). *The art of watching films* (5th ed.). Mountain View, CA: Mayfield Publishing.

Campbell, J. (1968). *The hero with a thousand faces.* (2nd ed). Princeton, N.J.: Princeton University Press.

_____, & Moyers, B. (1991). *The power of myth.* New York: Anchor Books.

Cotterell, A. & Storm, R. (1999). *The ultimate encyclopedia of mythology.* London: Lorenz Books.

Del Toro, G. (2006). *El laberinto del fauno.* London: Picturehouse.

Edwards, J., & Klosa, B. (2010). The complexity of evil in modern mythology: The evolution of the Wicked Witch of the West. In J. Perlich & D. Whitt (Eds.), *Millennial myth-*

making: Essays on the power of science fiction and fantasy literature, films and games. Jefferson, NC: McFarland Publishing.

Erikson, E. (1950, 1963). *Childhood and society.* New York: W. W. Norton.

Goertz, D. (2010). The hero with the thousand-and-first face: Miyazaki's girl quester in *Spirited Away* and Campbell's Monomyth. In J. Perlich & D. Whitt (Eds.), *Millennial mythmaking: Essays on the power of science fiction and fantasy literature, films and games.* Jefferson, NC: McFarland Publishing.

Hart, R. (1990). *Modern rhetorical criticism.* New York: Harper/Collins.

Leinenweber, C. (1977). Socialists in the street: The New York City Socialist Party in working class neighborhoods, 1908–1918. *Science and Society, 41,* 152–171.

Maines, D. (1989). Further dialectics: Strangers, friends, and historical transformations. In J. Anderson (Ed.), *Communication Yearbook, 12* (pp. 190–202). Newbury Park, CA: Sage.

McLuhan, M. (1964). *Understanding media: The extensions of man.* Corte Madera: Ginko Press.

Montgomery, B. (1993). Relationship maintenance versus relationship change: A dialectical dilemma. *Journal of Social and Personal Relationships, 10,* 205–223.

Mulvey, L. (1975). Visual Pleasure and Narrative Cinema. *Screen 16*(3), 6–18.

Navarro, B., Cuaron, A., Torresblanco, F., & Augustin, A. (Producers), del Toro, G. (Director). (2006). *Pan's labyrinth* [Film]. Picturehouse.

Pearson, C., & Pope, K. (1981). *The female hero in American and British literature.* New York: R. R. Bowker Co.

Perlich, J., & Whitt, D. (2008). Prologue: Not so long ago…. In D. Whitt & J. Perlich (Eds.), *Sith, slayers, stargates, & cyborgs: Modern mythology in the new millennium.* New York: Peter Lang.

Rawlins, W. (1989). A dialectical analysis of the tensions, functions, and strategic challenges of communication in young adult friendships. In J. Anderson (Ed.), *Communication Yearbook, 12* (pp. 157–189). Newbury Park, CA: Sage.

_____. (1992). *Friendship matters: Communication, dialectics, and the life course.* Hawthorne, NY: Aldine De Gruyter, Inc.

Rychlak, J. (1976). The multiple meanings of dialectic. In J. F. Rychlak (Ed.), *Dialectic: Humanistic rationale for behavior development* (pp. 1–17). New York: Karger.

Smith, P. J. (2007). Pan's labyrinth (El laberinto del fauno). *Film Quarterly, 60* (4), 4–9.

Werner, C., & Baxter, L. (1994). Temporal qualities of relationships: Organismic, transactional, and dialectical views. In M. Knapp & G. Miller (Eds.), *Handbook of interpersonal communication* (2nd ed.) (pp. 323–379). Newbury Park, CA: Sage.

Whitt, D. (2010). The odyssey of Madame Souza: A heroine's quest in *The Triplets of Belleville.* In J. Perlich & D. Whitt (Eds.), *Millennial mythmaking: Essays on the power of science fiction and fantasy literature, films and games.* Jefferson, NC: McFarland Publishing.

7

Actors and Their Mythic Heroes: From the Doctor to Captain Kirk

DJOYMI BAKER

When actor George Takei appeared on the NBC television series *Heroes* it was as Kaito Nakamura, the father of *Star Trek* fan Hiro. At the same time Takei also resonated with his former *Star Trek* character, Lt. Hikaru Sulu, from the original series. In other words, at first glance he is at once Takei/Sulu/Kaito. While television actors from series and serials frequently find it difficult to overcome the audience's association with their former characters, in programs such as *Heroes* and ABC's *Boston Legal* this resonance is not a problem to be overcome but rather an integral function of the show and its intertextual references. Combining and building on the work of classicist Ken Dowden (1992, 1996) and cinema academics Richard Dyer (1987) and Richard de Cordova (1990, 1991), this chapter argues that the mythic hero is not simply a function of any individual text but rather is a function of connections across texts and between actors and the characters they play. These connections build a mythic intertext that has synergies with ancient oral forms of Greek mythology and yet is specific to twenty and twenty-first century forms of media stardom.[1]

THE MYTHIC INTERTEXT

The earliest surviving use of the word *mythos* in the Greek epics of Homer (c. 700 B.C.E.) centred on the act of storytelling itself (Edmunds, 1997, pp. 415–418, 420). For this reason I have been interested in examining approaches to myth from within classical studies and exploring their application to contemporary entertainment texts (Baker, 2005). Classicist Lowell Edmunds (1997) argues that myth is a traditional story but one that must be kept alive by being retold in new ways that continue to have relevance to a society. Ken Dowden takes this further by arguing:

> Greek Mythology is an "intertext," because it is constituted by all the representations of mytho over experienced by its audience and because every new representation gains its sense from how it is positioned in relation to this totality of previous representations [1992, p. 8].

The intertext, then, refers to a complex interrelationship of stories. Dowden (1996) suggests that his model applies to early oral forms of myth and later literary versions.

A new version of a myth always sits in relation to older stories, through audience memory, direct reference or even by an obvious omission (Dowden, 1996). For example, in Homer's *The Odyssey*, Odysseus visits places and meets characters also featured in the story of Jason and his ship the Argo, whose adventure, we are told, "is in all men's minds" (Homer, trans. 1975, 12.70). This allows the audience to recall the story and compare Odysseus with a hero from a previous generation. Dowden (1992) notes that in some cases we can even trace family sagas across generations. Because myth survives by constant retelling and addition there will always be numerous older versions and related stories, even if not all of them survive today.[2] All of this jostling knowledge constitutes an intertextual understanding of Greek mythology.

In Greek mythology, intertextual connections could be made by overt references to other stories or even by short, repeated phrases known as epithet formulas that sum up a particular hero's characteristics (such as "swift-footed Achilles"). John Foley argues the mere use of this brief formulaic code reminds the audience of an entire heroic tradition, with all its related versions and contradictions (1997, pp. 167–168). As with Edmunds and Dowden, the meaning of the myth is an exchange between the heroic, mythic tradition and the new story being forged.

Although these scholars formulated their theories by examining traditional myths in ancient Greece, they all suggest that this 'tradition' is itself changeable. The Greeks not only played with their traditional stories, altering them over time, but also changed their minds about what myth meant as a concept (Baker, 2005, pp. 14–20). Taking this inherent instability into account, we can see myth as the interplay between traditional stories and the retelling of those stories. Each new storytelling technology enables the next phase in the mythic process. What constitutes 'tradition' may need to be rethought in this context, as each medium gradually builds up its own storytelling traditions. Thus a long-lasting, successful television franchise establishes a popular culture tradition that can stretch over decades and generations, as in the case of the BBC series *Doctor Who* (1963–1989, 1996, 2005-present) (see Rafer, 2007) or the various *Star Trek* shows (Baker, 2005). Or a mythic intertext might revolve around a cross-media hero such as James Bond (Bennett and Woollacott, 1987), or Batman (Collins, 1991). To retell such a hero's story is at once to recall his or her entire heroic background, as an integral part of the new story (Collins, 1991). Indeed, Collins (1991) argues that contemporary Batman texts highlight this history, revelling not only in the similarities but also the inconsistencies across Batman stories.[3] I would argue that this self-reflexive, cross-media hero myth becomes the most recent instalment in what Robert Parker (in the context of older works) has called the continual "succession of periods or styles" of myth (1987, pp. 188–189).

ACTORS AND MYTHIC HEROES

Drawing on the work of Richard de Cordova (1990, 1991) and Richard Dyer (1987) on the star as intertext, I want to suggest that actors become enmeshed in the mythic intertext of the heroes they portray. De Cordova notes how in cinema serials around the 1910s, actors would play the same character over and over, so that actors became closely associated with a specific role. This was encouraged by the fact that "the leading characters in the serials usually bore the same first name as the actors playing them" (de Cordova, 1990, p. 89). In television series and serials, actors may play the same role for several seasons over several years, even taking those characters across into spin-off programs and feature films. John Langer argues:

> An actor going from one long-running series where identity is well established to a new series in order to "play" a new character may encounter reluctant acceptance from the television audience. Any straightforward "reading" of the new programme is complicated by the lingering residue of the earlier show's "personality" [1981, p. 360].

Yet the "lingering residue" of an actor's past, iconic role has become part of the very fabric of contemporary television. Just as the mythic resonances of heroes in contemporary texts is often a deliberate writing strategy (drawing on Campbell-inspired guides such as Vogler's 1998 *The writer's journey: Mythic structure for storytellers and screenwriters*), so too programs ranging from *Heroes* to *Boston Legal* consciously invoke the mythic aura that an actor carries from a previous role. In this sense Langer (1981) underestimates the audience when he suggests that they remember only the fictional television character, and not the actor. Langer predates fan studies that were initiated in the 1990s which illustrate how fans follow an actor's career beyond their favored program (Jenkins, 1992; Pearson, 2004), or how the relationship between the actor and the role they play becomes central in some fan debates (Tulloch and Jenkins, 1995). The actor becomes so associated with a long-term television character that they become a melding of the two in the consciousness of the audience. Just as Foley (1997) notes the way a brief heroic epithet in Greek myth is enough to conjure up the memory of an entire heroic tradition, actors who have played iconic heroes on television series evoke that past as they appear in new roles. Rather than a "complication" to be overcome, in programs such as *Heroes* and *Boston Legal*, this shorthand resonance becomes one of the methods for building up new heroic stories in a similar mold.

NEW HEROES

Heroes charts the adventures of a disparate group of otherwise ordinary individuals who discover they have super-human abilities. Early in the first season, Japanese office worker Hiro Nakamura is established as a *Star Trek* fan. In "Genesis" (Kring and Semel, 2006), Hiro and his friend Ando continually compare his emerging abilities to control space and time with *Star Trek* aliens and technology. Hiro proclaims that he wants to "boldly go where no man has gone before," quoting Captain Kirk's opening monologue to the original series of *Star Trek*, a phrase retrospectively revealed in the UPN series *Star Trek: Enterprise* to be a quote from warp-creator Zefram Cochrane ("Broken Bow" Berman, Braga and Conway, 2001). When Hiro's father Kaito is first introduced in "The Fix" (Chaidez and O'Hara, 2007), I would argue that he appears as simultaneously George Takei, Lt. Sulu and Kaito Nakamura. The *Star Trek* fan has a *Star Trek* father, giving Hiro an heroic lineage that connects across texts and cuts across the distinction between the actor and the characters he plays. Later in "Distractions" (Green and Szwarc, 2007) the number plate to Kaito's Limousine reads NCC-1701, the service number for the original USS Enterprise on *Star Trek* where Takei played Lt. Sulu. Hiro is called Sulu by Hope just before she punches him out in "Run!" (Armus, Foster and Dawson, 2007)— directed by former *Star Trek: Voyager* (Berman and Braga, 1995–2001) actor Roxann Dawson.

Beyond a fun fan game of spot-the-*Star Trek*-reference (although this is the subject of fan web sites), the Takei/Sulu/Kaito heroic intertext is part of an older generation of heroes both within the *Heroes* story and within popular culture. That is, Takei's *Star Trek* past is used as an heroic epithet to help create his new character as an extension of that past. As noted earlier, in Greek mythology new heroic stories were framed in relation to the heroes who had come before. The multi-generational, intertextual heroic myth that we find in archaic Greece finds new expression in the actor/hero intertext of contemporary television.

Generations

Greek mythology is preoccupied with issues of genealogy and succession. Hesiod's *Theogony* (c. 700 B.C.E.) charts the history of existence itself as the conception of different generations of gods, many of whom overthrow the rule of the previous generation. The succession ends only when Zeus is able to assert his authority over the other gods and prevent the birth of a god powerful enough to dethrone him (Apollonius of Rhodes, trans. 1993, 4.790–809). This story of succession is a resonating background to the heroic epics of Homer, particularly as its greatest human hero—Achilles—might have been this new leader of gods if only Zeus had not intervened to ensure his mortality (Slatkin, 1991, pp. 7, 14).[4] In the human world, succession between generations of Greek heroes, and between fathers and sons, sets up an heroic template for behavior. In Homer's *Odyssey*, just as Odysseus is compared with Jason, an older generation of hero, so too Odysseus' son Telemachus must demonstrate his worthiness in the light of his father's heroic reputation (Jones, 1988, pp. 500–505). Even when not explicitly referenced, tales of different generations of gods and heroes inform the entire spectrum of Greek mythology,[5] giving a richness to new stories through the memory of the audience.

In *Heroes*, the passing from one heroic generation to the next is similarly a source of both friction and inspiration. By referencing the life histories not only of characters but of the actors who play them, *Heroes* asks the audience to understand this succession in terms of a broader mythic intertext beyond the program itself. In his heroic quest, Hiro is both defying his father's will and yet fulfilling the heroic values that Kaito has instilled in him from an early age. Hiro initially keeps his powers from his father, and for his part, Kaito appears stubbornly resistant to his son's quest and refusal to come home ("The Fix," Chaidez and O'Hara, 2007 and "Distractions," Green and Szwarc, 2007). However, in "Landslide" (Alexander, Adelman, and Beeman, 2007) it is revealed that Kaito is fully aware of his son's abilities, and has been watching his progress. In order to help his son on his quest to save the world, Kaito teaches Hiro his considerable sword-fighting skills. Kaito hints that he, too, had once been involved with a group on a similar heroic quest to save the world.

Like the gods of ancient Greece, the older generation in *Heroes* is powerful, enigmatic, and somewhat capricious. The Greek gods interfere in the lives of humans, many of whom are their own hybrid offspring, as in the case of Achilles in Homer's *The Iliad*, the son of the goddess Thetis and the human Peleus. Although Kaito has no apparent superhuman abilities of his own, in "Cautionary Tales" (Pokaski and Yaitanes, 2007) he says to his son: "We have the power of gods. That does not mean we can play God." This suggests that like his son, Kaito may himself have had a special power. Thus Kaito passes onto his son his learned skills in sword-fighting, and perhaps also an inherited genetic code for special abilities. Kaito's comments also reflect his remorse for his youthful actions. Earlier, in "Four Months Later..." (Kring and Beeman, 2007), he had talked to fellow elder Angela Petrelli about "the people we have killed.... I sought redemption by helping Hiro fulfill his destiny to save the world." With Kaito's death, Hiro is left alone to live up to the expectations of his father.

Heroes is the latest in a long line of intergenerational hero myths. Kaito and Hiro Nakamura—father and son—are newly invented characters for the *Heroes* television series. The ancient storytelling practice of deliberately linking new heroes to *pre-existing* ones finds a different form of expression in contemporary media. In the case of television, these prior heroes exist in earlier shows and are manifest through the physical body of the actor as much as through intertextual references. Indeed, the bodily presence of the actor *becomes* the intertextual reference, as work on stardom in the context of cinema has argued (Dyer, 1987; Maltby, 2003). This provides a new facet to the mythic intertext in its contemporary guise.

Thus Kaito is both a member of the older generation of heroes within Kring's *Heroes*, and of the older generation of *Star Trek* heroes, of which the program constantly reminds us. The hint of Kaito's own heroic quest can be understood purely within the *Heroes* story but gains deliberate resonance with our knowledge of his heroic exploits as part of another group of heroes on board the Enterprise.

Of course, the fictional world of *Star Trek* is its own cross-generational set of heroic stories, spanning different futuristic decades, programs, heroes, and different generations of viewers. Episodes and marketing have explicitly connected *Star Trek* with the older realm of mythic heroes. In the original series of *Star Trek*, the crew of the Enterprise discovers a planet that is home to a lone alien who asserts that he is the god Apollo, worshipped by the ancient Greeks on Earth ("Who Mourns for Adonais?" [sic], Ralston, Coon and Daniels, 1967). As twenty-third century space-farers, Captain Kirk and his crew are not in the least inclined to become his new worshippers. But for his part, Apollo sees in these latter-day humans the qualities that he so admired in the ancient heroes Agamemnon, Hector, and Odysseus. It is perhaps only with the retrospective knowledge of *Star Trek*'s revival and survival over more than 40 years that we might find his comparison compelling (Baker, 2001). While the entire *Star Trek* franchise has been called mythic in its own right, its programs and advertisements frequently and increasingly use references to older heroic traditions — including Greek mythology, King Arthur, the Medieval epic *Beowulf*, and Robin Hood, to name but a few — in order to deliberately bolster this association (Baker, 2001, 2005). It is only after *Star Trek* has become established in popular culture history that its references to heroic myth, legend and saga take on a new resonance.

Newer programs such as *Heroes* lack a history of their own and must instead endeavour to create one, through internal narrative development and flashbacks, and through references to older traditions such as *Star Trek*.[6] In terms of television and popular culture history, the use of *Star Trek* actors George Takei and Nichelle Nichols (Lt. Uhura from the original series) establishes a lineage to which *Heroes* can be added. Conversely, actor Zachary Quinto (who plays the arch enemy Sylar on *Heroes*) plays a young Spock in the 2009 *Star Trek* film, which (re)charts the beginnings of the original series characters. However it is the original Spock, actor Leonard Nimoy, who provided a voice-over on the first official trailer for "Space ... the final frontier" (Paramount, 2008). Thus the desire to flesh out the back-story of these fictional worlds creates a multi-directional set of associations through the figure of the actor, in this case through a Quinto/Sylar/Spock/Limoy amalgam in the minds and memories of the viewer.

Doctor Who? Regeneration and Disappearance

This strange actor/character amalgam across different fictional worlds can also be seen in the use of *Doctor Who* actor Christopher Eccleston as a man with the power (or curse) of invisibility in *Heroes*. As a member of the older generation of superhumans, he uses his invisibility to lead a reclusive life until discovered by Peter Petrelli, a young man having difficulty controlling his new-found ability to absorb the special powers of others. In "The Fix" (Chaidez and O'Hara, 2007), Eccleston's ostensibly unnamed character tells Peter "Me? I'm no one. I'm the Invisible Man. I'm Claude Rains. Now get away from me. Forget you ever saw me." Eccleston's character eventually agrees to help Peter learn to control his powers. Despite the acerbic outburst, *Heroes'* invisible man does indeed become known as Claude — a reference to the actor Claude Rains from the famous 1933 film *The Invisible Man*. Like the *Star Trek* references, Eccleston's dialogue functions both as a simple in-joke and as a means of establishing a tradition for the character.

But for fans of the even longer-running *Doctor Who*, this casting has an additional resonance, for the Doctor has himself been invisible for a time. In "The Celestial Toymaker" (Hayles, Tosh and Sellars, 1966), an alien forces the Doctor and his companions to play out a series of games, and renders the Doctor invisible as a punishment for not observing the rules. It was, of course, a *different* Doctor — the first Doctor played by William Hartnell. But the Doctor is an alien capable of delaying death by 'regeneration,' a form of rebirth during which the Doctor changes form but retains his memory. Thus all Doctors are both the same character yet different, by virtue both of the different actors who play him, and the different nuances they bring to that character in the fictional world.

The invisibility sub-plot in "The Celestial Toymaker" occurred for the entirely pragmatic reason to give its lead a holiday (Newman, 2005, p. 53). But it had been toyed with — and dismissed — as a means of bringing in a new actor after the Doctor regained visibility (Newman, 2005, p. 53). By fashioning a central character capable of regenerating and in the process changing his appearance, *Doctor Who* enables practical production issues of casting to be seamlessly integrated into its fictional world. In other words, changing actors does not disrupt *Doctor Who*'s self-defined science fiction logic.

Although the Doctor begins as a rather vague, mysterious figure, as his story develops he is revealed firstly as an "exile" and then as a "renegade," disenchanted with his home world (Newman, 2005, p. 60). As a result, he wanders through time and space with various companions traveling in his vessel, the TARDIS. With the 2005 revival of the program, his fellow Time Lords and their home planet Gallifrey are gone as a result of an extensive war with arch enemies, the Daleks. Thus, for Christopher Eccleston's incarnation as the ninth Doctor, the character is a somewhat haunted, lone survivor with genuine but strained connections with his traveling companions. Kim Newman argues that as the Doctor's original companion was his granddaughter, "the inference is that *all* the temporary traveling companions who come and go throughout the series are substitutes for the lost Susan" (emphasis in original, 2005, p. 44). In the current series, this loss of connection with the Doctor's race, home, and family is more profoundly felt. Newman notes that in the Christopher Eccleston episode "The Empty Child" (Moffat and Hawes, 2005), a "tiny, easy-to-miss, affecting moment" occurs when "an elderly man ... lament[s] that he started World War II 'as a father and grandfather but now I am neither.'" The Doctor replies, "I know the feeling" (Newman, 2005, p. 45). Newman's contention perhaps simplifies the Doctor's relationships with his various companions, which have toyed more overtly with romantic possibilities (and impossibilities) in the newer series. But the Doctor's status as a loner has never been more keenly felt now that it is not by choice.[7]

As the ninth Doctor, Eccleston became part of a "long-running series" with a "well established" character, and therefore becomes embroiled in the "lingering residue" of that character, to use Langer's terms (1981, p. 360). Each Doctor may be different, but he is still the Doctor. As Eccleston stayed in the role of the Doctor for only one season, he is arguably less associated with that character than other actors who have chosen to play him longer — most notably the fourth Doctor, Tom Baker, who remained into a seventh year. John Tulloch notes that in the United States, Baker "was the first Doctor screened, and so did become '*the* Doctor' there" (emphasis in original, 1995, p. 159). By comparison, it is entirely possible that when viewers come across Eccleston in other work, they may miss, forget, or disregard his role on *Doctor Who*, or recall other performances instead. But as a *Doctor Who* fan, for me Eccleston comes to *Heroes* at once as the invisible man and as the Doctor.

Thus, to stretch the metaphor somewhat, the mythic intertext to which both the Doctor and Eccleston belong may or may not be visible to the viewer. When brought into play, Claude's estrangement from those with special abilities (and the world in general) jostles with the Doctor's estrangement from his own race, and isolation once they have gone; Claude's reluctant acceptance of the role as Peter Petrelli's temporary mentor bounces off the Doctor's function as guide through time and space for his various companions; Claude's status as a member of the older generation of heroes resonates with the Doctor's age of some 900 years plus. I do not mean to make too much of such connections here precisely because as the potential interrelationships present themselves during or after viewing, they may be similarly fleeting.

This instability is a feature of all mythic intertexts, but becomes particularly evident in the case of actors. Writing on Hollywood stardom, Richard Maltby writes:

> The audience experiences the presence of the performer as well as — in the same body as — the presence of the character. The bodily presence of the performer is at the same time a distraction from the fiction and one of the principal means by which viewers invest in the existence of characters as if they were real people ... our impressions of

an actor's presence and his or her "disappearance" into character readily alternate with each other [2003, pp. 380–381].

Drawing on performance theory, Maltby argues that while watching a film, viewers remain in a contradictory state whereby we know that an actor is, well, acting, and yet we also choose to believe in their character. These states may shift through the course of the viewing experience, but in the case of established stars an emphasis on the actor will always be present (Maltby, 2003). Thus Maltby argues that Moses, Michelangelo and Ben-Hur all "become Charlton Heston" rather than the other way around (2003, p. 380). Langer (1981) argues that in television this formula is directly reversed, so that the character dominates and actors are forever associated with their fictional identities.[8] But if the character is paramount in a long-lasting series such as *Doctor Who*, does the Doctor-for-a-year Christopher Eccleston become and remain forever the Doctor? While the character has gained a veneer of permanence, the actor/character/program intertext has not.

Doctor Who outranks *Star Trek* in longevity, having premiered in the United Kingdom in 1963. Its central character, the Doctor, is also incredibly long-lived, both in terms of production and within its fictional world, such that David Rafer argues that the Doctor has himself become "a mythic hero" (2007, p. 123). Further, Rafer notes that over its extensive history *Doctor Who* has incorporated many references to mythology and makes the Doctor part of that mythology. However, as with more traditional forms of the mythic intertext, this relationship with older stories relies both on direct reference and audience knowledge. In "The Myth Makers" (Cotton and Leeston-Smith, 1965), it is the Doctor and not the Greek gods who helps the Trojans bring about the fall of Troy. Indeed, as Rafer notes, the Doctor "takes on a mythic role when he is identified with Zeus" (2007, p. 133).[9] "The Horns of Nimon" (Read and McBain, 1979–80) refashions the story of the Minotaur on an alien world. Rafer notes that elements from the original myth are retained while others are dropped, so that "whilst there's no mention of Pasiphaë's liaison with a bull resulting in the Minotaur, the Nimon are bull-headed half-humanoid aliens" (2007, p. 132). Just as the full circumstances that lead to Achilles' mortality are unspoken but ever-present in *The Iliad* (namely, Zeus' desire to keep him from being born a full god more powerful than himself), so too the mythic background to the Minotaur story in "The Horns of Nimon" remains just that — an intertextual background about which the audience may have varying degrees of knowledge.[10]

The mythic intertext is therefore highly dependant on memory, operating within and beyond any individual program. Just as I have argued that *Star Trek*'s status as a popular culture mythology is born partly out of its ability to draw upon the longevity and complexity of its fictional world (Baker, 2001, 2005), so too John Tulloch and Manuel Alvarado suggest that *Doctor Who* is capable of emphasizing its own "mythic reality" by drawing on its history

(1983, p. 89). In turn, Rafer suggests that "this sense of the programme's mythic reality ... is reinforced with Christopher Eccleston's Doctor confronting Autons and Daleks"—old adversaries of former incarnations of the Doctor (2007, p. 128). As Jim Collins has argued, "popular culture has a *history*," and our "cultural memory" is integral to our experience of new versions of old stories (emphasis in original, 1991, pp. 170–171). The audience's memory may be incomplete, imperfect, and may vary considerably, but it is always present in some form, creating intended and unintended intertextual connections between newer and older works, whether from last year, decade, century, or millennium. Collins' observation is but a contemporary extension of Dowden's argument (1992) that Greek mythology functions as an intertext, the mish-mash of stories past and present all jostling together.

It is in this sense that through the figure of the actor, *Heroes* becomes as much a *Doctor Who* outpost as a *Star Trek* one, creating the Eccleston/Doctor/Claude hero. This becomes the next installment of a refashioned hero myth, made out of both an actor and their characters. Both similar to and different from Greek myth in which the process of retelling was central, the intertexual hero myth becomes the next 'period or style' of myth in Parker's terms (1987, pp. 188–189).

This hybrid heroic identity is part of the sometimes surreal intertextual existence of actors. Richard Dyer (1987) argues that the star image is a contradictory bundle of information gathered from the roles actors play, their public appearances, and the 'real' person behind those roles. This star image becomes a form of marketing, a promise of what kind of film (or television program) you can expect to see (Dyer, 1987). In this sense, typecasting is an integral feature of the star system (Maltby, 2003, p. 387). The BBC (*BBC News*, 2005) initially reported that Eccleston had quit *Doctor Who* after only one season for fear of being typecast (which had haunted the career of Tom Baker for some time), but was forced to retract the statement after Eccleston complained they had not actually consulted him about it. Reporting on Eccleston's departure, *BBC News* (2005) added: "Bookies have tipped *Casanova* actor David Tennant as the hot favorite to replace Eccleston as the Time Lord," along with a still of Tennant as the "legendary lover." Given the romantic undercurrents between the Doctor and his companion Rose in season two,[11] and the unrequited attraction that his next companion Martha has for the Doctor in season three, the choice of Tennant carries over both a resonance and renouncement of his previous lead role in the BBC television series *Casanova* (Davies, 2005), written by Russell T. Davies—the executive producer and writer of the *Doctor Who* revival. Similarly, Tulloch and Alvarado (1983, p. 67) argue that the choice of Peter Davison to replace Tom Baker brought with it resonances of Davison's role as Tristan in *All Creatures Great and Small* (Sellars, 1978–1990), evident in his performance style. Thus he was touted in the press as "Like Tristan, but brave" (quoted in Tulloch and Alvarado, 1983, p. 203). Publicity along these lines asks us to relate roles and programs that may not otherwise seem at all related. The intertext is invoked as a matter of memory *and* marketing in forming new heroes in relation to an actor's old ones.

Marketing of the star image can also obscure any sense of a "real" person behind it. *Doctor Who*'s then producer, John Nathan-Turner, said: "I wanted basically 'Peter Davison/Doctor' with added attributes" (quoted in Tulloch and Alvarado, 1983, p. 197). As Tulloch and Alvarado note, the notion that an actor is in effect just "playing themselves" undermines their acting abilities and can compromise their ability to gain different roles (1983, p. 199). Conversely, we may abandon the search for the authentic person behind the star persona and instead revel in the artifice itself (Dyer, 1987, p. 16). Indeed, our enjoyment may lie precisely in the overt acting out of the persona and the social conventions they both embody and parody (Dyer, 1987, p. 16). It is this appreciation of the artificiality and inherent instability of the heroic intertext that I wish to explore in relation to William Shatner in *Boston Legal*.

Six Degrees of William Shatner

The inclusion of *Boston Legal* in this anthology may at first strike the reader as an odd one — it is not, after all, a science fiction or fantasy program. But just as *Heroes* becomes inflected with *Star Trek* and *Doctor Who* by virtue of its actors, so too *Boston Legal* becomes both a type of *Star Trek* reunion and an overt acting out of the Shatner/Kirk/Crane persona.

Shatner plays the egotistical, eccentric Dennis "Denny" Crane, first seen in the last season of *The Practice* and carried over into the new show based around his firm Crane, Poole and Schmidt. Along with Shatner, *Boston Legal* becomes littered with former *Star Trek* actors in lead and guest roles, including Rene Auberjonois (Paul Lewiston in *Boston Legal* and Odo in *Star Trek: Deep Space Nine*); John Larroquette (Carl Sack in *Boston Legal* and Maltz in *Star Trek III: The Search for Spock*); Scott Bakula (Jack Ross in *Boston Legal* and Captain Jonathan Archer in *Star Trek: Enterprise*); Ethan Phillips (Michael Schiller in *Boston Legal* and Nelix in *Star Trek: Voyager*); Jeri Ryan (Courtney Reese in *Boston Legal* and Seven of Nine in *Star Trek: Voyager*); Armin Shimerman (Judge Brian Hooper in *Boston Legal* and Quark in *Star Trek: Deep Space Nine*).... As with *Star Trek* references in *Heroes*, we become lost in a game of spot-the-former-*Star-Trek*-actor. An audience listening to Homer's *Odyssey* may well have had the older stories of Jason on their mind, but it is equally difficult to forget former *Star Trek* heroes when the actors who embody them keep turning up on *Boston Legal* to encounter Shatner/Crane/Kirk.

Boston Legal makes passing references to Shatner's *Star Trek* past, with Shatner/Crane saying "I once captained my own spaceship" in the third season finale episode "Trial of the Century" (Kelley and D'Elia, 2007). *Star Trek* references such as this draw attention to Shatner as Shatner, the actor playing Denny Crane, which in turn become part of a broader set of methods for highlighting the artificiality of the show. Thus Denny's frequent direct addresses to the camera and overt references to *Boston Legal* as TV program become tied in with Shatner's acting out of Shatner/Kirk/Crane. James Naremore (1988) distinguishes between presentational styles of acting, which acknowledge the audience, and representational styles, which pretend the audience does not exist. While *Boston Legal* spends most of its episode duration in a representational style, Denny consistently breaks this realist illusion, commenting to his friend Alan Shore "Ah, there you are. I've hardly seen you this episode" in "Too Much Information" (Kreisberg, Broch, and Robin, 2006). In "New Kids on the Block" (Kelley and D'Elia, 2006), Crane welcomes the firm's new lawyers by saying "welcome to Boston Legal," referring to the program's title rather than the fictional firm of Crane, Poole and Schmidt, and then commands, "Cue the music!" In "Mad About You" (Kelley, Broch and Verica, 2008), Denny comforts his neighbour after she has killed her husband and says: "Denny Crane. Ready for my close-up." These moments are played for humour both as an acknowledgment of the program as a program, and as indicative of Denny's egotism and eccentricity. Yet the commands to an off-screen crew are, of course, also suggestive of Shatner in his function as an actor.

Commenting on Naremore, Maltby argues that "there is ... a substantial element of the presentational in the constant by-play between star performance and role" (2003, 381).[12] In other words, the star's very presence is a constant reminder to the audience of their existence outside the fictional world in which they are acting, and that star persona is always a part of any character they play. Shatner recalls in his autobiography that David E. Kelly wrote the part of Crane specifically for Shatner. The character was to be:

> A pompous, eccentric, unpredictable, outrageous attorney. Denny Crane. Now, why would he think of me for that role? ... [Shatner's wife] Liz believes that sometimes I experiment with Denny Crane at home. And as he is a broad exaggeration of what I am, and she knows me so well, it's difficult for her to separate Shatner from Crane [2008, pp. 320, 327].[13]

Although Shatner was at first reluctant to include any references to his role as Captain James T. Kirk in the original series of *Star Trek*, with the success of *Boston Legal* in its own right this view softened and *Star Trek* references began to appear (Shatner, 2008, p. 327). But Shatner's self-deprecating remarks about similarities between Crane and himself draw on a public persona born partly from criticisms made by his former *Star Trek* cast members that he was "completely self-absorbed" (Shatner, 2008, p. 148). In Crane we might also see Captain Kirk's irreverence and swagger, or shades of Shatner's role as an arrogant womanizing alien leader known as The Big Giant Head in NBC's *3rd Rock from the Sun* (1996–2001). What we get in Crane is the acting out of a character and of a star persona, melded together and yet highlighted by self-referential asides—prompting the alternating audience awareness of which Maltby speaks.

CONCLUSION

Myth is a type of traditional story that nonetheless finds itself retold and reworked over generations. In each new story only the merest mention is needed to invoke in the audience a remembrance of broad heroic tradition, however complex or contradictory (Foley, 1997, pp. 167–8). It is this process of retelling that is central in both ancient and contemporary storytelling, and it is through the actor/character amalgam that the heroic, mythic intertext is refashioned in the contemporary era. Shatner himself writes:

> I was going to begin my autobiography this way:
>   Call me ... Captain James T. Kirk or Sergeant T. J. Hooker or Denny Crane Denny Crane [*sic*] or *Twilight Zone* plane passenger Bob Wilson or the Big Giant Head or Henry V or the Priceline Negotiator or ... [2008, p. 1].

Programs such as *Heroes* and *Boston Legal* ask their viewers to recall television history and our knowledge of the careers of actors, while at the same time choosing to ignore those industry factors just enough to be taken in by the fictional worlds they present. We might wonder why Hiro, if he is such a fan of *Star Trek*, never thinks, "Isn't it cool that my dad looks just like George Takei/Sulu?"

An intertextual approach to myth is useful for bringing in some of the industry aspects (of which the actor is but one) that inform our storytelling traditions in the twentieth and twenty-first centuries. Television may present us with a type of contemporary "myth" presented knowingly in quotation marks,[14] but perhaps this has always been the case to one degree or another. As new stories were added to the vast corpus of Greek mythology, Jan Bremmer (1987) argues that audiences must have recognized that they were recent inventions. And yet by adding to the storytelling tradition they soon became part of that tradition. The actor/character/hero revitalizes our understanding of how a hero is built up over a succession of stories spanning generations in the fictional world and generations of audiences. To rephrase Dowden, every new role gains its meaning in relation to every other previous role, building up a storytelling intertext brought to life both by references within the story and the memory of the audience.

NOTES

1. I would like to thank Professor Charles J. Stivale of Wayne State University for suggesting that my work on myth and *Star Trek* might have interesting applications to actors, and Dr Diana Sandars of the University of Melbourne for her comments.

2. Indeed, although Jason is a hero from an older generation, his story comes to us from a later text, Apollonius of Rhodes' *The Argonautica* of the third century B.C.E.

3. The Batman story continues to be retold in the recent *Batman Begins* and *The Dark Knight*.

4. It was prophesised that Achilles' mother, the goddess Thetis, would bear a son greater

than his father. Although the gods Zeus and Poseidon had been her suitors, Zeus forces her to marry a mere mortal in order to prevent an upending of his divine rule (Slatkin, 1991, pp. 96–99).

5. To gain a sense of the complexity of this generational tradition, one need only glance at the 3,673 names sorted into family trees in Newman and Newman's (2003) *A genealogical chart of Greek mythology*.

6. This is by no means restricted to *Star Trek* references, and as a whole *Heroes* spends far more time making connections with the extensive comicbook superhero tradition. Superheroes themselves owe much to the older mythological gods and heroes, in some cases being explicitly compared with them (Reynolds, 1992).

7. In "The Doctor's Daughter" (Greenhorn and Troughton, 2008), a daughter is created from the Doctor's cells against his wishes. She may or may not be a true Time Lord, but in any case the Doctor loses her also, incorrectly believing her to be dead.

8. Roberta E. Pearson argues that this 'entanglement' is particularly evident in cult television, examining the case of Patrick Stewart/Jean-Luc Picard (2004, p. 62).

9. See Cook (2001) for a more extended analysis of this episode with reference to original versions of the myth.

10. The potential address to different audience members based on their knowledge of mythology can be seen in a number of television programs, including those that pre-date *Doctor Who* (Baker, 2006).

11. This culminates in the season four episode "Journey's End" (Davies and Harper, 2008) with the romantic union of Rose and a human copy of the Doctor.

12. See also a similar discussion with regards to Hollywood style/Broadway style and impersonation/personification in Geraghty (2006).

13. Richard Dyer argues: "Star biographies are devoted to the notion of showing us the star as he or she really is," the authentic person "behind the scenes" (1987, p. 11). Shatner's autobiography, and my use of it here, clearly works in this fashion, while also perpetuating the Shatner/Crane/Kirk hybrid through the use of the *Star Trek* font on the front cover with a Crane-style photo, and a still as Kirk on the back.

14. As Collins (1991) has argued and I have extended upon (Baker, 2001, 2005).

REFERENCES

Abrams, J. J. (Producer and Director). (2009). *Star Trek* [Film]. United States: Paramount Pictures.

Alexander, J., and Adelman, B. (Writers) and Beeman, G. (Director). (2007). Landslide [Television series episode]. In A. Armus and K. Foster (Producers), *Heroes*. New York: NBC.

Apollonius of Rhodes (1993). *Jason and the golden fleece (The Argonautica)* (R. Hunter, Trans.). Oxford: Clarendon Press.

Armus, A., and Foster, K. (Writers), and Dawson, R. (Director). (2007). Run! [Television series episode]. In J. Chory (Producer), *Heroes*. New York: NBC.

Baker, D. (2001). 'Every old trick is new again': Myth in quotations and the *Star Trek* franchise. *Popular Culture Review, 12 (1)*, 67–77.

_____. (2005). *Broadcast space: TV culture, myth and Star Trek.* Unpublished doctoral dissertation, The University of Melbourne, Australia.

_____. (2006, February). 'The illusion of magnitude': Adapting the epic from film to television. *Senses of Cinema, 41.* Retrieved October 17, 2007, from http://www.sensesofcinema.com/contents/06/41/adapting-epic-film-tv.html

BBC News. (2005, March 31). Eccleston quits Doctor Who role. Retrieved July 28, 2008, from http://news.bbc.co.uk/1/hi/entertainment/tv_and_radio/4395849.stm

Bennett, H. (Producer), and Nimoy, L. (Director). (1984). *Star Trek III: The search for Spock* [Film]. United States: Paramount Pictures.

Bennett, T., and Woollacott, J. (1987). *Bond and beyond: The political career of a popular hero*. New York: Methuen.

Berman, R. (Producer). (1993–1999). *Star Trek: Deep Space Nine* [Television series]. Hollywood: Paramount.

_____, and Braga, B. (Producers). (1995–2001). *Star Trek: Voyager* [Television series]. Hollywood: Paramount.

_____, and Braga, B. (Producers). (2001–2005). *Star Trek: Enterprise* [Television series]. Hollywood: Paramount.

_____, and Braga, B. (Writers), and Conway, J. L. (Director). (2001). Broken bow [Television series episode]. In R. Berman and B. Braga (Producers), *Star Trek: Enterprise*. Hollywood: Paramount.

Breech, R., and Kelley, D. E. (Producers). (1997–2004). *The Practice* [Television series]. New York: ABC.

Bremmer, J. (Ed.). (1987). *Interpretations of Greek mythology*, London: Croom Helm.

Chaidez, N. (Writer), and O'Hara, T. (Director). (2007). The fix [Television series episode]. In A. Armus and K. Foster (Producers), *Heroes*. New York: NBC.

Collins, J. (1991). Batman: The movie, the narrative, the hyperconscious. In R. E. Pearson and W. Uricchio (Eds.), *The many lives of the Batman: Critical approaches to a superhero and his media* (pp. 164–81). New York: Routledge and London: BFI.

Collinson, P. (Producer). (2005-). *Doctor Who*. Cardiff: BBC Wales.

Cook, A. L. (2001). The Doctor and Odysseus: The fall of Troy in ancient times and Now. Retrieved July 26, 2008, from http://homepages.bw.edu/~jcurtis/Cook_1.htm

Cotton, D. (Writer), and Leeston-Smith, M. (Director). (1965). The myth makers [Television series episode]. In Wiles, J. (Producer), *Doctor Who*. London: BBC.

Davies, R. T. (Producer). (2005). *Casanova* [Television series]. Cardiff: BBC Wales.

_____. (Executive Producer). (2005-). Doctor Who [Television series]. Cardiff: BBC Wales.

_____. (Writer), and Harper, G. (Director). (2008). Journey's end [Television series episode]. In R.T. Davies (Executive Producer), *Doctor Who*. Cardiff: BBC Wales.

de Cordova, R. (1990). *Picture personalities: The emergence of the star system in America*. Urbana and Chicago: University of Illinois Press.

_____. (1991). The emergence of the star system in America. In C. Gledhill (Ed.), *Stardom: Industry of desire* (pp. 17–29). London and NY: Routledge.

D'Elia, B. (Producer). (2004-). *Boston Legal* [Television series]. New York: ABC.

Dowden, K. (1992). *The uses of Greek mythology*. London and New York: Routledge.

_____. (1996). Homer's sense of text. *Journal of Hellenic Studies*, cxvi, 47–61.

Dyer, R. (1987). *Heavenly bodies: Film stars and society*. London: MacMillan.

Edmunds, L. (1997). Myth in Homer. In I. Morris and B. Powell (Eds.), *A new companion to Homer* (pp. 414–441). Leiden and New York: Brill.

Foley, J. (1997). Oral tradition and its implications. In I. Morris and B. Powell (Eds.), *A new companion to Homer* (pp. 146–173). Leiden and New York: Brill.

Franco, L. J. (Producer), and Nolan, C. (Director). (2005). *Batman Begins* [Film]. United States: Warner Bros.

Geraghty, C. (2006). Re-examining stardom: Questions of texts, bodies and performance. In S. Holmes and S. Redmond (Eds.), *Stardom and celebrity: A reader* (pp. 98–110). London: Sage.

Green, M. J. (Writer), and Szwarc, J. (Director). (2007). Distractions [Television series episode]. In A. Armus and K. Foster (Producers), *Heroes*. New York: NBC.

Greenhorn, S. (Writer), and Troughton, A. (Director). (2008). The Doctor's daughter [Television series episode]. In R.T. Davies (Executive Producer), *Doctor Who*. Cardiff: BBC Wales.

Hayles, B. and Tosh, D. (Writers), and Sellars, B. (Director). (1966). The celestial toymaker [Television series episode]. In I. Lloyd (Producer), *Doctor Who*. London: BBC.

Hesiod. (1914). *Theogony, the Homeric hymns and Homerica* (H. G. Evelyn-White, Trans.). Cambridge, MA: Harvard University Press and London: William Heinemann Ltd. Retrieved June 29, 2002 from http://www.perseus.tufts.edu/cgi-bin/ptext?lookup=Hes.+Th.+5

Homer. (1965, 1975). *The Odyssey of Homer* (R. Lattimore, Trans.). New York: Harper Perennial.

Jenkins, H. (1992). *Textual poachers: Television fans and participatory culture*. New York: Routledge.

Jones, P. V. (1988). The kleos of Telemachus: Odyssey 1.95. *The American Journal of Philology*, *109*, 4, 496–506.

Kelley, D. E., and Broch, L. (Writers), Verica, T. (Director). (2008). Mad about you [Television series episode]. In S. Robin (Producer), *Boston Legal*. New York: ABC.

_____. (Writer), and D'Elia, B. (Director). (2006). New kids on the block [Television series episode]. In S. Robin (Producer), *Boston Legal*. New York: ABC.

_____. (Writer), and D'Elia, B. (Director). (2007). Trial of the century [Television series episode]. In S. Robin (Producer), *Boston Legal*. New York: ABC.

Kreisberg, A., and Broch, L. (Writers), and Robin, S. (Director). (2006). Too much information [Television series episode]. In S. Robin (Producer), *Boston Legal*. New York: ABC.

Kring, T. (Producer). (2006-). *Heroes* [Television series]. New York: NBC.

_____. (Writer), and Beeman, G. (Director). (2007). Four months later... [Television series episode]. In T. Kring (Producer), *Heroes*. New York: NBC.

_____. (Writer), and Semel, D. (Director). (2006). Genesis [Television series episode]. In T. Kring (Producer), *Heroes*. New York: NBC.

Laemmle, Jr. C. (Producer), and Whale, J. (Director). (1933). *The Invisible Man* [Motion picture]. United States: Universal Pictures.

Lambert, V., Wiles, J., Lloyd, I., Bryant, P., Sherwin, D., Letts, B., Hinchcliffe, P., Williams, G., and Nathan-Turner, J. (Producers). (1963–1989). *Doctor Who* [Television series]. London: BBC.

Langer, J. (1981). Television's 'personality system.' *Media, Culture and Society*, *4*, 351–365.

Maltby, R. (2003). *Hollywood cinema* (2nd ed.). Malden MA: Blackwell Publishing.

Moffat, S. (Writer), and Hawes, J. (Director). (2005). The empty child [Television series episode]. In R.T. Davies (Executive Producer), *Doctor Who*. Cardiff: BBC Wales.

Naremore, J. (1988). *Acting in the cinema*. Berkeley: University of California Press.

Newman, H., and Newman, J. (2003). *A genealogical chart of Greek mythology*. Chapel Hill and London: The University of North Carolina Press.

Newman, K. (2005). *Doctor Who*. London: BFI.

Paramount. (2008). *Star Trek movie*. Retrieved July 28, 2008 from http://www.startrekmovie.com/

Parker, R. (1987). Myths of early Athens. In J. Bremmer (Ed.), *Interpretations of Greek mythology* (pp. 187–214). London: Croom Helm.

Pearson, R. E. (2004). "Bright particular star": Patrick Stewart, Jean-Luc-Picard, and cult television. In S. Gwenllian-Jones and R. E. Pearson (Eds.), *Cult television* (pp. 61–80). Minneapolis and London: University of Minnesota Press.

Pokaski, J. (Writer), and Yaitanes, G. (Director). (2007). Cautionary tales [Television series episode]. In T. Kring (Producer), *Heroes*. New York: NBC.

Rafer, D. (2007). Mythic identity in *Doctor Who*. In D. Butler (Ed.), *Time and relative dissertations in space: critical perspectives on* Doctor Who (pp. 123–137). Manchester and New York: Manchester University Press.

Ralston, G. A, Coon, G. L. (Writers), and Daniels, M. (Director). (1967). Who mourns for Adonais? [Television series episode]. In Coon, G. L. (Producer), *Star Trek*. New York: NBC.

Read, A. (Writer), and McBain, K. (Director). (1979–80). The horns of Nimon [Television series episode]. In G. Williams (Producer), *Doctor Who*. London: BBC.

Reynolds, R. (1992). *Super heroes — A modern mythology*. London: B.T. Batsford.

Roddenberry, G. (Producer). (1966–1969). *Star Trek* [Television series]. New York: NBC.

Roven, C. (Producer), and Nolan, C. (Director). (2008). *The Dark Knight* [Motion picture]. United States: Warner Bros.

Sellars, B. (Producer). (1978–1990). *All Creatures Great and Small*. London: BBC.

Shatner, W., and Fisher, D. (2008). *Up till now: The autobiography*. London: Sidgwick and Jackson.

Slatkin, L. M. (1991). *The power of Thetis: Allusion and interpretation in* The Iliad. Berkeley: University of California Press.

Tulloch, J., and Alvarado, M. (1983). *Doctor Who: The unfolding text.* London: MacMillan Press.

_____, and Jenkins, H. (1995). *Science fiction audiences: Watching* Doctor Who *and* Star Trek. London and New York: Routledge.

Turner, B., and Turner, T. (Producers). (1996–2001). *3rd Rock from the Sun* [Television series]. New York: NBC.

Vogler, C. (1998). *The writer's journey: Mythic structure for storytellers and screenwriters.* Studio City CA: M. Wiese.

Ware, P. (Producer), and Sax, G. (Director). (1996). *Doctor Who* [Film]. UK: BBC.

8

Running Free in Angelina Jolie's Virtual Body: The Myth of the New Frontier and Gender Liberation in Second Life

ELLEN GORSEVSKI

Second Life is an expansive virtual world that implicitly promises personal liberation from the everyday woes we experience in our modern lives. Much like other interactive virtual reality spaces/places such as the Sims, *Second Life* (hereafter *SL*) conjures a new life for the person who navigates in these cyberspace worlds via an avatar. An avatar is the virtual world equivalent of the interactive user's body. It is something akin to a 'second' self or representational body through which one gains access and navigates around the eerie, video-game-like world of *SL*. Put another way, an avatar is "a graphical depiction of a digital persona" (Williams, 2007, p. 61). *SL*, like the burgeoning virtual universe from which it springs, is what Dave Antonacci and Nellie Modaress (2005) call a "massively multiplayer virtual world (MMVW)" (¶ 2). Today *SL*, among many other forms of digital platforms or tools, is being touted at numerous universities and colleges by their Centers for Teaching, Learning and Technology (CTLT) for the many "educational possibilities of these emerging technologies" (Antonacci and Modaress, 2005, ¶ 3). Because a person "cannot be passive in a game or simulation" such as *SL*, these forums enable "students [to be] engaged in educational games and simulations [for] interpreting, analyzing, discovering, evaluating, acting, and problem solving" (Antonacci and Modaress, 2005, ¶ 6). Anthony Fontana (2008), an administrator of the *SL* Virtual Campus of Bowling Green State University (BGSU) describes the educational benefits in this way:

Second Life offers educators and students an online space to meet face to face, dramatically changing the dynamic of online meetings and education. Since people all over the world use *Second Life*, it presents an opportunity to engage in cross-cultural networking and research within a global community. The *Second Life* virtual world is also a dynamic 3-D space and immersive learning environment that is entirely created by the user [p. 6].

Such sunny discourse is employed to characterize the endless possibilities of virtual realms like *SL*, giving it an ambiance of being pragmatic and useful in multiple contexts, including education. Some scholars of cyberspace such as Mark Poster are "optimistic about the possibilities for community in ... contemporary technological society" because they see it as "enabling the freeing up of social roles and the multiplication of worldviews" (Willson, 2006, p. 179). There is no doubt that there are many beneficial possibilities for interacting in cyber worlds like *SL*.

At the same time, however, the rhetorical tropes promising a glorious, utilitarian virtual world for its users, whether they be students, soldiers or housewives, need to be examined as a specific persuasive discourse that has a long and troubling history. Any time human beings are lured by potent rhetoric that promises new, exciting, uncharted terrains—whether they are geographical, psychological, or now, cybernetic—usually two opposing camps arise. In the case of cyberspace, neo-luddites such as Neil Postman caution us that we are *Amusing Ourselves to Death*, whereas proponents like Richard Lanham have more optimistic things to say about the new interactive medium (Snyder, 2000). Both sides of the debate have valid perspectives worth considering.

In terms of resisting new, visually based forms of propagandistic communication, Neil Postman has offered the worrying view that "two great technologies confront each other ... for the control of students' minds" (as cited in Synder, 2000). Postman presents the hand-wringing scenario of an either-or communicative world of the visual versus the verbal, in which one must attain primacy over the other; the visual is associated with the fluff of television whereas the verbal is linked to logic and critical thinking (as cited in Synder, 2000). In contrast, Richard Lanham has expressed no such fear of technology, for he envisions a creative matching of visual and verbal, each informing and enhancing the processes of the other (as cited in Synder 2000). The following discussion treads the ground of this debate while respecting both Postman's and Lanham's views, and provides the additional insights of feminist theory.

What feminist perspectives add to the discussion of communicative interaction in cyber worlds is an awareness that avatars and "virtual humans" present a naturalized, normalized characterization of what it means to be a woman, all while this essentialized feminine persona of the avatar is actually a highly artificial construct (Zdenek, 2007, p. 397–398). Although the computer programmer designs and controls the rhetorical experience of the user of a "virtual human" or avatar in artificial worlds or interfaces, the direct role that the programmer has in creating the experience remains hidden or naturalized:

> [Avatars] ... designed for the Web enact familiar scripts about women's work, circum-
> scribe the range of possible roles and personalities for women, invoke service to others
> as the primary context for women's work (at the expense of other ways of inscribing
> social experience and human labor), and objectify women through a not-so-subtle
> process of linking technology-as-tool to the ideal that women are tools, fetishized
> instruments to be used in the service of accomplishing users' goals [Zdenek, 2007, p.
> 398].

Thus Zdenek (2007) contends that when people operating inside of virtual worlds encounter and use programmer prescribed "virtual characters" they "interact with [these characters] as social actors" even though they believe they are only engaging in artificial and therefore impact-free activities (p. 398). Moreover Zdenek (2007) posits these interactions are highly rhetorical since they foster both constitutive and socially reiterative behaviors (pp. 401–403). Zdenek (2007) also confirms that because avatars constitute "the rhetoric of virtual characters" they merit further examination (p. 399).

The discourses surrounding *SL* draw upon a rich vein of rhetoric that mines the myth of freedom offered by earlier narratives and rhetorics of the frontier of the Old West. Today participants to *SL* are lured by a scientific, virtual world of digital precision that is ostensibly free from disease, aging, violence and death, pollution, global warming, and myriad other problems we humans, plus all forms of plant and animal life, face here on earth (Wallace, 2005, ¶ 6). *SL* is a rhetorical experience with its own "rhetorical climate" (Gorsevski, 2004, p. 126 –133). *SL* purveys a specific rhetorical climate in its cyber world, as evidenced by its being advertised with persuasive flourishes that evoke a new digital frontier and cyber-Manifest Destiny. Linden Lab, the company that created *SL* in 2003, describes it in this way: "From the moment you enter the World you'll discover a vast digital continent, teeming with people, entertainment, experiences and opportunity. Once you've explored a bit, perhaps you'll find a perfect parcel of land to build your house or business" (*SL*, 2008, ¶ 1). It is easy to see that the rhetoric used to market *SL* liberally uses terms that evoke nineteenth century homesteading: "vast," "continent," "teeming" "opportunity," "parcel of land," "build," "house," and of course, "business." But once inside *SL*, what is it really like to experience this "world"? Also, is the *SL* experience consistent with the rhetoric used by Linden Lab in its marketing, or by others such as administrators in higher education urging faculty and students to use *SL* as a teaching/learning tool?

In this chapter I explore some of the ways that the rhetoric used by the creators of this artificial world reinforce predetermined morés, attitudes and actions among many of the avatars that represent real people who walk, run, fly or Segway their way through *SL*. This chapter will explore the ramifications of the myth of gender liberation that the new digital frontier offers, particularly for women who operate with female avatars. To be sure, many women use avatars that enable them to feel free and liberated; this discussion does not take issue with that fact. However, myth operates as a rhetorical narrative which is built upon layers of discourse and meanings. Such a complex and layered narrative creates contradictory representations of "women's liberation" as women navigate and exist in a fluid state between real and artificial worlds. This discussion helps unfurl and explicate the backstory to the myth.

The layered narrative of the myth of freedom on the frontier, and the specific ways that notion of freedom conceptualizes and represents women in *SL*, is what is being examined in this chapter. There is a mythic discourse, both visually and discursively in the *SL* world. As only one component of the new digital frontier, *SL* features strange paradoxes when one is, through one's gendered avatar, simultaneously both embodied and disembodied. Experiential engagement with *SL* is both an existential and constitutive rhetoric with a teleology resulting from the issuing of bodies of gendered and highly idealized avatars.

This study opens with a review of the salient literature on the rhetoric of the new digital frontier that reinforces earlier tropes of Manifest Destiny. This chapter will focus on two interrelated problems: I will discuss the (dis)embodied rhetoric of normed, gendered experiences that tend to occur in a uniform way for women using female avatars since their virtual reality is shaped by online network communication communities. Such virtual communication communities, or "network socialities" (Wittel, 2001 as cited in Williams 2007, p. 64) are considered here within the context of the multi-user dimension (MUD); such communities are conceptualized as groups of communicators who control programming, design or movement and communicative interaction of avatars in virtual worlds such as *SL*. I also offer a short sketch of my own experience as a typical novice, or "newbie" as a woman user being initiated into *SL*. In addition, I will briefly address the occurrences of violence, or "griefing" as it is called in *SL*, focusing specifically on feminine gendered avatars *owned* as it were by women in the real (non-digital) world. Gender-based griefing is tantamount to virtual-world sexual harassment and violence that parallels that which is frequently experienced by women in the real world.

In exploring both the communicative and the embodied dimensions of *SL*, *it* is not to be understood as a strictly terrible place that offers nothing redeeming; I do view *SL* as a virtual space and place of great possibilities and experiences, existing on the Postman-Lanham continuum between problematic and redeeming. I have used *SL* as a teaching tool myself-so in this discussion my aim is *not* to make a throw-the-baby-out-with-the-bathwater kind of argument. By highlighting the two entwined issues of virtual forms of communication and embodiment, however, I do wish to foster a more sober understanding of this peculiar and increasingly popular cyber world. This discussion builds upon the work of scholars such as Wajcman (2004) and Miller (2005) in asserting that "virtual humans are not natural, objective, or transparent ... they are designed and persuasive" (Zdenek, 2007, p. 400). In addition, because *SL* deeply invokes "the frontier myth," which is "a powerful and value laden embodiment of ... cultural identity, it is important for the rhetorical critic to trace its changes" (Rushing, 1991, p. 244) up through to today's cyber world interactivity. In short, this discussion aims to heighten the awareness of how discourse and visual rhetoric of the mythical Wild West frontier has implications for the agency of women operating female avatars in *SL.*

THE NEW DIGITAL FRONTIER

The staying power of the deeply entrenched myth of the nineteenth-century's discourses of Manifest Destiny is not limited to the United States. White Americans have been led by the rhetoric of leaders such as Thomas Jefferson with his ethnic cleansing plans for native Americans, onward to Theodore Roosevelt with his Rough Rider imperialism, and later, to Dwight D. Eisenhower's and John F. Kennedy's calls for astronauts to rocket into outer space, which eventually happened alongside deepening American involvement in the Vietnam war under presidents Lyndon B. Johnson and Richard M. Nixon. Such rhetorics spring from a tradition of colonial domination over native peoples that was excused in both official and popular discourses as being divinely and politically preordained. Meanwhile, Western European nations such as England, France, Germany and the Netherlands purveyed similarly intoxicating discourses for the purposes of taming their respective colonial peoples through processes of religious, socio-cultural, political and economic domination.

Today, not coincidentally, the technosavvy descendants of all of these Western nations comprise large numbers of users of *SL.* James McDaniel (2002) explains the enticing draw of such New Frontier rhetoric in the digital context, which harkens back to its antecedents because "current new frontier rhetoric ... articulates itself frequently in terms of nineteenth-century fantasies and tropes of Manifest Destiny, in which God's will was invoked to justify and motivate the stretch westward" (p. 94) in the American context, and outward in all directions of the compass, in the European context. This rhetoric, adds McDaniel, "remodels [such fantasies] for present use by combining pastoral with technological imageries. Yesterday's theological-religious sense of 'destiny' becomes today's cult of techno-determinism...." (p. 94). He calls it "cyber rhetoric" (p. 94). Examples of cyber rhetoric include the terms noted earlier that Linden Lab offers to describe *SL,* such as "vast," "continent," "teeming" "opportunity," "parcel of land" (*SL,* 2008, ¶ 1). This cyber rhetoric of the frontier myth, then, is the mainstay of *SL.*

Further, McDaniel highlights the embodied aspect of the rhetoric of the new digital frontier by observing, "Public discourses that constitute new frontiers characteristically evoke novel senses of place and displacement as well as subjectivities capable of flourishing in these sense-spaces" (p. 91). McDaniel maintains that New Frontier rhetoric plays out in cyberspace through its connection to the "curious genre [of] tall tales, and the oral fantasies that illuminate the nineteenth century's expansionist ideology" (p. 91). He argues,

Because it is so highly stylized, tall talk is a potent mode for collective memory ... [such exaggerated discourse carries over the] nineteenth-century U.S. oral fantasy ... and in the ... early twenty-first century ... [which is] increasingly optical-visual, a sense of space as inexhaustibly vast and subjectivity as equally enormous or as radically displaced... [pp. 91–92].

Thus seemingly vast, virtual worlds such as *SL* exploit "today's postmodernist ethos and aesthetic sensibility [to] reconstitute public fantasy..." (McDaniel, 2002, p. 93). Similarly, Janice Hocker Rushing's analysis of science fiction films provides further visual foregrounding for what a three dimensional, interactive cyber frontier and its rhetorical precursors invoke. Rushing (1991) observes that "'The New Frontier' of space ... [has] remained central to our mythic consciousness" (p. 243). Importantly, Rushing avers that heroic and symbolic interaction with "The New Frontier" of cyber space lacks substantive engagement with the "inner space" of the "psyche" because we are not attuned to the "*quiet contemplation*" that is necessary for ethical interaction with others (p. 244). Rushing maintains that "recent versions of the American frontier myth in popular film deal with the impulse toward introspection by co-opting it to further traditional, outward-directed action" (p. 244), which applies just as easily to the rhetoric of *SL* as a virtual space as it does to filmic representations of outer space. Rushing believes that in many science fiction films, such as the *Alien* franchise, the "forgotten feminine ... myth" becomes "subsumed by an explosive reenactment of exploitative frontierism that co-opts the heroine for its patriarchal mission" (p. 244). As this chapter will show, it is precisely this kind of narrative of the new frontier and its cooptation that carries over seamlessly into the cyberspace of *SL*.

Just like its colonial precursors the rhetoric surrounding the cyber myth of the new digital frontier is deeply rooted in transnational discourses of globalization. Virtual spaces and places such as *SL* display and rely upon mythic discourses, which help to both link and intoxicate users whose intercultural avatars traverse virtual "countries" in which real languages are spoken, and which are metaphorically rooted in histories of domination of real, physical places and peoples, such as the Western European nations noted above: England, France, Germany and the Netherlands, as well as the United States.

Another underlying aspect of the mythic fantasy is the "utopian celebration of the liberating possibilities of the new electronic frontier [that] promotes an ecstatic dream ... a fantasy of escape" (Nye, 1994, as cited in McDaniel, 2002, p. 93). *SL* can be seen in this light as an experiential rhetoric that is both embodied and disembodied, "cybernetic and organic material, human with machine" (p. 93). Thus *SL* may be viewed as a venue within the new digital frontier that evinces the same persuasive "master tropes" as its "precursors," particularly when it comes to "images of sexual and social intercourse that produce new beings or modes of being, alliances, friendships, partnerships" (p. 93). The simple act of creating an avatar in *SL* is one such form of production of a "new being." There is also a feature in *SL* that enables a user to create a list of "friends" for the user's avatar, friends with whom one's avatar may regularly converse both inside *SL* or outside it, via regular emails.

With regard to gendered forms of "intercourse" in *SL*, one may also purchase for one's avatar sexual body parts through which one's avatar may engage in virtual sexual intercourse. Lynn (2006) emphasizes that a featured speaker at the *SL* Convention in San Francisco was a man who goes by the avatar pseudonym "Stroker Serpentine of Strokerz Toys.... [He is] famous for creating avatar genitals and sex animations and other complex in-world sex tech (¶ 1). This virtual world, produced and replicated mostly by male/masculine programmers as a masculine reiteration of the earlier machismo of Manifest Destiny, offers endless opportunities for a gendered experience for its "cyber-colonists" (Vlahos as cited in McDaniel, 2002, p. 94). The role of women as the feminine avatar and archetypal "Eve" in the "Frontier Myth" is crucial for the new digital frontier to flourish (Georgi-Findlay, 1996, p. 4).

Hence, just as Rushing (1991) saw in its science fiction forbears, *SL* becomes a "*rhetorically* significant [cultural document] ... that ... concerns the history of cultural values" since it "represents a significant prototype in the ongoing evolution of the American frontier" myth (p. 245). *SL* exists and is experienced as a highly realistic, interactive cyber world in no small part because of its reliance upon the familiar "dramatizations of the old west" which "are as plentiful as the buffalo before" the arrival of the white settlers (Rushing, 1991, p. 245). Because *SL* is a cyberworld that is like a science fiction film come to life, its reliance upon the masculinity of what Rushing (1991) calls the "old western hero" (p. 245) holds ramifications for how interaction in the cyber world plays out for feminine gendered women participants.

To better understand the ways that gender operates in mythic contexts, "scholars deconstructing the frontier myth tend to ignore the ... significance of women as readers as much as they tend to ignore the potentially symbolic significations of gender within a text" (Kolodny as cited in Georgi-Findlay, 1996, p. 5). In the *SL* context, women are likewise "readers" of *SL* rhetoric through their roles as active participants who are being portrayed and represented by avatars. The frontier myth, then, is an ideological one comprised of a "web of rhetoric, ritual, and assumption through which society coerces, persuades, and coheres" (Bercovitch as cited in Georgi-Findlay, 1996, p. 5). In the digital context of *SL*, the ideological entailments of the frontier myth are as problematic for women with female avatars as they were for the actual women who were lured into nineteenth-century frontiers in "a symbolic role as the hero's other, made to stand for the repressive rules and constraints of white civilization, inimical to adventure, independence, and freedom ... [which] ... denies women active, heroic roles but defines them as obstacles to the male hero's freedom" (Georgi-Findlay, 1996, p. 6). In *SL*, however, since female avatars are so highly sexualized and are unanchored from the repressive connotations of the Old West myth, in the new digital frontier, feminine avatars (even the standard-issue white ones) operate rhetorically so as to symbolically replace the exoticism of the sexualized native peoples who were portrayed, in earlier frontier mythology, as savages to be conquered in missionary style, and converted.

In many ways *SL* fundamentally reproduces for its users, through their gendered avatars, a gendered cyber society that echoes its Davy Crockett-as-frontiersman antecedent to "rearticulate structures of gender" in which the most empowered "subject [is] male, mobile, nomadic, robust, cunning, violent ... as a [rhetorical] figure, Crockett prefigures today's cyborg ... in virtual reality" (McDaniel, p. 100). In the next section I consider the question that flows from this troubling cybernetic virtual existence of raw masculine power. This masculine power stems, in part, from the inexorable rhetorical magnetism of the frontier and Manifest Destiny. These rhetorics are further heightened by the intractable problem of the dearth of women and feminine gendered programmers for the new digital frontier: where, then, does that leave a woman who navigates through *SL* with a feminine gendered cyborg or avatar? Donna Haraway has embedded into her definition of "cyborg" the deeply felt linkage between the woman who is using a computer or other advanced technological tool to meld her sense of being into a liminal space (pp. 150–153). Haraway asserts that this fluid state of the cyborg can be empowering to feminists but also empowering to oppressors such as the military or capitalist establishments (pp. 160–164). If a female avatar is rhetorically constituted so as to preference the interpretation of her through new frontier discourses as a prostitute, then the woman-as-cyborg who is navigating in *SL* via a female avatar is in some way liable to being viscerally affected by this status.

THE GENDERED EXPERIENCE OF *SL*

As one leader of the *SL* business community puts it, new participants in *SL* "are all shocked how real it feels" (King as cited in Wetzler, 2007, ¶ 15). *SL* features a (dis)embodied rhetoric of normed, gendered experiences that tend to occur in a uniform way for women using female avatars since their virtual reality is shaped by masculine communication communities. Charlotte Krolokke and Anne Scott Sorensen (2006) call for "feminist communication scholars ... to explore how gender performativity emerges from the tension between agency and ... underlying norms, which are frequently unconscious and appear natural, thus preceding the subject" (p. 40). Notably, the groundbreaking work of Sandra Bem (1974) and others (Butler 1990; Halberstam, 1998; Davies, 2004; Krolokke and Sorensen, 2006; Zdenek, 2007; Wood, 2008;) view gender as existing along a continuum, rather than in a binary of male-female. There are myriad possibilities, constrained only by one's abilities to use advance computer programming skills, to create more androgynous and gender-continuous identities via avatars in *SL*.

But the problem faced by many, if not most, female users of *SL* is that women's socialization and constrained emplacement within the societal structure currently results in advanced computer programming skills being less common and less rewarded among female than male users (Turkle, 1995; Hapnes and Sorensen, 1995; Consalvo, 2006; Zdenek, 2007). Consalvo emphasizes that "production processes are gendered" and that cyber "culture has come to be seen as masculine and overwhelmingly male" (p. 362). Antonacci and Modaress (2005) confirm that "some aspects of *Second Life*, such as building and scripting, have steep learning curves" (¶ 31). Edward Davies' (2004) expansive conceptualization of gender as "gender mobility" or "gender migration" or "gender transgression" in virtual spaces is simply more circumscribed for women (as cited in Krolokke and Sorensen, 2006, p. 41). Stephen Webb (2001) underscores the fact that "humanoid avatars are heavily stereotyped along lines of gender and ethnicity. They usually appear as ethnically white with mundane aspects of masculinity and femininity being vividly marked out. Avatars are often significantly sexualized and glamorized" (p. 563). Since sexuality for women relies on physical prowess that relates to appearing sexualized, it is telling that the female avatars featured in the marketing web page "What is *Second Life*?" appear physically as idealized prostitutes highly reminiscent of the nineteenth-century Wild West. They wear get-ups worthy of Victoria's Secret television commercials, including thigh-high stockings and merry-widow bustiers (see http:// SecondLife.com/whatis/). While Linden Lab would not permit me to show that highly sexualized image here, anyone can view less suggestive pictures on the website, and they are still indicative of the typical, buxom female avatars that are ubiquitous in *SL*.

Indeed, Virginia Sharff's (1998) work has highlighted how the marketing of new technologies often relies heavily on Victorian mores of "separate spheres" between "masculinity and femininity" (as cited in Zdenek, 2007, p. 401). Thus, the promise of a new digital frontier in which "a plethora of gender possibilities" exists remains, in the context of *SL*, a strong means to create the illusion of gender liberation, when in actuality, for women using female avatars, it seems far more elusive to attain (Krolokke and Sorensen, 2006, p. 42). In the frontier myth "feeling" is associated with "the province of the woman," which, while "not necessarily [being] ridiculed or evil," is "primarily an inferior *supplement* to the masculine hero" (Rushing, 1991, p. 247). So the implicitly male hero in this new cyber plain is enabled to "transition from horse to spacecraft ... from gun to laser" (Rushing, 1991, p. 247) and from character in a science fiction film to an avatar flying through a cyber world. The male gendered avatar is the hero; the female gendered avatar is merely his "*supplement*."

Because communication among avatars in *SL* is text based, other problems emerge for women operating in *SL*. Megan Boler (2007) writes that "while marketing hypes and cyber-enthusiast hopes actively mythologize the potentials of disembodied (computer mediated communication) CMC with promises of anonymity and fluid identities, the actualities of the way in which users interpret and derive meaning from text-based communication often involve reductive bodily markers that re-invoke stereotypical notions of racialized, sexualized and gendered bodies" (p. 140). So in addition to the visual pornification of the feminine body through the standard-issue female avatar in *SL*, the Angelina Jolie look-alike cyberdrone, women assuming female personas in virtual spaces can be vulnerable to communicative exchanges that are hyper-sexualized and potentially degrading. Again, this is not to say that sexuality in *SL* is exclusively problematic, nor is it to posit that cyber sexuality cannot bring sexual liberation, which for some users it may. Rather, what is noteworthy here is that the experience of women using prostitute-like female avatars in *SL* hinges on a kind of impersonal, dehumanizing, "replicant" sexuality that the film *Blade Runner* (1992) displayed, and which other science fiction films and their old western precursors celebrated. This kind of dehumanization can limit women's agency in *SL* while also reconfirming the Wild West stereotype that most women in frontier towns should serve as anonymous workers in the sex trade.

Indeed, in the nineteenth-century lexicon, actresses were equated with prostitutes. This Old West era rhetoric fluidly migrates into the new digital frontier when women avatars are portrayed as looking like the actress Angelina Jolie, and wearing the most suggestive of costumes. In the next section, the discussion turns to examining the implications of how a gendered cyberspace play out, along with an analysis of some of the ramifications for the real world women users of *SL*.

AN EDUCATION IN *SECOND LIFE*

I became aware of and involved in *SL* because my employer, a state university, had, for an undisclosed sum, "purchased" an "island" of space (note the rhetoric of capitalism and colonialism) in the *SL* virtual world as a space and place to connect with students, faculty and staff for pedagogical and extracurricular activities (Fontana, 2008, p. 6). Because my department was working on creating more plugged-in forms of outreach for alumni and today's millennial students, I, as a newly arrived assistant professor, volunteered to set up a virtual office space in *SL* for our department's high-tech outreach purposes.

I dutifully attended the *SL* workshop offered by our Center for Teaching and Learning, whereupon the student facilitator informed us that *SL* is a fun place, but that, unlike a video game, it is primarily a location for communicating and interacting with others. For those on the cutting edge of teaching and learning practices at many large colleges and universities, *SL* is billed as a place to foster pedagogy, so that all manner of teaching exercises can be offered (particularly those that might be infeasible in real life). For example, a Psychology professor in England set up a virtual location in *SL* to show students how it feels to have schizophrenia, so that once one's avatar enters the special room, crazy voices and spirits pop out of walls and come shrieking at one's avatar while in the room. Another professor had her students go to one of the ubiquitous night-club dance floors in *SL*. The hitch was that her students' avatars would be wearing giant Kool-Aid mascot outfits reminiscent of old Kool-Aid commercials on television. As soon as the Kool-Aid avatars entered the dance floor, their enormous outfits had the digital effect in the real world of bogging down the vast amount of computer memory needed to run the computers of the other avatars who were in the s/place. Suddenly the Kool-Aid kids were being verbally assaulted and insulted as a result of the frustration of the other avatars in the nightclub. The teaching/learning objective was to show students what it feels like to experience discrimination based upon one's size and physical appearance. All of this sounds wonderful, and is consistent with the new digital frontier myth of hope and opportunity for betterment, at least on the surface. Indeed, Donna Haraway's "Cyborg Manifesto" proffers a belief, shared among some scholars, that virtual worlds offer opportunities for "constitutive" rhetoric to expand with "meta-narratives of technoculture," which yield "more equitable, democratic, and socialist-feminist terms" (McDaniel, 2002, p. 105). Haraway's belief is that "cyber-sociality prefers femininity" (p. 105). Haraway describes myth as it relates to the cyborg woman in this way:

> Communications technologies and biotechnologies are the crucial tools recrafting [women's] ... bodies. These tools embody and enforce new social relations for women world-wide. Technologies and scientific discourses can be partially understood as formalizations, i.e., as frozen moments, of the fluid social interactions constituting them, but they should also be viewed as instruments for enforcing meanings. The boundary is permeable between tool and myth, instrument and concept, historical systems of social relations and historical anatomies of possible bodies, including objects of knowledge. Indeed, myth and tool mutually constitute each other [p. 164].

For Haraway, this blend of "myth and tool" tend to lead to liberation. Haraway argues that "science and technology provide fresh sources of power" for women, and that "rearrangements of race, sex, and class rooted in high-tech-facilitated social relations can make socialist-feminism ... [and] progressive politics" possible (p. 166). To be sure, technologies that blend "myth and tool" can be used in positive ways. To her credit, Haraway has implicated the military industrial complex's uses of technology in perpetuating systems of violence. Still, Haraway appears to mainly view technology as a beneficial force for exerting women's agency. However, in the case of *SL*, my experience has led me to investigate, and, to the extent possible in this chapter, expose this discourse of gender liberation as being rooted in a consciousness of feminist possibility while the experience of some women does not live up to the idealized myth.

Following the *SL* workshop, and with the help of a colleague whose research emphasis is cyberspace, I was ready to obtain an avatar and gain access to explore *SL* for the first time. This is where the experience of gender comes in. When initially signing up to get an avatar in *SL*, one may select a male or female avatar, and then outfit him or her as one sees fit from the menu of standard-issue garb. When one first gets the avatar body, it is fully nude, which was quite awkward as I was sitting next to a senior faculty member who was guiding me through the process. Embarrassingly, the nude avatar has to stand in a queue behind others who enter "Orientation Island," whereupon the avatar is prompted through a series of tasks to enable one to learn how to get one's avatar to move about in *SL* by walking, running, flying, or even using a Segway, the two-wheeled standing mobility device, one of which President George W. Bush famously fell off of in 2003.

Although most users are probably less conscious of it than I was at the time, "creating an avatar is a rhetorical act, and the parameters of that virtual self also establish communicative limits" (Kolko, 1999, p. 183). After selecting a female as my avatar, I (through my new virtual entity) entered the rather bleak, gray, ghetto that is the environment of Orientation Island. Immediately, I was hit on by a male avatar who was also going through the Segway part of the tutorial. He first tried talking to me via dialogue boxes. When I disregarded his attempts at conversation, he then stalked me. As my avatar was ready to board the Segway, the male avatar cut in front of me and sat down on it, which by default forced me to share the Segway ride with him — tight quarters, even by virtual world standards. He kept trying to chat with "me" when I wished to be left alone to focus on my orientation tasks. The anonymous quality of avatar communicative exchange itself sets up conditions that are not always benign; such interactions can facilitate certain behaviors. It is irrelevant here whether or not the male avatar was being operated by a man or a woman because either way, he or she was using both verbal and nonverbal forms of communication that are indicative of masculine communication communities, which will be discussed in more detail below.

This brief orientation episode reinforced to me the distinct impression that *SL* is a world that is structured in many respects as a masculine communication community. *SL* is designed primarily by male computer programmers for an entrepreneurial venture capital company that, like *eBay*, earns real dollars in the real world by selling virtual real estate in its virtual *SL* world (Wetzler, 2007, ¶ 7; Bugeja, 2007, ¶ 8). The gendered nature of *SL* is mirrored in the gendered nature of the industry of information technology (IT) at large. This is especially true with respect to vendor user interfaces that rely upon women portrayed as female avatars or "virtual humans" to market and sell products (Zdenek, 2007, p. 398).

Gender roles are naturalized through discourses that hide the masculinized design behind much new technology (Zdenek, 2007, pp. 405–407). Masculine design stems in part from the difficulty women have had in breaking into or sustaining satisfaction from careers in IT. For instance, Hadfield (2005) reported that "a survey of 100 female computer science graduates from the UK's top 20 [programs] ... showed 39% opted for a career *outside* IT because companies recruiting graduates for IT roles only gave women junior positions" (¶ 1). Likewise Levesque and Wilson (2004) report that "evidence of gender imbalance is corroborated by ... the ratio of male to female authors or the gender ratio of speakers at [IT] conferences" (p. 40). There is a link between women's experiences of the programming side of IT to the user end of the spectrum, so my experience of *SL*, like any of its other novice users, was gendered through and through. The feeling of freedom that I had initially felt that was propelled by the myth of a new digital frontier bumped up almost viscerally with the more problematic reality in my brief opening foray into *SL*.

Therefore, this critique focuses on the implications for women users of standard-issue female avatars who all, at least initially, resemble the Oscar-winning actress, Angelina Jolie: complete with a slim body, large breasts, and a young face featuring make-up, high cheekbones, full, pouty lips slicked with lip gloss, and a thick head of hair. Beth Kolko (1999) has given critics good reason to consider that "avatar design ... is an important enterprise ... because it directly affects the nature of 'real' interaction online" (p. 184). Similarly, Zdenek (2007) has shown that due to the disproportionately male gender imbalance in programming and the naturalization of the sexist portrayals of women which are a direct result of that structural inequity, "the majority of animated Web characters reinforce rather than challenge traditional gender hierarchies" (p. 422). Kolko (1999) also avers that "gendered considerations are at the forefront of the social and rhetorical implications of avatar design" (p. 184.) Again, the aim here is not to deny any liberating possibilities exist for some users of such highly idealized gender representations of femininity. Rather, the purpose of this discussion is simply to draw attention to some of the possible problems that may arise from using an Angelina Jolie-like avatar as the immediate and most accessible option for women to use for self-representation of a virtual self in feminine form in the cyber world of *SL*.

Just as the American dream is a myth for those who are socially, economically and culturally disenfranchised, so is the new digital frontier exposed as a myth once the lopsided realities of gendered politics within virtual reality are grappled with. I join other scholars in expressing the need to be "concerned to identify material disadvantage and structural inequalities, focusing on the collectivities of class, gender and ethnicity" as they appear not only in the real world, but importantly, in cyber worlds that mirror real life (Wyatt, 2008, ¶ 28). Clearly, the experience of technology is "both a source and a consequence of gender relations" (Wajcman as cited in Zdenek, 2007, p. 400). Communication practices online can frequently duplicate real world communication, so any promises of virtual worlds that flout real world oppressions should be regarded not only with hope, but also with a critical lens (Zdenek, 2007, p. 424; Wyatt, 2008, ¶ 28). The next section of this chapter thus considers some of the more serious and problematic aspects of virtual world interactions that

Linden Lab or the typical university's Center for Teaching and Learning do not at present actively encourage us to reflect upon.

GENDERED NORMS OF VIOLENCE
AND SEXUAL HARASSMENT IN *SL*

The rhetoric of the new digital frontier heavily exudes the same kind of safe "fun" that echoes nineteenth-century travel literature. Take, for instance, Linden Lab's marketing web page about *SL* titled, "Have Fun," which states, "In the *Second Life* world, there's something new around every corner. The world is filled with hundreds of games, from multi-player ... to puzzles and grid-wide contests. There are also dance clubs, shopping malls, space stations, vampire castles and movie theatres" (*SL*, 2008, ¶ 1). Compare that to the travel writing of author Charles Goodrich (1838), whose readers could, from the "comfort and security of [their] homes ... visit the most savage tribes.... Indians, Algerines, New Zealanders, barbarians, cannibals" (as cited in Harvey, 2001, p. 9). Thus *SL* becomes the more updated, interactive version of being an "armchair traveler," whether it is for viewing mythic vampires or cyber savages (Harvey, 2001, p. 9).

The powerful constitutive rhetoric of the myth of the new digital frontier fosters the belief that one's subject, as represented by one's avatar in virtual places such as *SL*, "unfolds into the subject-as-'free agent,' the robotic figure" that is both embodied in the avatar yet remains, through its virtual world boundedness, as a "disembodied signifying apparatus ... capable of radically rewriting and reproducing itself" (McDaniel, 2002, p. 107). Yet clearly, despite its pixilated representation of perfection, *SL* is not a perfect world. *SL* mirrors the gendered postmodern society and culture in which computer users live in the twenty-first century. For instance, there is much visual similarity and therefore there is a potent symbolic and representational relationship between and among the virtual worlds that technosavvy users variously engage with on a regular basis. *Grand Theft Auto (GTA)*, a video game that portrays a post-punk cyber world, has the exact same look and feel as *SL*. *GTA* players use avatars to score points for raping and killing prostitutes. Whereas *SL* is not a game and no such scorecard is actually kept, there exists nonetheless the possibility for gender-based violence to occur, such as avatars acting uninvited upon other avatars; my own experience of my avatar having been forced into sharing tiny Segway with a pursuing male avatar is one example of this.

Also, in "computer-mediated communication (CMC) such as chat rooms, female participants ... get more responses, but since these are often harassing and sexist in nature, they serve to mute female participation..." (Krolokke and Sorensen, 2006, p. 79). Such gender inequities are built into the design system, and "because gender becomes invisible within a larger focus on humanness, critics and designers may not be sensitive to how gender stereotypes and other cultural values are inscribed" within the avatars and forms of communication as rhetorical "artifacts" (Zdenek, 2007, p. 406). Thus, unless women users resort to assuming masculine avatars, "gender-neutral user names" and discourse styles (Krolokke and Sorensen, 2006, p. 79), the lure in *SL* of an idealized gender liberation coming to fruition does not pan out.

Even worse, there are instances of virtual violence, or "griefing" as it is called in *SL*. Virtual or "computer-mediated environments are ... found to convey a gendered reality: cyber-anonymity encourages sexual harassment and even virtual rape" (Krolokke and Sorensen, 2006, p. 79). In their research, Krolokke and Sorensen (2006) relied upon feminist communication theories and media studies that confirm the linkages between violent portrayals of women in the media and actual violence against women in the real world (p. 79). In examining violence in cyber worlds, Krolokke and Sorensen (2006) drew upon Laura Mulvey's (1975) landmark essay, "Visual Pleasure and Narrative Cinema" in which Mulvey posits that visually mediated worlds such as film, and Krolokke and Sorensen add, cyber worlds, yield a specifically "male gaze" that objectifies and disempowers women (pp. 78–79). Krolokke and Sorensen (2006) also rely on the respected work of feminist media scholar Bonnie Dow (1996), who has shown that women are "portrayed in the media ... in pornographic ways" (p. 79). These "stereotypical portrayals," Krolokke and Sorensen (2006) conclude, "serve to normalize violence against girls and women" in real life (p. 79). Thus, aggressive or otherwise amoral relationships portrayed in various media can bleed over into gendered interactions between avatars in *SL*. There has recently even been a case of a real life divorce instigated by the erotic cyber affair of a husband whose avatar was having graphic cyber sex with another woman's avatar in *SL* (De Bruxelles, 2008).

Krolokke and Sorensen (2006) find additional support for their conclusions drawn from visual media research with existing research on sex-based linguistic differences in online chat room exchanges from studies by Herring (1999; 2003). Krolokke and Sorensen (2006) conducted a follow-up case study on 40 chat room participants, with 57.5 percent male and at least 25 percent confirmed female (the sex of the remaining participants was undetermined); the follow-up case study was based on Herring and Panyametheekul's (2003) male to female conversational excerpts from online chat rooms. In revisiting this study, Krolokke and Sorensen (2006) found "that women and men have recognizably different communication styles and men not only dominate women in online discussion groups and chat rooms, but women are frequently alienated from online communication opportunities and forced to create communities of their own" (pp. 85–86). Male chat room participants would often opt for more verbally aggressive or socially violent strategies, such as "kicking out" women participants from the chat, whereas women in conflict would behave in more accommodating ways (p. 85). Thus, for women the anonymous and mediated environment of cyber worlds can pose obstacles to which male participants are often both impervious and oblivious.

Webb (2001) has also observed that "exchanges in virtual environments can be painful and ugly and often amount to ... 'virtual carnage'" (p. 581). For instance, Bugeja (2007) reports that "in the wake of the shootings at Virginia Tech, a visiting avatar entered [Ohio University's] *Second Life* campus and fired at other avatars" (¶ 3). Incidents such as this can actually elicit in users of MUDs the effects of post traumatic stress disorder, so there is a deep, visceral connection between the virtual world and the real beings who are interacting there via their avatars. While griefing in *SL* may not be gender-specific, as it can happen to male avatars as well as female ones, there are histories that link violence and technology and their discourses to the victimization of women. This discussion explores specifically the implications of the experience of women in the real (non-digital) world who operate feminine gendered avatars in the virtual world of *SL*.

Tom Boellstorff (2008), who completed an extensive ethnographic study of *SL*, defines griefing as an incidence of "disinhibition" in which the anonymity of *SL* enables some pranksters to behave in ways that "disrupt the experience of others" (p. 187). Griefing can range from verbal abuse to "repeating" an act of "antisocial behavior," ranging in severity from sexist humor, such as "building giant dildos in the Welcome Area" to more serious acts such as "bombing events" or other actions resulting in "terrible consequences, including financial and emotional harm" (p. 188). Boellstorff notes the long tradition of griefing through technology in everything from rude male teenaged operators of early telephone switchboards in 1878 to text-based "virtual worlds like LambdaMOO in which ... repeated sexual harassment" or "cruelty" occurs (Curtis as cited in Boellstorff, 2008, p. 188–189). Many anonymous communication environments such as talk radio or blogging web sites often foster aggressive behavior and *SL* shares this pitfall (Whitt, 2008). While stalking and virtual rape can and does occur in virtual worlds like *SL*, Boellstorff maintains that the most common form of griefing is usually visual or "verbal harassment" such as "sexually explicit images" being placed "on the sides of buildings" (p. 189). Cyber-physicality is yet another form of griefing, in which "walking up to an avatar and pushing it with one's own avatar" occurs so as "to intimidate or trap" the targeted avatar (p. 192).

In addition, advanced computer programming "scripts can also be used to animate avatars against the wishes of their owners" (Boellstorff, 2008, p. 192). He quotes one female user's experience in SL of conversing with a group of "people, and somehow one of them was able to [move] my avatar. All of a sudden, I'm walking toward him [against my will]" (p. 192). Given that advanced computer programming skills are gender biased in favor of men, women's agency in such situations is often greatly circumscribed (Consalvo, 2006, p. 362). *SL* may also be considered as being structurally biased against women users because instances of griefing are "too numerous to be addressed in every case by Linden Lab, a source of frustration to many residents" (p. 195). Another interesting aspect of griefing is that its forms and interventions mirror the violence and the discourses of the Old West. Williams (2007) notes for example that currently the prevalent strategy for intervening against griefers in cyber worlds is often to "adopt vigilante-style justice" (p. 66). Also, "long established members of the [cyber] community [are] often referred to as 'old timers'" (p. 66) Thus, the familiar terms of the Old West are rehearsed and recycled in the new digital frontier, continually refreshing and reminding users of the narrow, gendered roles of actors who are presented in that rhetorical framework.

Overall, "griefing [is] a highly emotional issue for residents" (p. 196). Indeed, "assault" that occurs "in a text-based environment" to "female avatars" means that the women who operate these avatars really do "experience virtual sexual harassment and ... report suffering real-world anger and grief" (Reuveni as cited in Bugeja, 2007, ¶ 10). Griefing is a gendered issue, one which further implicates the macho discourses of the Old West as they play out in the new digital frontier. In addition, griefing done to female avatars that are 'owned' by real-world male users of *SL*, and also "political homophobia" griefing (p. 196) present other possible fruitful future directions of this study. Avatars portrayed as gay men who are feminized in virtual spaces can also be seen through frontier discourses as potential targets of violence in conveniently anonymous incidents of virtual gay bashing. Even Linden Lab has "acknowledged 'a definite creep factor' when the harasser is anonymous" (Bugeja, 2007, ¶ 11). Clearly, further exploration and study is warranted into who is being victimized in cyber worlds, why they are targeted, and what can be done to prevent or mitigate such violence.

CONCLUSION

This chapter has covered some of the more deleterious entailments of *SL*, the ramifications of which may be applied and used for comparison to other, similar virtual worlds through which computer users navigate. *SL* and other cyber worlds like it are complicated virtual spaces and places that merit further critical examination. While proponents and advertisers of cyber worlds like *SL* tend to use rhetorics that emphasize the "commonality" among all users, critics need to be attuned to the "virtual community" issue of "fleeting bonds," that is, brief, often superficial communicative exchanges (Willson, 2006, p. 189). So while optimism about such technology has come from noteworthy scholars such as Mark Poster, Willson (2006) points out that

> Poster does not examine the way in which technology enables the occlusion of the Other through the seeking out and maintaining of relations with those who are the Same. The potential to isolate and protect the individual from disruptive or alternate subjects and social forms does not bode well for the celebration of difference or for the ability to interact sensitively and compassionately with those who are different [p. 189].

This chapter has introduced the implications of this relative lack of "difference" as it relates to gendered representation of female avatars as well as the comparative lack of agency in numerous areas, including programming that many women users of avatars in *SL* often have as compared to their male counterparts.

The monotonous, soul crushing sameness that average women users of *SL* find in the standard-issue female avatar is the Hollywood image of female perfection: the visual equivalent of Angelina Jolie's *Tomb Raider* character. The highly standardized, highly sexualized portrayal of women as avatars in cyber worlds like *SL* needs to be considered given the context of alluring linguistic and visual rhetorics that stem from potent nineteenth-century discourses. Experiential rhetorics translate easily to the new Wild West, the digital terrain of cyberspace. Just was the Old West was 'won' by white males, it was lost in equal measure by its aboriginal native peoples, and by women of all races, ethnicities, and backgrounds who were forced into specific forms of menial and violent labor, including the sex trade.

While *SL* and cyber worlds like it afford us the temporary ability to escape our normal, everyday lives and the imperfections of our ever aging, sagging bodies, we need to engage in these technologies with a sense of awareness of the burden of inhumane practices that we inherit from historical frontier discourses. The myth of the new digital frontier is encased in a Panglossian sense of openness and expansiveness, which needs to be cracked so that we seek for more aware ways to explore these strange, new spaces. While this chapter has emphasized the problems that women users of stereotyped avatars experience, much more research and discussion remains to be done on the equally problematic portrayals of the wide gamut of human beings and creatures that fall under the category of Other.

In closing, surely there is some potential for a measure of feminine gender liberation in *SL*, for "as individuals come to own the means of production, their inner sanctums can be recoded as public spectacles for consumption, at once democratizing and capitalizing the available means of representation" (McDaniel, 2002, p. 103). But there is a long way to go before such mythic ideals are met. The point of this discussion has not been to demonize this technology, but rather to emphasize that if universities like mine are pushing us as educators to use *SL* as a teaching tool (Fontana, 2008, p. 6), we need to do so in an ethical way that is fully cognizant that our students, especially those who are women, may be implicitly disadvantaged in some ways. Bugeja (2007) reminds us that:

> When it comes to *Second Life*, we're not only talking about money. We're talking about whether you as a professor or administrator will be held accountable for introducing your students and/or employees to a virtual world that accepts little responsibility for anything that happens among avatars, including online harassment and assault [¶ 9].

Nonetheless, while this chapter has focused with great intensity on some of these deleterious implications of *SL*, I fully acknowledge that its use is complicated and can be "both liberating and hegemonic at the same time" (Perlich, 2008).

The main aim of this chapter has been to foster a greater critical awareness of some of the pitfalls of *SL* as it relates to gender and mythology of the new digital frontier. Equipped with such knowledge, critics and users of cyber worlds like SL can be in a better position to actively demand redress of patriarchal, masculine tendencies that are left over from potent Old West frontier rhetorics so as to disrupt or prevent their hyperduplication in the new digital frontier. This is crucial because rhetorics surrounding cyber worlds foster the mythically based illusion that technology is "objective," "neutral" and therefore "natural" (Zdenek, 2007, p. 400) while in fact it impacts users in both psychosocial and material/physical ways because "online and offline lives are inexorably connected" (Williams, 2007, p. 72). The fable of the convenient separation of electronic from real world spheres of existence needs to be further studied, but so far, evidence indicates that such a separation is nonexistent (Bugeja, 2007). That means that representations and interactions of people in virtual worlds that are designed to occur in circumscribed ways have effects on people in the real world.

By becoming more cognizant of the kinds of obstacles presented by *SL* to a gender-sensitive virtual landscape and interactive cyber world, perhaps its users can lobby for, and its creators and maintenance crew can endeavor to foster, a less biased, less structurally violent, hence more inclusive, peaceful virtual world. Feminist scholars of new technologies such as Beth Kolko (1999) and Mia Consalvo (2006) have emphasized the critical "importance for women to have a role in [virtual reality] design" and usage (p. 181). Further, Sean Zdenek urges teachers, designers, students and users of cyber worlds to foster IT pedagogy that is "centered around the *rhetoric* of virtual characters" that enables us "to unpack the constellation of assumptions that drive the development and marketing of [avatars], and to critically interpret them" (p. 424). Ideally, by creating a more ethical virtual world, perhaps it can be a more helpful milieu that enables and guides its users in how we behave in our real world, our first life.

REFERENCES

Antonacci, D. M., and Modaress, N. (16 Feb., 2005). Second Life: The Educational Possibilities of a Massively Multiplayer Virtual World (MMVW). EDUCAUSE Southwest Regional Conference, February 16, 2005, Austin, Texas. Retrieved 30 April, 2008 from http://www2.kumc.edu/tlt/SLEDUCAUSESW2005/ SLPresentationOutline.htm

Bem, S. L. (1974). The measurement of psychological androgyny. *Journal of Consulting and Clinical Psychology. 42*, 155–62.

Boellstorff, T. (2008). *Coming of age in Second Life: an anthropologist explores the virtually human.* Princeton: Princeton University Press.

Boler, M. (2007). Hypes, hopes and actualities: new digital Cartesianism and bodies in cyberspace. *New Media and Society, 9* (1), 139–168.

Bugeja, M. J. (2007). Second thoughts about Second Life. *Chronicle of Higher Education.* Sept. 14, 2007. Retrieved 1 November, 2008, from http://chronicle.com/jobs/news/2007/09/2007091401c.htm

Butler, J. (1990). Performative acts and gender constitution: An essay in phenomenology and feminist theory. In S. Case (Ed.), *Performing feminisms: Feminist critical theory and theater* (pp. 270–282). Baltimore, MD: Johns Hopkins University Press.

Consalvo, M. (2006). Gender and New Media. In B. Dow and J. Wood (Eds.), *The Sage handbook of gender and communication* (355–369). Thousand Oaks, CA: Sage Publications, Inc.

De Bruxelles, S. (2008). Second Life affair leads to real-life divorce for David Pollard, aka Dave Barmy. *The Times Online.* 14 Nov. 2008. Retrieved 1 January, 2009, from http://women.timesonline.co.uk/tol/life_and_style/women/relationships/article5151126.ece

Dow, B. J. (1996). *Prime-time feminism: Television, media culture, and the women's movement since 1970.* Philadelpia: University of Pennsylvania Press.

Fontana, A. (2008). The state of our *Second Life*: Part I. *Connect: The Newsletter of the Office of the Chief Information Officer, Bowling Green State University (BGSU),* 6 (1), 6–7.

Georgi-Findlay, B. (1996). *The frontiers of women's writing: women's narratives and the rhetoric of westward expansion.* Tucson: The University of Arizona Press.

Gorsevski, E. (2004). *Peaceful persuasion: The geopolitics of nonviolent rhetoric.* New York: State University of New York Press.

Gruber, S. (1999). Communication Gone Wired: Working Toward a 'Practiced' Cyberfeminism. *Information Society,* 15 (3), 199–209.

Guadagno, R.E., Blascovich, J., Bailenson, J. N., and Mccall, C. (2007). "Virtual Humans and Persuasion: The Effects of Agency and Behavioral Realism." *Media Psychology,* 10 (1), 1–22.

Hadfield, W. (2005). Females opt against a career in IT. *Computer Weekly,* Sept. 27, 2005. Retrieved July 7, 2008, from EBSCOhost.com

Haraway, D. (1991). A Cyborg manifesto: Science, technology, and Socialist Feminism in Late Twentieth Centure. In *Simians, cyborgs and women: The reinvention of nature.* London: Free Association Books.

Harvey, B. (2001). *American geographics: U.S. national narratives and the representation of the non–European world, 1830–1865.* Stanford: Stanford University Press.

Herring, S., and Panyametheekul, S. (2003). Gender and turn allocation in a Thair chat room. *Journal of Computer Mediated Communication,* 9 (1), 1–21.

_____. (1999). The rhetorical dynamics of gender harassment online. *Information Society,* 15 (3), 151–167.

Kolko, B. (1999). Representing bodies in virtual space: the rhetoric of avatar design. *Information Society,* 15 (3), 177–186.

Krolokke, C., and Sorensen, A. S. (2006). *Gender communication theories and analyses: from silence to performance.* Thousand Oaks: Sage Publications.

Lamont, I. (2007, 19 May). Teaching in Second Life: One instructor's perspective. Terra Nova. Retrieved 30 April, 2008 from http://terranova.blogs.com/terra_nova/2007/05/teaching_in_sec.html

Levesque, M., and Wilson, G. (2004). Open source, cold shoulder. *Software Development,* 12 (11), 40–43.

Lynn, R. Second Life gets sexier. *Wired.com.* Aug. 25, 2006. Retrieved 27 Oct. 2008 from: http://www.wired.com/gaming/virtualworlds/commentary/ sexdrive/2006/08/71657

McDaniel, J. P. (2002). Figures for new frontiers, from Davy Crockett to cyberspace gurus. *Quarterly Journal of Speech,* 88 (1), 91–111.

Michele, A. W. (2006). *Technically together: Rethinking community within techno-society.* New York: Peter Lang Publishing.

Miller, C. R. (2000). *Writing in a culture of simulation: Ethos online.* Paper presented at Rhetoric Society of America biennial conference, May 25–28, Washington, D.C.

Mulvey, L. (1975). Visual pleasure and narrative cinema. *Screen,* 16 (3), 6–18.

Perlich, J. (2008). Correspondence with author. Sept. 30, 2008.

Rushing, J. H. (1991). Frontierism and the Materialization of the Psyche: The Rhetoric of Innerspace. *Southern Communication Journal, 56*, 243–256.

Second Life (2008). "What is Second Life?: What Is?" Second Life.com Retrieved July 7, 2008, from http://Second Life.com/whatis/

_____ (2000). "What is Second Life?. Have Fun." Second Life.com Retrieved July 23, 2008, from http://Second Life.com/whatis/fun.php

Snyder, M. (2000). Broadening the interdisciplinary approach of technology education: connections between communications, language, and the literary arts. *Journal of Industrial Teacher Education, 37* (4). October 27, 2008, from: http://scholar.lib.vt.edu/ejournals/JITE/v37n4/snyder.html

Turkle, S. (1995). *Life on the screen: Identity in the age of the Internet.* New York: Simon and Schuster.

Wallace, M. (2005, August 21). Letting your fingers do the running. *The New York Times.* Retrieved July 17, 2008 from LexisNexis.com.

Wajcman, J. (2004). *TechnoFeminism.* Malden, MA: Polity Press.

Webb, S. (2001). Avatar Culture: Narrative, power and identity in virtual world environments. *Information, Communication and Society, 4* (4), 560–594.

Wetzler, C.M. (2007, September 16). Exploring the vast business potential of the metaverse. *The New York Times.* Retrieved July 17, 2008 from LexisNexis.com.

Whitt, D. (2008). Correspondence with author. Dec. 15, 2008.

Williams, M. (2007). Policing and cybersociety: the maturation of regulation within an online community. *Policing and Society. 17* (1), 59–82.

Willson, M. (2006). *Technically together: Rethinking community within techno-society.* New York: Peter Lang Publishing, Inc.

Wyatt, S. (2008). Feminism, technology and the information society: learning from the past, imagining the future. *Information, Communication and Society, 11* (1), Retrieved 7 July from: http://0-www.informaworld.com.maurice.bgsu.edu/ smpp/section?content=a 790637676&fulltext=713240928

Zdenek, S. (2007). "Just roll your mouse over me": Designing virtual women for customer service on the Web. *Technical Communication Quarterly. 16* (4), 397–430.

9

So Where Do I Go from Here? Ghost in the Shell *and Imagining Cyborg Mythology for the New Millennium*

JAY SCOTT CHIPMAN

Two interesting news events concerning technological advances for athletes appeared in the months prior to the 2008 Summer Olympics in Beijing, China. The first detailed the situation of South African sprinter Oscar Pistorius, a double amputee who races with carbon-fiber "Cheetah" flex-foot prostheses. Pistorius was banned from participating in the Olympics following a hearing in which the International Association of Athletics Federation (IAAF) claimed that the Cheetahs gave him "an unfair advantage over able-bodied athletes by allowing him to use less energy as he ran" (Springer, 2008, p. 26). The ruling was eventually reversed when evidence was presented that effectively disputed the IAAF claim.

One of the experts who testified on behalf of Pistorius at the appeal hearing was Dr. Hugh Herr, a professor of biomechatronics at MIT and also a double amputee. Although Herr's goal is to "one day reach the point where artificial limbs improve upon human design," he testified that, to date, there "has never been a prosthesis developed that's been shown to decrease energy requirements to walk or run." Herr also suggested that "pop culture and Hollywood" had contributed to the initial ruling against Pistorius, stating, "people believe things exist that don't" (Springer, 2008, p. 26).

The other news event involved controversy about the LZR Racer full-length competition swimwear manufactured by Speedo. The suits feature fabric that is "ultrasonically welded rather than sewn" and contain "compression panels placed along the chest, thighs and buttocks, plus a corset-like 'core stabilizer,'" all features designed to minimize drag due to skin movement and "maximize streamlining" (Powers, 2008, p. A15). The garments helped account for numerous world records being broken in meets prior to the Games, accompanied by a desperate rush by athletes to switch equipment. Although the swimwear was approved by the Federation Internationale de Natation (FINA), the official sanction did not deter complaints of "technological doping" by coaches and competitors not using the suits. It also prompted lawsuits filed against teams and individual swimmers who opted out of wearing suits contracted through other companies.

John Powers (2008) comments that swimmers fortunate to have access to wearing the suit describe it "as if it's a supernatural skin." Backstroke world champion Ryan Lochte, in an interview with Powers, stated: "When I put it on, I feel like some kind of Action Hero, ready to take on the world" (p. A1). Essentially, the suit, which often takes fifteen minutes or longer to put on, can be viewed as a wearable, light-weight machine designed to allow the swimmer to move faster. "I dive in, and I feel like I'm shooting through the water," states world individual medley medalist Katie Hoff, a feeling Powers compares to being a "Master of the Universe" (p. A15).

Both stories demonstrate technology's potential to enhance human performance as well as the suspicions and insecurities such technology sometimes engenders. They serve, as well, as reminders of what Anne Basalmo (1996) has described as "the merger of the biological and the technological" that has "infiltrated the imagination" of Western culture. The "technological human," she asserts "has become a familiar figuration of the subject of postmodernity" (p. 5). This entity, evidenced by the rhetoric of the interviewees and writers cited above, often emerges in popular cultural artifacts such as film, television programs, toys, and comic books. The cybernetic organism, or cyborg, is one manifestation of this impulse that has been notably persistent in these media.

The cyborg has been defined in many ways. Balsamo (1996) succinctly offers what is, perhaps, the most common delineation, that of "a coupling between a human being and an electronic mechanical apparatus," a hybrid species that is "neither wholly technological nor completely organic" (p. 11). Such a species confounds, as N. Catherine Hayles (1999a) suggests, "the dichotomy between natural and unnatural, made and born" (p. 157). The result is what Sharalyn Orbaugh (2002) refers to as an "embodied amalgam," whose interfacing biotic and techno-mechanical components interface seamlessly and inextricably as a functional unit (p. 436, 439). Olympic-hopeful sprinter Oscar Pistorius may surely be viewed as an example of such an amalgam.

Balsamo (1996) also, however, posits a second kind of cyborg identity, that of "organisms embedded in a cybernetic information system," in which "the boundary between the body and technology is socially inscribed, at once indistinct and arbitrary, but no less functional" (p. 11). Basalmo's suggestion is provocative and far-reaching. She is implying that human social interaction with increasingly sophisticated technologies associated with automobiles, computers, cellular telephones, digital gaming devices, global positioning systems, mp3 players, etc., produces cyborg identities. This exigency greatly expands the continuum of what might be viewed as cyborg, multiplying the possibilities to include a range of virtual and/or material entities within social and informational cybernetic network systems (p. 11). It also encompasses Carl Silvio's (2006) suggestion that the definition of cyborg can be extended to include "humans who extensively use or rely heavily on advanced technology, despite the fact that this technology may not actually be integrated into their corporeal form" (p. 115). To text message, to word process, to download music, to network on Facebook or Twitter, to purchase online or to simply surf the internet is to celebrate cyborg identity. The LZR Racer-garbed Olympic swimmer certainly emerges as a cyborg as well.

It is of little wonder then that, within the scope of these definitions, the cyborg has become a resonant reflection of the contemporary state of being. It is, as Donna Haraway (1991) asserts, "a creature of social reality as well as a creature of fiction" (p. 149). In its persistence, potency and proliferation, it is also reasonable to venture that the cyborg has entered the realm of myth, despite Joseph Campbell's (1988) claim that, in contemporary times, "[t]hings are changing too fast to become mythologized" (p 31).

Jon Wagner and Jan Lundeen (1998) have written extensively about myth and its functions in contemporary culture. They describe myths as "a people's deep stories—the narratives that structure their world view and that give form and meaning to the disconnected data of everyday life" (p. 3). Myths are particularly effective, they suggest, in their investigation of "life's ambiguities in a way that preserves our appreciation of their complexity while at the same time allowing for a sense of enhanced understanding, and perhaps even personal or collective empowerment" (p. 4). Elaborating upon these pedagogical and political functions, Wagner and Lundeen further contend that "[m]yth confronts problems that in real life are the most unmanageable; it mediates in narrative terms the conflicts of cultural ethos that seem unbridgeable in practical life. It opens a space for human creativity within and between the irreconcilable polarities of human existence" (p. 5).

What unmanageable real life problems or conflicts do cyborg myths potentially confront or mediate? Problems, Silvio (2006) suggests, involving "our collective anxieties, hopes, and expectations concerning the posthuman condition" (p. 117). Contemporary individuals, Orbaugh (2002) notes, are "compelled daily to face the breakdown of the distinction between the mechanical/technological and the organic/biotic" (p. 436). Cyborg myths embedded in cultural products, Orbaugh stresses, "help us to come to terms with the meaning of ... new relationship[s] between the human body and technology *as th[ese] relationship[s] unfold*: narrative helps us to work through the fears and desires of a particular historical-cultural moment" (Orbaugh's emphasis,

p. 436). Our particular historical-cultural moment in the first years of the new millennium, it would seem, is characterized by the tensions associated with both technophobia and technophilia, and the acknowledgement that the two are rarely mutually exclusive.

One fundamental, and potentially troubling and/or perplexing and/or enticing aspect of the posthuman condition, as posited by Hayles (1999b), is the configuration of the "human being so that it can be seamlessly articulated with intelligent machines" (p. 3). This configuration is achieved, according to Silvio, when the privileged status of the human body as a site of intelligence is surrendered. Instead, the body is regarded more simply as being "made of information that just happens to reside in a given material context" (p. 116). Once this shift consciously or unconsciously occurs, Silvio contends, contemporary individuals increasingly come to experience "overt instances of human-machine interfacing, both real and imagined, as something plausible" (p. 116). Cyborg mythology narratively and visually participates in the mediation of the plausibility factor, interrogating the liminal spaces of what is and what is not currently occurring in the human-machine interface and daring to suggest worlds of possibility.

Ghost in the Shell (frequently abbreviated as *GITS*) is a visionary Japanese narrative that depicts a dystopian future society in which all humans have been equipped with cyberbrains (or e-brains) that enhance their "original" brains to allow almost instant access to information on a digitalized network as well as the ability to communicate with others by thought rather than voice or text. Human culture in *GITS*, thus, has been completely cyborgized and questions of identity partially center around what percentage of human flesh remains in the individual body. The storyline of *GITS*, which originated as a manga series published in 1989, written and drawn by Masamune Shirow, follows the activities of agents employed by Section 9 of the National Public Safety Commission, an elite, top secret, covert operations squad that specializes in cyber-crime investigations, many involving cyberbrain ethics violations.

One of the main story threads of the manga follows top agent Major Motoko Kusanagi, a cyborg whose body has been almost completely mechanized, and her encounter with a notorious cyber-criminal, the Puppeteer. The manga was adapted for a theatrical amine film (also titled *Ghost in the Shell*) by Kazunori Ito, directed by Mamoru Oshii, and released to considerable acclaim in 1995. Shirow continued to explore the character of Major Kusanagi and the ethical and philosophical ramifications of the merging of humanity and technology, publishing a sequel, *Ghost in the Shell 2: Man-Machine Interface*, in 2002. He also collected and published several *GITS* stories, intended for but ultimately not included in the sequel, in a separate volume titled *Ghost in the Shell 1.5: Human Error Processor* in 2003. Oshii wrote and directed *Ghost in the Shell 2: Innocence*, a sequel to the anime released in 2004, based upon a subplot in Shirow's original manga dealing with the illegal duplication of cyberbrains.

These five related *GITS* works (as well as the popular animated series *Stand Alone Complex*), in spite of tensions involving different authorship and creative media, provide a substantial foundation for cyborg myth analysis. To facilitate such an analysis, it is essential to first propose a theoretical model for cyborg mythologies as a point of departure. As a next step, then, some aspects of the texts of *Ghost in the Shell* (focusing primarily on the original manga and anime and *Man-Machine Interface*) may be utilized to both illustrate and test the limitations of the model. Finally, building upon Wagner and Lundeen's (1998) assertion that the technological prowess that permits the formulation of the "superpowerful and potentially immortal being" (such as the cyborg) also "opens new vistas for the mythic imagination" (p. 55), it is possible to suggest how *Ghost in the Shell* opens new possibilities for imagining cyborg myths for new millennia.

TOWARD A CYBORG MYTH

Numerous scholars have found the character of Frankenstein's creature, as presented in Mary Shelley's gothic novel *Frankenstein, or the Modern Prometheus*, published in 1818, to offer a compelling starting point for analyzing cyborg narratives. Gray, Mentor, and Figueroa-Sarriera (1995), for example, insist that Victor Frankenstein's creation is "the first true cyborg" (p. 5). Whitt (2002), as well, claims that Shelley's *Frankenstein*, drawing as it does upon the machine mythology of the Industrial Revolution, is "undoubtedly the seminal mythic cyborg text" (p. 43), particularly as the "questions of identity, responsibility, and power" raised by Shelley continue to resonate (p. 43). "Not only did Shelley imagine the potential of science to create and sustain life," Whitt states, "she also addressed the ethical questions of this process" (p. 43).

The complex, cautionary tale of Victor Frankenstein's arduous, ultimately successful quest to generate an "artificial" life form and the resultant existential anguish (and revenge plots) of both creator and creation has become, according to Wagner and Lundeen, "one of the great myths of modern times" (p. 52). And like all great myths, they suggest, the story "lends itself to a variety of revisionings and adaptations" (p. 52). Rushing and Frentz (1995), significantly, reshape the Frankenstein story into the technological hunter myth where an "ego-driven, exploitative hunter" fashions beings (often in the form of cyborgic weapons) in his own image (p. 5). The hunter either "remak[es] a human being into a perfected machine or [makes] an artificial 'human' from scratch" (p. 54). These technological beings "demand to be cared for, to be given a legitimate and valued place in human society" and, when denied, "develop a desire for complete freedom" and turn against their maker (p. 55). The result is a "technological apocalypse in which humanity is replaced or destroyed by what it has made" (p. 5). In this revisioning of the Frankenstein myth, the creature may become a cyborg as one manifestation of the obsession to create (android, robot, or other entirely artificial entity being others). It may be tempting, therefore, to regard the Frankenstein myth as sufficient for critically examining cyborgs. It is more advantageous, however, to advocate for cyborg myths absorbing Shelley's Frankenstein myth as a constitutive foundation as well as a specific narrative option.

Drawing as it does, as Lykke and Braidotti (1996) suggest, upon "feelings of fear and aversion to the non-human/human boundary figure" (p. 15), *Frankenstein*'s dominant critical employment in science fiction literary analysis has been to investigate the adverse, dystopian, impact of "modern science monsters" (p. 15). Whitt (2008) reminds, however, that Frankenstein's creature is "a product of humanity's faith in science and technology ... making him the embodiment of our contemporary digital culture reflected through the image of the man/machine cyborg" (p. 34). As an integral part of cyborg myth, a cyborg creature's journey of self-discovery and interaction with its human maker must have a full range of imaginable outcomes.

Sharalyn Orbaugh's genealogy of cyborgs in Japanese popular culture as well as her close readings of Japanese cyborg narratives provides a foundation upon which to build. In contrast to many Western references, Orbaugh (2002) notes, "Japanese social discourse incorporates robots and cyborgs with little of the implicit dread" (p. 437). From childhood onward, the Japanese encounter and enjoy "a wide range of characters that mix human and machine elements" in a variety of media (art, prose fiction, film, manga, and anime) (p. 437). Many of these representations (such as *Mobile Police Patlabor, Macross, Neon Genesis Evangelion, Mobile Suit Gundam*, and *Guyver*), Orbaugh (2005) argues, are "complex and thoughtful, and their sheer quantity means that the various issues at the heart of the new cyborg paradigm are explored in Japanese popular culture perhaps more thoroughly than anywhere else" (p. 56).

Tracing the "interplay of discursive streams from both foreign and native sources" Orbaugh articulates how Japan's particular historical, political, and cultural circumstances of modernization produce diverse, sophisticated cyborg discourses and narratives (2005, p 71). Orbaugh cites a variety of influences, many with their roots in the late nineteenth century, for what she terms the "hardware-technophilic stream of Japanese cyborg narrative" (p. 61). These include the novels of Jules Verne, popular techo-adventure novels (*boken shosetsu*) for boys often incorporating transportation technology (submarines, ships, and airplanes; these become futuristic battle machines with the rise of militarism in the 1930s), and science novels (*kagaku shosetsu*), imaginative and fantastic stories featuring both realistic science and technology and representations of experiments, including ideas of scientifically modified humans, artificial humans or robots, that sometimes result in "monstrous embodiments occurring through accident or design" (p. 64). These works inspire cyborg narratives both cautionary and, importantly, celebratory.

Orbaugh also mentions a story in the *Senshusho* folktale collection (compiled sometime between the twelfth and fourteenth centuries) that indicates fascination with the concept of an artificially created human predates the modern Japanese period by at least 500 years. In this story, a revered poet successfully uses Buddhist mystical techniques to (re)create "an exact, functioning replica" of a friend who has recently died. Conflicted about what he has done, the poet goes for advice to a hermit who, he finds, "admits to having produced many artificial humans himself, all of whom are currently living happily in the world undetected" (p. 65). Although the poet ultimately decides not to experiment further, the story offers a sympathetic, affirmative view of the impulse to do so.

Frankenstein, as well, comes into Orbaugh's cyborg genealogical pursuit, but in the form of what she terms "the Frankenstein syndrome."

> Like the monster in *Frankenstein*, rejected first by his creator and eventually by all the other humans with whom he tries to establish contact, the people of modernizing Japan were forced time and again to recognize that even their complete acquisition of the "godlike science" of language — in the form of the discourses of industrial, post-enlightenment modernism — was not enough to save them from the curse of monsterism in the eyes of the West. All modern Japanese literature and art have been, and continue to be, produced under the shadow of this recognition, leading to a marked concern with monstrous or anomalous bodies/subjectivities and a range of attendant issues [p. 62].

One significant impact of this syndrome on Japanese cyborg narratives (such as *Guyver* or *Neon Genesis Evangelion*), Orbaugh stresses, "is the tendency to explore monstrous subjectivities from a sympathetic, interiorized point of view" (p. 62). This results in a shift in emphasis to an "intense exploration of the experience of monstrous embodiment" focusing both on "the nature of cyborg (or android) subjectivity, experienced from the inside" and "the ramifications to society of our impending (or already accomplished) posthuman condition" (p. 63–64). Within such explorations, cyborgization may even be viewed as a potentially positive, even ideal, outcome.

Orbaugh's ideas, the full scope of which cannot be adequately summarized here, enlarge cyborg myth far beyond representation of the cyborg as a threatening presence antithetical to humans. In the merging of Orbaugh's two conceptual streams of cyborg discourse, hardware technophilic and monstrous embodiment, self-aware cyborgs utilize their enhanced brains and bodies to demonstrate a more utopian vision of technology's positive potential. The terrors and delights of the human-machine interface, the simultaneous processes of organic and inorganic colonization, lead Orbaugh to envision a "next stage of posthumanity" in which embodiment is discarded altogether, and in which cyborgian consciousness actively embeds itself into digital information systems (2006, p. 104).

Finally, Donna Haraway's (1985) "A Cyborg Manifesto: Science, Technology and Socialist-Feminism in the Late Twentieth Century" must also be acknowledged in any attempted articulation of cyborg myth. Haraway's influential essay may be viewed, as Silvio (1999) suggests, as an "ironic polit-ical myth" theorizing "the liberatory potential inherent in women's interac-tions with information technology" (p. 54). While recognizing the cyborg's potential for patriarchal deployment as a device for oppressive social control, Haraway, to quote Silvio, also simultaneously endorses the cyborg "as an imag-inary figuration of a posthuman, postgendered subject who has slipped the bonds of dominant culture" (p. 54). The political struggle, as Haraway her-self advocates, "is to see from both perspectives at once because each reveals both dominations and possibilities unimaginable from the other vantage point" (p. 154).

Conceptualizing the cyborg as "resolutely committed to partiality, irony, intimacy, and perversity" and as "oppositional, utopian, and completely with-out innocence" (p. 151), Haraway invents a cyborg myth she describes as "about transgressed boundaries, potent fusions, and dangerous possibilities which progressive people might explore as one part of needed political work" (p. 154). In Haraway's myth the cyborg is "a condensed image of both imagina-tion and material reality," engaged in a "border war" or "revolution of social relations" in which "the territories of production, reproduction, and imagi-nation" are at stake (p. 150–1). In such conflicts, as Karen Cadora (2005) has stated, cyborgs may well hold "high-tech keys for survival," given that they are "multiply positioned" subjects enabled by technology (p. 360).

Haraway's manifesto has continuing appeal for its astonishing scope, vision, and rhetoric. Overtly political, openly subversive, deliberately disrup-tive, the cyborg imagined by Haraway is a potential device for challenging norms, destabilizing identities, and celebrating virtually unlimited dimen-sions of radical hybridity. Though articulated as an ideal, a means for possi-ble resistance and eventual political action, the dynamic rhetoric of Haraway's myth still encourages revolutionary, ever-expanding avenues for imagining cyborg subjectivities, quests and myths. By fusing Haraway's theories with the potent narrative structures of Frankenstein myth and the productive dual streams associated with Japanese cyborg genealogy, the foundation of a flexi-ble model for cyborg myth emerges. It is a model best illustrated by examin-ing cyborg narratives such as *Ghost in the Shell*, where elements of the myth are concretely manifested in character and plot.

GHOST IN THE SHELL AND
TWO FOUNDATIONS OF CYBORG MYTH

Major Motoko Kusanagi may be considered the character of central con-cern in the *Ghost in the Shell* narratives of Shirow and Oshii. This is true even in *Innocence*, the second anime, where though "physically" absent she contin-ues to inspire action and discourse, and plays a crucial, "embodied" role in the film's climactic battle scene. The character of Kusanagi, therefore, will provide the point of entry in this analysis, for she represents a kind of archetypal cyborg entity, poised in the ever-shifting boundaries and borders between human and posthuman, technophilic and technophobic, utopian and dystopian, ordinary and extraordinary, conservative and radical.

This complex subjectivity is established, narratively, early in the first manga and anime. The reader/viewer immediately encounters Kusanagi in her occupation as a highly competent Section 9 operative fighting technological terrorism. Cloaked in a 2902 Thermo Optical Camo[flage] garment, Kusanagi dives from the top of a skyscraper and interrupts a corporate crime in progress, assassinating a corrupt diplomat. Oshii follows the startling, somewhat disorienting opening scene with the film's title sequence in which Kusanagi's "birth" as a cyborg is represented. Attention is first focused on the being's brain, it's only biological element, encased in a metal shield, then further protected within a titanium skull and digitally scanned to make sure it is functioning. The viewer then is permitted to see the fully-assembled cyborg body frame in its raw interior form, a combination of metal, electronic, and flesh-like parts. This frame is then submerged in a series of liquids to coat to machinery with layers of "skin," after which the outermost layer flakes off in large pieces to reveal the finished "creation." Orbaugh (2006) stresses, importantly, that it is impossible in this sequence to tell whether Kusanagi is being created, recreated, or replicated (p. 93). Nor is there any indication of who or what is creating the cyborg.

Shirow does not include a parallel representation in the manga. He does, however, have Kusanagi serve as "official observer" for the making of a female cyborg, in order to verify that "everything was done correctly" and "to ensure her rights" (p. 106). The implication is that this is how Kusanagi, also, came into being. The cover of the manga in addition, graphically represents Kusanagi's status as cyborg with its visually perplexing layers of "skin," gaping patches of internal machinery, and wiring connecting the cyborg to microchip circuitry. Kusanagi appears to hover within the chip, effectively complicating time, place, and ontology.

Early in the film, as Silvio (1999) points out, Kusanagi "undergoes a profound humanist crisis concerning her cybernetic construction and what it suggests about her identity" (p. 59). She has persistent concerns about whether or not she is being manipulated to believe, or is deluding herself, that any part of her is not artificial. It is also troubling that the entirety of her cyborgic "shell" is actually owned by Section 9, thus restricting her options for change and control of self-destiny. Her body, therefore, "does not exist as an ontologically stable presence that guarantees her identity, but as an ensemble of parts" that circulate within a larger bureaucratic organizational system (Silvio, 1999, p 60). Kusanagi realizes that, at any moment, any or all parts of her being could be "re-coded, exchanged for another, or discarded entirely" (Silvio, 1999, p. 60).

In the manga, Kusanagi voices these concerns to a technician from the cyborg manufacturing center, with whom she is having dinner in a restaurant. "Sometimes I wonder if I've really already died," she says, "and what I think of as 'me' isn't really just an artificial personality comprised of a prosthetic body and a cyberbrain" (Shirow, 2004, p. 108). Oshii, in the anime, permits Kusanagi a moment of philosophical reflection on her cyborg identity crisis. After a scuba-diving session, she openly acknowledges to her colleague Batou that Section 9 owns their "cyborg shells—and the memories they hold." All the same, she insists,

> Just as there are many parts needed to make a human a human ... there's a remarkable number of things needed to make ... an individual what they are. A face to distinguish yourself from others. A voice you aren't aware of yourself. The hand you see when you awaken. The memories of childhood, the feelings for the future. That's not all. There's the expanse of the data net ... my cyber-brain can access. All of that goes into making me what I am. Giving rise to a consciousness that I call "me." And simultaneously confining "me" within set limits [Oshii and Ito, 1995].

It is a moment remarkable for articulating cyborg subjectivity.

Kusanagi, then, may be seen to represent a pivotal aspect in cyborg myth-making. She is a manufactured entity (like Frankenstein's creature) that demonstrates aspects of both hardware technophilia and the intense personal investigation of individual cyborg subjectivity associated with monstrous embodiment discourse. There are also implications that she exceeds conventional cyborgian constructions, in terms of ability, multiplicity, anonymity, and imaginative transformation. Another comment Kusanagi makes to Batou in the scuba-diving scene also foreshadows what Silvio describes as "liberatory possibilities associated with technology's intersection with the body" (1999, p. 60). "As I float up towards the surface," she states, "I almost feel as though I could change into something else" (Oshii and Ito, 1995).

Liberation

It soon becomes evident that the primary focus of *GITS* is Kusanagi's gradual liberation from the limitations, uncertainties, and anxieties of cyborg existence circa the year 2029. Instrumental in this process is the entity that comes to be known as Project 2051, nicknamed the Puppeteer (translated as Puppet Master in Oshii's first anime), that is engaged in its own liberatory quest. It is this narrative arc of liberation that is an essential element of cyborg myth.

The Puppeteer is initially encountered by Kusanagi (and the reader) as a somewhat conventional science-fiction antagonist. It is perceived to be "a cyber-terrorist who commits acts of international theft and sabotage while masking his identity by ghost-hacking into other cyborgs and using their shells [and memories] as platforms from which to access the various information systems that he has targeted" (Silvio, 1999, p. 60). It is soon discovered, however, that Project 2051 is actually a top secret computer program devised by the Ministry of Foreign Affairs, a "precious tool" with which to commit acts of espionage that will "grease the wheels of foreign diplomacy" (Silvio, 1999, p. 60; Cavallaro, 2006, p. 189). Though the Puppeteer is coded male, vocally in the film and by pronoun choice in both manga and film, it is actually a sexless, genderless, bodiless, newly sentient being, a new life form circulating "within the data matrices of the net" (Silvio, 1999, p. 60).

In the sudden process of becoming self-aware, the Puppeteer has managed to elude the control of its creators, throwing the Ministry into a panic and prompting them to initiate a specialized virus attack that will either destroy or temporarily disable the renegade project. Unable to resist the attack barrier and fearful of being placed back under tight control and surveillance, the Puppeteer generates the construction of a robot female prosthetic body into which it can enter (or be forced to enter) and endeavors to have it fall into the hands of Section 9, where it requests political asylum as a "self-aware life form" that was "spontaneously created from the sea of information" (Shirow, 1995, p. 250–1). This strategy also places the Puppeteer in close proximity to Kusanagi with whom, perhaps perceiving her ontological discontent, it attempts to establish rapport.

Responding to the Puppeteer's appeal, in both senses of the word, Kusanagi arranges to secure the remains of the robotic torso in which the Puppeteer is embedded. She then "brain-dives" into the Puppeteer to assess the situational circumstances of the curious surrender and to ascertain why it has selected her as a potential ally. This happens only once in the film, but Shirow has it occur twice in the manga, so that Kusanagi can begin to grasp the complexities of the Puppeteer's subjectivity before she chooses to participate in an action that potentially will liberate them both. She wants to know whether this entity is a cyborg? An AI? Some new hybrid? Or something completely unique? Her first "brain-dive" serves to liberate her thinking and to illustrate, for the reader, the surprisingly intimate experience of cyber-communication.

Visually depicted first as a complex of digital circuitry, as Kusanagi dives deeper the recognizable elements drop away, replaced by structures that are by turns ambiguously wall-like, cloud-like, tree-like, mist-like, map-like, blinding light-like, and, ultimately, what the Puppeteer communicates as "a vacuum filled with virtual particles" (Shirow, 2004, 271–278). Suspended in this vacuum Kusanagi encounters what is intended to represent the "core" of the Puppeteer's "being," what may be described as a simultaneously branch-like, artery-like, wire-like, spider-like, yet somewhat simple mass (Shirow 2004, p. 279). Cajoled by the Puppeteer to "cast off all restrictions and shells and shift to a higher level system," Kusanagi is depicted, suspensefully, as almost touching the mass with her foot just before her "dive" is forcibly ended by her colleagues (p. 279). She has clearly been intrigued both by this process of cybernetic exchange and immersion, exploring much deeper than she had anticipated, and by the potential opportunity to escape contemporary institutions of power.

As Silvio notes, the Puppeteer represents "a truly technologized, posthuman subject, an example of a non-human cyber-consciousness whose computerized existence enables rather than limits" (1999, p. 60–61). Though initially viewed, like Frankenstein's creature, as an artificial being turning against its maker, the Puppeteer, through an examination of its monstrous interiority, emerges as a radical, sympathetic entity embroiled, like Kusanagi, in a struggle for freedom.

Transformation

The "fusion" or "merging" of Major Motoko Kusanagi and the Puppeteer into one new "being" must be regarded as the defining moment of the first *GITS* manga and anime. Positioned as the focus of the final "chapter" in the manga and emphasized as climax in the film, this dramatic action functions both as a moment of closure and a moment that will initiate new beginnings, new stories, new challenges. In terms of cyborg myth, the fusion is a concrete representation of transformation as a second, possibly most vital, foundation. It is in this possibility for transformation, whether the opportunity is actually realized or not, that emergent beings, subjectivities, and identities may be imagined and developed. This act of imagining must be considered one of the primary functions or outcomes of cyborg myth.

Oshii and Shirow, significantly, construct the events leading to the fusion of Kusanagi and the Puppeteer each in their own way. Likewise, the pivotal moment of fusion reflects their individual artistic vision. Unique to the film is a short scene immediately prior to the Puppeteer's request for assistance from Section 9 that is designed to demonstrate Kusanagi's deepening crisis of identity. Alone with Batou, she ponders the actions of the Puppeteer, asking:

> And what if a computer brain could generate a ghost ... and harbor a soul? On what basis then do I believe in myself?" "Maybe all full-replacement cyborgs like me start wondering this. That perhaps the real me died a long time ago ... and I'm a replicant made with a cyborg body and computer brain. Or maybe there never was a real "me" to begin with [Oshii and Ito, 1995].

This important moment of doubt and existential angst is designed to haunt the viewer and serve as a source of motivation for Kusanagi's immediate course of action.

The scene is followed by the Puppeteer's pronouncement and request for assistance, during which Kusanagi becomes convinced that the Puppeteer may be able to provide assistance with or, at least, a new perspective on her personal anxieties. Kusanagi begins actively seeking an opportunity to communicate with the Puppeteer before the entity can be confiscated and circulated merely as a political "bargaining chip." When the Section 9 lab is suddenly ambushed, resulting in the theft of the robot torso containing the Puppeteer, Kusanagi seizes the chance to recover it for her own purposes.

Pursuing the thieves to a decrepit museum or conservatory, Kusanagi discovers the Puppeteer guarded by an enormous tank that she manages to successfully deactivate, causing extensive damage to her cyborg body in the process. With the assistance of her colleague, Batou, Kusanagi is able to directly interface with the Puppeteer. It is a two-way connection, however, as the cautious Batou observes when he begins to encounter interference in his monitoring process: "Hey! Are you going into him or is he coming into you?" (Oshii and Ito, 1995).

The Puppeteer acknowledges that it has had Kusanagi under close surveillance and has determined that they are kindred spirits with shared desires and discontents. Lacking a system of basic life processes, including those enabling death and reproduction, the Puppeteer views itself an incomplete life-form. In order to guard against deadly viruses or other unforeseen circumstances that might result in its solitary species extinction, it asks the favor of merging with Kusanagi. Though there is a degree of uncertainty about exactly what will occur in the process, the Puppeteer predicts that they "will both be slightly changed, but neither will lose anything. Afterwards, it should be impossible to distinguish one from the other" (Oshii and Ito, 1995). Kusanagi's apparent consent is spectacularly represented as an "angel" descending from overhead, white feathers whirling as the moment of merger approaches. Suddenly, however, the bodies are violently destroyed by government forces, effectively leaving some question whether the fusion of life forms has been accomplished or interrupted.

Shirow's manga leads to the moment of fusion or merger through different narrative means. First, Shirow gives Kusanagi additional incentive to consider the Puppeteer's proposal once it is ventured. She finds herself facing likely conviction on the charges of killing, while in the line of duty, a young boy whose cyberbrain has been hacked into by criminal masterminds, converting him into an innocent-looking, but deadly, renegade terrorist. The potential outcomes are bleak, she must either submit to imprisonment (and almost certain death or cyber-sabotage by government operatives) or Section 9 will be discontinued in the face of public outrage. Kusanagi engineers, therefore, a third option in which she becomes a fugitive from justice while awaiting the verdict in her trial and appears to die in a dramatic standoff with government soldiers. The reader learns, however, that what has actually been destroyed is Kusanagi's prosthetic body as modified by Batou to house a "dummy" brain. Her actual cyberbrain is being sustained in "autistic mode" by means of battery while Batou seeks another shell. Kusanagi complains, "I can't stand to have my body represented only by virtual signals" (Shirow, 2004, p. 328).

While Kusanagi is in this somewhat vulnerable condition, Shirow then has the Puppeteer initiate contact. This surprises Kusanagi because, although she has vaguely sensed the presence of the Puppeteer in the time since her first brain-dive, the government has been adamant in its claims that the Puppeteer is dead. This interface is visually represented in negative frame with white electronic outlines of Puppeteer circuitry and Kusanagi's brain and body — connected through cyberbrainwaves (Shirow, 2004, p. 337). The Puppeteer then presents its carefully prepared rhetorical argument, in which the dynamics of life and species survival are philosophically discussed in biological, theological and digital terms, accompanied with images by turns electronic, intergalactic, botanical, anatomical, molecular, and seismic (Shirow, 2004, p. 338–343). Although it has evolved rapidly as a life form, the Puppeteer feels it has reached a stage where it is stunted, unable to reach its full potential. "My system doesn't have any slack or 'play' in it; it doesn't have any protection against catastrophe," the Puppeteer explains (Shirow, 2004, p. 343). A single virus may destroy it as no diversity or individuality occurs during digital replication. The Puppeteer fears that eventually "the difference between a life form and an 'integration of information' would then disappear" and it would become "just a fragment of 'human'" (Shirow, 2004, p. 343).

The Puppeteer then asks "a small favor," to bond with Kusanagi in total fusion, a state of complete unification after which "it should be impossible for us to recognize each other" (Shirow, 2004, p. 344). The Puppeteer refers to the blended life form that will result as "the new, post-fusion you," a cyborg entity enhanced with the Puppeteer's "net," "data," and "functions" (Shirow, 2004, p. 344–5). Kusangi somewhat quickly agrees to "'marry' a life form consisting of nothing but intelligence" admitting that she has had a premonition about this happening and acknowledging the Puppeteer's claim of a "karmic connectivity" between them (Shirow, 2004, p. 346). Shirow depicts this fusion first as the Puppeteer circuitry sitting almost hat-like atop Kusanagi's head, Kusanagi's left hand extended upwards toward it as the Puppeteer says "Let's fuse together like flowing clouds, become a part of the uncertain but diverse world" (Shirow, 2004, p. 346).

Then, in the next frame, he captures the moment of fusion as an imploding burst of light emitting tendrils of digital energy integrating instantly into a web of ultra-thin fibers (Shirow, 2004, p. 346).

In both narratives Batou retrieves the fused entity into a prosthetic body. In the anime, he places what he believes to be Kusanagi into the shell of a young girl. It feels alienated within this body, telling Batou in an adult voice that "[h]ere before you is neither the program called the Puppet[eer] ... nor the woman that was called the Major" (Oshii and Ito, 1995). Batou, in the manga, places his friend's cyberbrain in what turns out to be the prosthetic form of a transgendered or transvestite male. Equally uncomfortable in this shell, the new entity describes itself as "the cosmic species—the seed," a "highly efficient package of information ... the greatness of life" (Shirow, 2004, 350). In both cases the descriptions of new, post-fusion self are notable. They feature affirmation of transformation, advanced technological sophistication inherent in the blended form, and demonstrate continuance of acute self-awareness of monstrous subjectivity. Consequently, the fused entity is positioned as a potential new post-human archetype that will open more vistas for the mythic cyborg imagination.

Manga and anime end with a similar image. The hybrid creature, ready to depart, stands looking over the city pondering where to go. The city sprawls as far as the eye can see. "The net is vast..." the entity exclaims, overtly drawing a parallel between city and cyberbrain network (Oshi and Ito, 1995; Shirow, 2004, p. 350). Transformation complete, arc of liberation accomplished, the image also implies a beginning as well as an end. New transformations and liberations most certainly lie ahead. Effectively, the reader/viewer is left to imagine what the post-fusion entity can and will do.

MAN-MACHINE INTERFACE: CYBORG, ADVANCING

A page of artwork preceding the prologue to Shirow's *Ghost in the Shell 2: Man-Machine Interface* presents what appears to be a young woman with reddish-orange hair seemingly floating in a vast digital universe, layers of networks surrounding her like galaxies or nebulas ripe for exploration. Her body is apparently unclothed (although the lack of anatomical detail adjusts perception to imagine a body covering of some kind), inverted, head and gloved hands apparently interfacing with her environment. Her eyes seem, at first glance, almost like marbles, but glowing. A close-up frame is then provided, emphasizing the woman's eyes, which are revealed to each contain the digital universe or e-brain network in which she is also suspended (Shirow, 2005, p. 7).

In the text accompanying the images, the woman is identified simply as Motoko, immediately forging an intertextual connection for the majority of readers to Major Motoko Kusanagi of *Ghost in the Shell*. Described as a "hyper-advanced cyborg," the being's body is said to consist of "all of her active drives; her memory of all of her active sources" (Shirow, 2005, p. 7). This type of cyborg, it is noted, experiences the reality of both the "physical world" and the "world of information," while retaining "bio-components" that "crave energy and sleep," always reminding her "of her basic identity-layer" (Shirow, 2005, p. 7). This, then, the reader speculates, is the post-fusion entity left wondering, at the end of *Ghost in the Shell* anime, "And where shall I go now?"

Interestingly this cyborg is then visually absent from the manga's prologue, occurring timewise four years and five months following the events of *Ghost in the Shell*. Instead, the reader is introduced to Tamaki Tamai, a "seeker" or psychic investigator from a "channeling agency," who has been engaged, under the careful supervision of a temple leader, by Section 9's Chief Aramaki to pursue an assignment regarding "the appearance of one of the most complex phenomena in the known universe" (Shirow, 2005, p. 10).

Although the specifics of the phenomena are withheld, it becomes immediately clear that it involves the cyborg that was once Motoko Kusanagi.

Tamaki, after reporting on the very recent death of hybrid life-form scientist Professor Rahampol (described as "said to be the creator of *those-who-are-complex*"), is asked about "the other '*creator*'*-like* spirit" [Shirow's emphasis] (Shirow, 2005, p. 11). That this spirit is Kusanagi is evident in Tamaki's reply, designed to provide a tiny snippet of exposition concerning Kusanagi's whereabouts in the preceding few years. She senses through her psychic powers that, although Kusanagi underwent temporary post-fusion chaos, her condition has now stabilized. Tamaki also reports that Kusanagi "has fused with four key spirits, the most recent being eighteen months ago" and that she is calling herself, after Section 9's Chief, "Motoko Aramaki" (Shirow, 2005, p. 11).

Though only a brief three pages in length, Shirow's prologue is significant for several reasons. Most importantly, it establishes the post-fusion Kusanagi as simultaneously creature and creator. Whether her self-created entity has been a productive or disruptive force remains tantalizingly ambiguous, although the connotations associated with chaos and stability suggest both may have occurred in the creature's "infancy" as it explored its identity and capabilities. It is also implied that the new cyborg being has continued to actively transform itself by merging with other "spirits." Although exactly what these spirits might be is left unknown, it can assumed that they are the consciousnesses of other sentient beings, whether cyborg or other intelligent life-form. Kusanagi, it is clear, has attained a somewhat legendary status (or notoriety) since her mysterious disappearance. But what, exactly, Kusanagi has become is far from certain — stimulating enigmatic possibilities for what the reader might encounter in the pages ahead.

In the remainder of *Man-Machine Interface*, beginning with the first chapter, Shirow depicts what it means to be a hyper-advanced cyborg by following the adventures of the somewhat mysterious, highly efficient, red-haired Motoko Aramaki. A large portion of these exploits, notably, occur in the aforementioned "world of information," providing readers imaginative (but plausible) glimpses of what it might be like to embed one's cyborgian consciousness (to use Orbaugh's phraseology noted above) into a cybernetic network system. In doing so, Shirow also continues to interrogate the scope of cyborg interiority, focusing on the subjectivity of disembodied intelligence, of personality without material personage, of the being-ness of awareness and emotion generated sans a human central nervous system. He also proceeds to illustrate, imagine, and expand the dynamics of cyborg mythology. Though space precludes in-depth discussion of the manga sequel, it is possible to suggest several salient features that cyborg myth scholars may find fruitful while simultaneously reiterating some of the points this essay has endeavored to explicate.

Post-Fusion, Hyper-Advanced

Man-Machine Interface devotes substantial frame space to representation of Motoko's life as a counter-terrorist security agent investigating violations of international e-brain ethics laws and consulting with corporate, scientific, and governmental organizations about the creation and deployment of information protection systems. Shirow illustrates the ease with which she navigates the net and her skill at infiltrating the most sophisticated information-protection barriers, all the while protecting her own e-brain system with an array of viruses, antibodies, decoys, mazes, and a variety of bombs (trash can, copy, toy) designed to confound or disable operating systems by delivering file elements pack with parts of compound viruses. To do so, Shirow gradually acquaints the reader with a visual vocabulary of Motoko's digitalized existence within an extensive system of information networks.

As in *Ghost in the Shell*, cyborgs can communicate thoughts e-brain to e-brain, in addition to spoken language. Shirow represents this aspect (or mode) of cyborg existence by showing characters costumed (they have unlimited choice of how they may construct a virtual visual representation of personal appearance), suspended within and surrounded by white-outlined spherical circuitry, usually against a blue and/or purple background. In a series of brief scenes, Motoko is seen communicating with a doctor who designs weaponry for her, her executive secretary, and with mini–AI assistants (their presence represented in bubble inserts) who provide instantaneous cyber-information about active cases on which she is working.

These "net communication" capabilities, however, are but one aspect of Motoko's post-fusion identity. She is also able to download her "self" into a series of remote-controlled humanoid terminals or decots (decoy rebots named Clarice, Chroma, etc...) that she has stashed in strategic locations (including within her giant robot bodyguards) all over the world for use when a material presence is advantageous to meet with clients or to fight enemies intent on human massacre or destruction of property. She can also, when necessary, occupy the bodies of other cyborgs, as evidenced by her inhabiting the shell of a female police officer while seeking the source of an attack on the president of a corporation.

Even more impressive is Motoko's ability to hack into the e-brains of other cyborgs in order to gather information and solve, or prevent, cyber-crimes. This becomes especially useful in her investigation of the Meditech case, in which a corporate clone-organ farm, in which pigs are utilized as vessels for human genetic material should a person need a transplant, has been destroyed. This terrorist event is the narrative's primary inciting incident, the basis for many of Motoko's actions for the remainder of the manga, including her decision to hack into the e-brain of Lebris, a technician she believes to be part of an enemy conspiracy with first-hand knowledge of the crime. It also facilitates Shirow's first illustration of Motoko's hacking skills that will play an important role in the final, climactic chapters. The hacking sequence is also important for several reasons beyond the narrative: the expansion of cyborg hero consciousness, the representation of cyborg existence, and presentation of a visual dimension of cyborg myth.

Shirow begins by representing this dramatic moment, visually, by showing Motoko, clad in skintight silver bodysuit and protective eye-ware, literally stepping into Lebris's cyber-brain, drawn as swirling, glowing, white-yellow layers of digital rings emerging almost cylindrically from his head (Shirow, 2005, p. 84). The frames that follow show Motoko, accompanied by mini–AIs (who help guide, deploy viruses and antibodies, and disable defense systems), rapidly hurtling ever deeper within the circuitry of Lebris's brain. This circuitry is now drawn in a rainbow of colors (first pink, then red-orange, then orange, then yellow)— in sharp contrast against the blues and purples of the "ordinary net" established earlier in the communication sequences.

As Motoko approaches Lebris's "ghost line" (the part of the e-brain housing the cyborg's human memory and active functions), the whirling circuitry is bright yellow with sudden bursts of flame-like sparks indicating an enemy attack barrier being activated (Shirow, 2005, p. 89–90). Upon deactivation of this barrier, she is plunged instantly into another digital matrix, olive green in color, devoid of circuitry, filled with white snake-like tendrils and firework-like explosions. Motoko describes this series of phenomena as akin to the "branching [of] an experimental neurochip with limits set to zero" (Shirow, 2005, p 91). Interestingly, she is no longer garbed in the bodysuit (appearing "naked," but again with no anatomical detail) and the color of her hair has changed from red to brown, more resembling Kusanagi in the first manga. No explanation is given for the transformation. Has Motoko Aramaki become Kusanagi?

It is at this point that Motoko and her AI companions realize that "something else" is also present is Lebris's e-brain system, actively trying to prevent them from going further. Motoko comments that she is still "baffled by this bizarre memory field," noting that "there's an awful lot of capillary netspace branching here" (Shirow, 2005, p. 92). Correspondingly, Shirow's frames become more complex, mold-like or sponge-like shapes begin to emerge amidst the snake-like firework shapes. Motoko then suddenly comes face-to-face with herself, or an image of herself, that rapidly fades from view. The AI asserts that this was a "mirror-type decoy," and that a segment of the enemy "has randomized and disappeared" (Shirow, 2005, p. 94).

Shortly afterward they are able to break through easily into Lebris's memory, where they uncover the sinister plot surrounding the Meditech crime: human brains are being grown in the pigs for some illegal purpose. Motoko also determines that they are dealing with two enemies, one enemy has committed the crime with human brains in pigs and another has infiltrated or "raided" the first company, possibly with good intentions of exposing the scheme, and possibly deliberately leading Motoko, herself, to the case (Shirow, 2005, p. 98–99). Back to her preferred, red-haired, prosthetic self, the perplexing circumstances stimulate Motoko's curiosity and outrage, and motivate her to pursue the perpetrators of the crime even more diligently.

In the character of Motoko, Shirow celebrates technology's positive potential while illustrating the tensions, dangers, temptations, and pleasures inherent in its employment. The discourses of hardware technophilia and monstrous embodiment emerge overtly in the series of astonishing, arresting images. The hacking sequence prepares the reader for what is to come by proving Motoko's integrity, determination and competence, by representing how she systematically operates in the digital realm, and by establishing a visual world of cyborg mythology within the digital information network, a world of circuitry, cyborg ghost line frontiers, attack barriers, and memory.

Self-Transformation, Species Transformation

So, too, does Motoko pursue a quest of self-discovery and liberation, although she only gradually becomes aware of this fact. The final chapter of *Man-Machine Interface* is set almost exclusively in the "net" as Motoko attempts to hunt down the Meditech criminals, only to find herself as she dives deeper and deeper into the digital universe, encountering "sibling" entities who construct considerable obstacles to Motoko's progress. She persists, however, finally arriving at "an orbiting body-deposit facility called Sleeping Universe" (Shirow, 2005, p. 242). There she finds the prosthetic body of Kusanagi suspended in a green liquid with connections to some kind of life-support machine for cyborgs spread over her body. Sensing this is where her long journey has been leading her, she attempts to infiltrate the inert Kusanagi's e-brain, the success of which is indicated by a frame of Kusanagi opening her eyes.

What follows is a virtual parent-child showdown with the "original" post-fusion Kusanagi. It is revealed that Motoko Aramaki is a digital descendant of the hybrid entity generated by the fusion of Kusanagi and the Puppeteer in the original manga. She is referred to as "Motoko 11 ... sort of an eleventh level isotope ... the type that ignores whatever cannot be scientifically proven" (Shirow, 2005, p. 253). Many replicant Kusanagi entities apparently exist, each of which carry, on their version of a species hard-drive, a set of "Kusanagi identity files" and each of which, independently, may choose to replicate or fuse with other beings. In fact, it is implied that fusion activity has been so plentiful that "entities with e-brains all become a subspecies of Mototko Kusanagi or become isotope fractions" (Shirow, 2005, p. 258). In connection with this increased power and influence, the rhetoric of fusion undergoes an interesting shift. The characters, toward the end of *Man-Machine Interface*, begin to describe the fusion activity as "brain expansion" and speak of the possibility of "infinite personalities encapsulataed in one" (Shirow, 2005, p. 257).

Motoko learns that Kusanagi has possibly lured her there in order to test her skill and knowledge and to acquire, hidden within Motoko's e-brain files, a blueprint for a silicon life-form developed by the creator of those-who-are-complex, Professor Rahampol. Kusanagi is quite interested in this blueprint as it represents potential for additional life-form continuity if she fuses with it. Kusanagi invites Motoko to join her in this brain expansion endeavor — bringing the element of potential species transformation once again into active play for cyborg myth-making.

By the end of the manga it is suggested that this brain expansion has, indeed, occurred. In the final pages, the story reverts back to psychic investigator Tamaki Tamai. Her mission is complete. Yet she has a final psychic vision in which she envisions Kusanagi's body duplicating. The process, then, rapidly accelerates in a starburst pattern with millions of Kusanagi extending outward from the center. "Flowers of light on the tree branches are blooming in huge numbers ... there are five colors..." describes Tamaki Tamai (Shirow, 2005, p. 299). The successive frames show replication continuing as the tree of Kusanagis appears to bloom and bloom until it resembles a universe of ever-expanding clouds (Shirow, 2005, pp. 300–303). "I'm seeing the tree in double," states Tamaki Tamai, perplexed, "No, wait ... perhaps there's two of *me*...? Everything looks like a double image, but it's stabilized. In terms of scale, it's the maximum possible visible space ... it's like a revolving mirror. The mirror seems asymmetrical and warped..." [Shirow's emphasis] (Shirow, 2005, pp. 301–302). Here, both in the choice of language and in the artwork, Shirow attempts to illustrate what the idea of brain expansion and species transformation might entail.

Unsure of what Tamaki Tamai is experiencing and concerned for her safety and well-being, the temple leader overseeing the psychic investigation discontinues the ritual and initiates procedures to bring her out of her trance state. Shirow concludes the story with a philosophical discussion between the temple leader, Section 9 Chief Aramaki and Batou about the meaning of her final words, followed by three close-up frames of Tamaki Tamai. The final frame is an image of her eyes with a similar glowing digital universe or e-brain network that was viewed, in the opening pages, in Motoko's eyes (Shirow, 2005, p. 308). The implication, from this visual representation, would seem to be that Tamaki Tamai has herself, whether willingly, by force, or by coincidence, become fused into the new Kusanagi-Motoko Aramaki-silicon life-form entity. It is also implied that a new journey of liberation and transformation has been initiated.

CONCLUSION

Man-Machine Interface is deserving of a much more in-depth cyborg myth analysis. This all-too-brief study demonstrates, however, how Shirow's *GITS* sequel, like the earlier *GITS* manga and anime, may be viewed within a flexible framework of cyborg myth. It has been presented as a model based in Frankenstein myth, Japanese cyborg genealogy, and Haraway's radical manifesto. It has been envisioned as a mythology that can stretch to accommodate a range of cyborg entities, identities, subjectivities and narratives involving liberation and transformation.

Man-Machine Interface reveals Shirow pushing cyborg identity to new imaginative limits, stretching conventions of character, narrative, and visual design. His starting point, of course, is the "cosmic species—the seed," that "highly efficient package of information ... the greatness of life" posited by the new life form as self-identification at the conclusion of *GITS* (Shirow, 2004, p. 350). Two of the defining primary characteristics of this hyper-advanced cyborg, it quickly becomes evident in *Man-Machine Interface*, are that it is continually transforming itself by fusing with other intelligent entities and that it is capable of rapid self-replication. These are, unquestionably, aspects of what the temple leader called, in the prologue, "the appearance of one of the most complex phenomena in the known universe" (Shirow, 2005, p. 10). These processes of fusion and replication, involving the weaving together and duplication of multiple-consciousnesses, apparently were initially accompanied by post-fusion and post-replication chaos and, what the temple leader terms, "the stress syndrome unique to cyborgs" (Shirow, 2005, p. 306). It is suggested by the end of the manga, as the story concludes, that these fusion side-effects may have been reduced, if not eliminated entirely. It is also implied that the new entity — a cyborg, advancing — has increased its intelligence, adjusted its worldview, and corrected some vulnerabilities inherent in its "design."

Shirow, then, offers a glimpse of this being, teasing the reader with a final image after he has formally "closed" the "control preferences" of his narrative interface mechanism (Shirow, 2005, p. 209). If the reader chooses to turn the page, s/he encounters a complex, visually-arresting image of what appears to be Motoko Aramaki clad in a skin-tight pink metal garment seemingly astride an apparatus that simultaneously appears to be both a piece of industrial hardware and a digital connection in process. On closer inspection, however, it becomes clear that Motoko is integrated into this combination material-virtual device. A pink, glowing halo indicating her on-line status rings her head. She has at least five visible arms. Above one hovers a ball of digital energy from which flows a continuum of electronic signals. From another emerges the barrel of a massive automatic rifle. Another appears to be reaching out from within the interior mechanism, almost as if the machine, itself, has sprouted an arm that can steer, hold, or activate its components (Shirow, 2005, p. 210). Almost Escher-like in its visual complexity and the way the eye is deceived by seemingly impossible, yet oddly plausible, architectural structures, this image may be viewed as a vivid example of Donna Haraway's potentially subversive cyborg in all of its radical-hybrid glory. It is a culminating image, deceptive, disruptive, and highly indicative of what has been experienced visually and narratively throughout the entire *GITS* series: multiply-positioned, techno-logically-advanced, politically-subversive cyborgs that challenge norms, desta-bilize identities, and celebrate differences.

Echoes of the Frankenstein myth narrative reverberate in surprising ways in the first *Ghost in the Shell* stories and in *Man-Machine Interface* as charac-ters grapple with both the impulse and ability to create or generate new life-forms (including self-generation) and with the outcome of those actions. This is especially evident in *Man-Machine Interface*, where the hyper-advanced post-fusion Kusanagi functions as both initiator of species creation and modification, as well as demonstrates willingness to utilize her own "self" as the raw material for experimentation. The entire Motoko Aramaki story line may even be viewed as the creator's "off-spring" or "creature" rebelling against or challenging its maker. In Motoko, Kusanagi wittingly or accidentally gen-erates a rival or sibling self of considerable skill and intelligence, who must ultimately be re-inscribed or re-incorporated. This act of fusion liberates both Kusanagi and Motoko Aramaki, as joining with the silicon life form appar-ently ensures greater species diversity as well as a "presence" in all cyborg e-brains.

Ghost in the Shell (manga and anime) and *Man-Machine Interface* all extend the hardware technophilic and monstrous embodiment streams of Japanese cyborg development. Shirow actively champions the wonders and fascinations of technology as he imagines the ranges, boundaries, and limits of cyborg identities. He also provides considerable frame space to investigat-ing the interior subjectivity of a wide variety of cyborgs including the hyper-advanced cyborg. In doing so, Shirow raises many questions. At what point is a cyborg so technologically advanced that it is no longer a cyborg, but some other kind of entity? What happens to the human component of cyborg embodiment as the cyborg merges with other life forms? What if the advanced cyborg hybrids no longer feel compelled to communicate or interact with the "human" population? How do these advanced entities communicate and nego-tiate with each other? Is there a protocol? How are disagreements resolved? And where shall the species go now?

Questions like these, clearly, are related to immediate concerns in the historical moment of the early twenty-first century, in which human and machine materialities are increasingly meshed due to rapid advances in tech-nology (as evidenced by the controversies surrounding "Cheetah" flex-foot prosthesis and the LZR Racer competitive swimwear). Often contemporary individuals are the recipients of mixed messages about new or impending relationships between the human body and technology, as well as a seemingly endless quantity of them. Daily life for most people is, essentially, cyborgian, celebrating and/or struggling with technology's impact upon or within one's corporeal self.

Frequent, ongoing decisions must be made about whether to enhance and/or extend one's life by means of a range of surgical implants, transplants, replacements, reconstructions, rehabilitations and body modification devices involving machines or incorporating machine parts. Mobile, interactive communication technology infiltrates almost every dimension of existence in the increasingly seductive quest to be and stay instantly connected. Should an identification microchip be implanted in the family pet? Should vision difficulties be corrected with laser surgery? What features should the next cell phone, computer, automobile, or cosmetic surgery upgrade include? It is evident that the post-human moment has been "this moment" for quite some time. It is also clear that inquiries involving questions of "Who am I?" "What am I becoming?" "What have I become?" "What can I become?" are increasingly involving incorporated and/or socially inscribed technology as a portion of the answers.

Tensions and anxieties about such matters are persistent. Contemporary mythology assists in addressing these concerns by providing narratives, particularly cyborg narratives, that help to make sense of past, immediate and anticipated experiences. As embedded within mythical stories, differing philosophies may be discussed, multiple options for solving problems may be generated, and those strategies and solutions may be practiced, rehearsed, enacted. Myths may also, it is important to note, stimulate action, whether internal or external, that can lead to personal, societal, and/or cultural clarifications and modifications.

Cyborg mythology, as seen in the various *Ghost in the Shell* stories, functions to help contemporary individuals address, confront, and accept or reject the possibilities for increased realization of hybrid beings in the developed world. Shirow and Oshii, admirably, do not minimize or attempt to simplify the complexities of cyborg subjectivity. Nor do they glorify or fetishize it. In encountering the multiple manifestations of the character of Kusanagi (the Major, the life-form resulting from fusion with the Puppeteer, Motoko Aramaki and other "offspring"), readers and film viewers are empowered to explore the celebrations, conflicts, advantages, limitations, and ethical concerns associated with an ever-developing cyborg identity operating within increasingly sophisticated cybernetic systems. It is difficult to not identify, as contemporary (literal, virtual and/or social) cyborgs, with Kusanagi. Her world and her actions are plausible enough within the context of current technological developments. Many of the freedoms and powers that she enjoys are seductively appealing. Yet it is a world fraught with dangers and anxieties that threaten those very same freedoms and powers. The tensions and celebrations surrounding cyborg identities embedded in the *GITS* narratives allow the contemporary individual to weigh options and devise strategies for coping with human-machine interfacing. They also stimulate the imagination, potentially generating new truths and stories involving questions of post-human subjectivities in this, and future, millennia.

References

Balsamo, A. (1996). *Technologies of the gendered body: Reading cyborg women*. Durham, NC: Duke University Press.

Brown, S. T. (2006). Screening Anime. In S. T. Brown (Ed.), *Cinema anime: Critical engagements with Japanese animation* (pp. 1–19). New York: Palgrave MacMillan.

Cadora, K. (2005). Feminist cyberpunk. *Science Fiction Studies, 22* (3), 357–72.

Campbell, J., and Moyers, B. (1988). *The power of myth*. New York: Doubleday.

Cavallaro, D. (2006). *The cinema of Mamoru Oshii: Fantasy, technology and politics*. Jefferson NC: McFarland and Company, Inc.

Gray, C. H. (Ed.) (1995). *The cyborg handbook*. New York: Routledge.

_____, Mentor, S., and Figueroa-Sarriera, H.J. (1995). Cyborgology: Constructing the knowledge of cybernetic organisms. In C.H. Gray (Ed.), *The cyborg handbook* (pp. 1–14). New York: Routledge.

Haraway, D. (1991). A cyborg manifesto: Science, technology, and socialist-feminism in the late twentieth century. In D. Haraway, *Simians, cyborgs, and women: The reinvention of nature* (pp. 149–181). New York: Routledge.

Hayles, N. C. (1999a). The life cycle of cyborgs: Writing the posthuman. In, J. Wolmark (Ed.), *Cybersexualities: A Reader on feminist theory, cyborgs and cyberspace* (pp. 157–173). Edinburgh: Edinburgh University Press.

_____. (1999b). *How we became posthuman: Virtual bodies in cybernetics, literature, and informatics*. Chicago: University of Chicago Press.

Levi, A. (2001). New Myths for the Millennium: Japanese Animation. In. J. A. Lent (Ed.), *Animation in Asia and the Pacific* (pp. 33–50). Bloomington: Indiana University Press.

Lykke, N, and Braidotti, R. (1996). *Between monsters, goddesses and cyborgs: Feminist confrontations with science, medicine, and cyberspace*. New Jersey: Zed Books.

Napier, S. J. (2000). *Anime from Akira to Princess Mononoke: Experiencing contemporary Japanese animation*. New York: Palgrave.

Orbaugh, S. (2002). Sex and the single cyborg: Japanese popular culture experiments in subjectivity. *Science Fiction Studies, 29* (3), 436–52.

_____. (2005). The genealogy of the cyborg in Japanese popular culture. In. W. K. Yuen, G. Westfahl, and A. K. Chan (Eds.), *World weavers: Globalization, science fiction, and the cybernetic revolution* (pp. 55–72). Aberdeen: Hong Kong University Press.

Orbaugh, S. (2006). Frankenstein and the cyborg metropolis: The evolution of body and city in science fiction narratives. In. S. T. Brown (Ed.), *Cinema anime: Critical engagements with Japanese animation* (pp. 81–111). New York: Palgrave MacMillan.

Oshii, M. (Director) and Ito, K. (Writer). (1995). *Ghost in the shell* [Film]. United States: Manga Video.

_____. (Director and Writer). (2004). *Ghost in the shell 2: Innocence* [Film]. United States; Dreamworks.

Power, J. (2008). For swimmers, new suit a stroke of genius. *Boston Globe*, 29 June, A1, 15.

Ruh, B. (2004). *Stray dog of anime: The films of Mamoru Oshii*. New York: Palgrave.

Rushing, J. H., and Frentz, T. S. (1995). *Projecting the shadow: The cyborg hero in American film*. Chicago: University of Chicago Press.

Shirow, M. (2003). *Ghost in the shell 1.5: Human-error processor*. Milwaukee, OR: Dark Horse Manga.

_____. (2004). *Ghost in the shell* (2nd Ed.). Milwaukee, OR: Dark Horse Manga.

_____. (2005). *Ghost in the shell: Man-machine interface*. Milwaukee, OR: Dark Horse Manga.

Silvio C. (1999). Refiguring the radical cyborg. *Science Fiction Studies, 26* (1), 54–72.

_____. (2006). Animated bodies and cybernetic selves: The animatrix and the question of posthumanity. In S. T. Brown (Ed.), *Cinema anime: Critical engagements with Japanese animation* (pp. 114–137). New York: Palgrave MacMillan.

Springer, S. (2008). Running strong. *Boston Globe* Magazine, 29 June, 26–7.

Wagner, J., and Lundeen, J. (1998). *Deep space and sacred time: Star Trek in the American mythos*. Westport, CT.

Whitt, D. F. (2002). "Resistance is futile": The rhetoric of the cyborg in the information age. Unpublished doctoral dissertation, University of Nebraska, Lincoln.

_____. (2008). Booyahs, sonic cannons, and a 50,000-watt power cell: Teen Titans' Cyborg and the Frankenstein myth. In D. Whitt and J. Perlich (Eds.) *Sith, slayers, stargates, and cyborgs: Modern mythology in the new millennium*, (p. 30–47). New York: Peter Lang Publishing.

Epilogue

"Always in Motion
Is the Future..."

In the first chapter of *The Power of Myth* (1991) titled "Myth and the Modern World," Joseph Campbell discusses with Bill Moyers the purpose of mythology. One particular exchange highlights Campbell's belief in the remarkable scope and influence of myth.

> MOYERS: Don't you sometimes think, as you consider these stories, that you are drowning in other people's dreams?
> CAMPBELL: I don't listen to other people's dreams.
> MOYERS: But all of these myths are other people's dreams.
> CAMPBELL: Oh, no, they're not. They are the world's dreams. They are archetypal dreams and deal with great human problems [p. 19].

Initially, Campbell's use of the word dreams may suggest an analysis of imaginings associated with sleep. However, a closer reading unveils a more pragmatic meaning, one that connects dreams with our present and the hopes and aspirations of our future. As the world's dreams myths are more than just stories about heroes, gods, and strange creatures, they are personal, social, and cultural maps guiding us through the unknown. In this way myths have transformative power in their ability to motivate, teach, and inspire. For example, Atkinson (1995) argues that Homer's *Odyssey* can be used a metaphor for spiritual development. He writes, "Odysseus's entire journey can also be understood literally and symbolically. On a symbolic level, all the external difficulties he encounters could signify character transformation and spiritual awakening he is experiencing internally" (p. 24). When compared to the two-thousand year old story of Odysseus the adventures of Harry Potter, Chihiro, Ofelia, and Madame Souza may not yet, or for that matter ever, carry the same timeless quality or epic weight of Homer's poem. However, this should not automatically exclude the examination of these characters and their stories from a mythic perspective.

While Campbell (Campbell & Moyer, 1991, p. 38), himself, points out that "we can't have a mythology for a long, long time to come," because "things are changing too fast to become mythologized," this is not to suggest that modern myth and mythology are obsolete — quite the contrary. New mythologies may, in fact, simply be old mythologies contextualized. In the words of Campbell, "[t]he individual has to find an aspect of myth that relates to his [or her] own life" (p. 38). Whether the myth resonates with classic themes and structures (e.g., the hero(ine) journey) or new frontiers (e.g., cyborg development), the value of myth comes from an ability to both represent and constitute our past, present, and future.

The meaning of myth is profound. Campbell (p. 38) articulated at least four succinct functions: the mystical, the cosmological, the sociological, and the pedagogical. Mystery, and "awe before this mystery," is the first function of myth — to help us explain those things that cannot be explained (nor, perhaps, should be explained). Seeing the *familiar* as *unfamiliar* may be the second function of myth, and is known as the cosmological function (using story, narrative, and tales to articulate the mundane physical reality in terms that resonate within us) — "what's fire? You can tell me about oxidation, but that doesn't tell me a thing" (p. 39). Myth varies enormously from place-to-place as a result of the sociological function, which supports and validates social orders — structures that are dated according to Campbell (p. 39). Ultimately, the most useful aspect of myth, the pedagogical function, relates to the individual — such stories teach us "how to live a human lifetime under any circumstances" (p. 39).

Many readers of this volume have made it this far because they inherently understand and value the role of myth and mythology — myths explain, elucidate, validate, and teach. There are, however, skeptical readers of this volume who undoubtedly have adopted a mindset that all this "stuff" is spurious. For them, we explain the value of *story* using the words of noted philosopher Kenneth Burke — wherein we substitute the word story (a.k.a. myth or rhetoric) with "substance."[1] Burke (1945) explains, "there is cause to believe that, in banishing the *term*, far from banishing its *functions* one merely conceals them. Hence, from the dramatistic point of view, we are admonished to dwell upon the word, considering its embarrassments and its potentialities of transformation, so that we may detect its covert influence even in cases where it is overtly absent" (p. 21). Simply put, myth and story is significant in both its presence and absence; we should be mindful of stories when we hear them, and skeptical when we do not. Stories, myths, and mythologies are, in fact, substance.

The essays in this book reflect a wide array of interpretations regarding myth applied to contemporary science fiction and fantasy. Like our first book on creative mythology the conclusions of some authors may generate new interest or appreciation for various films or television programs in this genre. No doubt the analysis and implications of other authors will also raise questions and provoke debate. We welcome such scrutiny and hope this work will inspire scholars from other disciplines to examine myth as it relates to twenty-first century texts not only within sci-fi/fantasy, but in other areas such as politics, sports, business, and the arts.

For us, our next quest will be to complete our "trilogy" of books on creative mythology. And, just like our previous publishing adventures, we will expect struggle and sacrifice throughout this journey, but once again are counting on hero partners to help us along the way. Having navigated the perilous seas of publishing, we are hopeful that the wellspring of mythology, as we labeled it in our last book, will not soon run dry. Campbell (1991) would seem to support our optimism stating, "You can't predict what a myth is going to be any more than you can predict what you're going to dream tonight" (p. 41). The linking of myth and dream by Campbell is deliberate as these distinct flights of imagination have been, and forever will be, inseparable making this volume not the end, but a new beginning.— David Whitt and John Perlich.

NOTES

1. The transposition of "story" with "substance" would not be considered an outrageous leap of logic for anyone familiar with either Burke or writings in the loosely related area of symbolic interaction.

REFERENCES

Atkinson, R. (1995). *The gift of stories: Practical and spiritual applications of autobiography, life stories, and personal mythmaking.* Westport, CT: Bergin and Garvey.
Burke, K. (1945). *A grammar of motives.* New York: Prentice Hall.
Campbell, J., & Moyers, B. (1991). *The power of myth.* New York: Anchor Books.

About the Contributors

Djoymi Baker (Ph.D., University of Melbourne) is a lecturer in cinema studies and cinema management at the University of Melbourne in Australia.

Richard Besel (M.A., University of Illinois–Chicago; Ph.D., University of Illinois–Urbana–Champaign) is an assistant professor of communication studies at California Polytechnic State University.

Jay Scott Chipman (M.A., Louisiana State University–Baton Rouge; Ph.D., University of Pittsburgh) is a professor of communication and theatre arts at Nebraska Wesleyan University.

Kirstin Cronn-Mills (M.A., University of Nebraska–Lincoln; Ph.D., Iowa State University) is an instructor at South Central College in Minnesota.

Jason Edwards (M.A., Minnesota State University–Mankato; Ph.D., Georgia State University) is an assistant professor of communication at Bridgewater State College in Massachusetts.

Sharon Dee Goertz (M.A. and Ph.D., University of Kentucky) is a professor of English at Hanover College in Indiana.

Ellen Gorsevski (M.A., Oregon State University; Ph.D., Pennsylvania State University) is an assistant professor of communication at Bowling Green State University in Ohio.

Brian Klosa (M.F.A., Minnesota State University–Mankato) is an instructor at South Central College in Minnesota.

John Perlich (M.A., Minnesota State University–Mankato; Ph.D., University of Nebraska–Lincoln) is a professor of communication studies at Hastings College in Nebraska.

Jessica Samens (M.A., Minnesota State University–Mankato) is an instructor in speech communication at Minnesota State University–Mankato.

Reneé Smith Besel is an M.F.A. candidate at Roosevelt University, and an account director for Marketing Direct Inc. in St. Louis, Missouri.

David Whitt (M.A. and Ph.D., University of Nebraska–Lincoln) is an associate professor of communication studies at Nebraska Wesleyan University.

Index